DEVELOPING THE CORE CURRICULUM

DEVELOPING THE CORE CURRICULUM

ROLAND C. FAUNCE · *Professor of*
Education, Wayne State University

NELSON L. BOSSING · *Professor of*
Education, University of Minnesota

SECOND EDITION

1958

PRENTICE-HALL, INC. · *Englewood Cliffs, N. J.*

Library of Congress
Catalog Card No.: 58-6203

20476

*To the many core teachers
who have advanced the educational
frontier by their persistent search
for the better way*

Preface

Within the past four decades there has been a widespread effort to redefine and to reconstruct the school curriculum. At the present time the definition of the curriculum in terms of the learning experiences of the child is generally accepted. Many curriculum patterns have been developed as educational workers have tried to translate the new conception of the curriculum as experience into practical forms for school usage. The curriculum pattern now rapidly coming into favor is known as the core curriculum. It appears to offer the greatest possibilities of developing a curriculum in harmony with modern conceptions of experience learning and is equally consistent with the kind of behavior competencies needed in our democratic society.

For some time many educationally minded, adventurous administrative leaders and teachers have been pioneering with the core curriculum. Out of their extensive experiences are now emerging practical suggestions for the initiation, organization, and conduct of the core curriculum within the school.

Unfortunately, prior to this time, this body of valuable experience data has not been brought together in such a way as to be a resource aid to educational workers who desired to introduce the core curriculum into their schools. A few valuable sources of help have come from centers where the core curriculum has been in operation. It is the purpose of this book to bring together and present in extended form some of the results of the rich experience of many who have successfully experimented with the core curriculum. It is hoped that the information and suggestions gleaned from many sources and shared in this book may prove of inestimable value to administrators who wish to introduce the core curriculum into their schools and to the alert teachers who desire to create more vital and effective learning situations for their pupils. They should also prove useful to the educational aspirant in training who wishes to become informed on the basic principles underlying the core curriculum concept, and on practical methods for its effective use in the school and classroom.

The first five chapters of the book present the definition and underlying educational basis of the core curriculum within our democratic society. The remaining chapters are devoted to the implementation of the core curriculum within the community, the school, and the classroom. Many practical suggestions with a wealth of illustrations from many sources have been given in the hope that the experiences of others may offer helpful suggestions to the administrator and the classroom teacher.

A book of this kind of necessity lays heavy tribute upon the experiences and judgments of others. The authors are conscious of their obligations to those who have pioneered the core curriculum and thus made available the wealth of practical experience so freely drawn upon in the pages of this book. Many have read portions of the manuscript and offered valuable suggestions. Their help is greatly appreciated. Particularly, the authors desire to acknowledge their obligation to and appreciation of the help of Dr. Rosalind Zapf, core teacher at Edwin Denby High School, Detroit, who contributed much to Chapter 6, "The Core Class in Action."

R. C. F.
N. L. B.

Contents

ix

10. Using Resources in Core Classes (Cont.)

11. Learning How to Teach Core Classes 248

12. The Role of the Administrator 263

13. Procedures in Developing a Core Curriculum . . 281

14. The Community Can Help 311

14. The Community Can Help (Cont.)

15. Evaluating Progress in Core Classes 339

Chapter 1

Education Confronts New Challenges

Our culture is in a state of rapid and profound change. On every side the old gives way to the new. It is true that some form of change has always characterized society, however imperceptible the modifications might at times have seemed to be; but never in the history of man has this change been so swift or so revolutionary. A recent writer asserts that because of the discovery of steam and electricity, there has been more alteration in technology in two generations than in all previous history.[1] Rugg and Withers suggest the uniqueness of contemporary cultural change thus:

Two generations have slipped by since John Dewey opened his pioneering Laboratory School and he and Francis Parker organized the first School of Education at the University of Chicago. *These six decades have witnessed the swiftest cultural change in the 800 years during which modern society has been founded.* . . . So drastic were the changes precipitated by

---

[1] Norman Cousins, *Modern Man Is Obsolete.* New York: The Viking Press, 1945, p. 16.

1

the passage from the crude "Machine Age" of the nineteenth century to the efficient "Atomic Age" of today, and so crucial were the problems that emerged, that it deserves the name, "The Great Transition." [2]

Even more startling and pointed is the statement of another writer, who declares that, because of the unprecedented rapidity of social change characteristic of our age, we are living in the first period of human history in which it is not possible for one generation to assume that the conditions under which it lives can be transmitted substantially unchanged to the next generation.[3] A casual survey of the contemporary scene clearly indicates that change is a major aspect of our age, and that future generations must face new and baffling problems not contemplated by their predecessors.

In such a culture, education is presented with difficult challenges. In a democracy the responsibility for the determination of broad policy rests squarely upon the citizen. To discharge this obligation successfully each citizen must be fully aware of the nature of the changing world in which he lives, and must be equipped with the understandings and skills necessary to solve intelligently the strange new problems that confront him. It is the task of education, then, to insure that every citizen understands, as far as possible, the nature of the changes taking place in his culture and possesses the requisite skills to make effective adjustments to the new situations.

How Do Cultural Changes Create New Challenges?

1. the challenge of changes in population

"Go West, young man," was the familiar admonition of grandfather's day. It was the challenge to those who sought new adventure and the possibilities of creating homes, fortunes, and spe-

---

[2] Harold Rugg and William Withers, *Social Foundations of Education*. Englewood Cliffs, N. J.: Prentice-Hall, Inc., 1955, p. 6. Italics quoted.

[3] Alfred North Whitehead, *Adventures of Ideas*. New York: The Macmillan Company, 1933, p. 117.

cial niches for themselves in yet undeveloped territory. It was likewise a device by which crises caused by maladjustments in the cultural pattern were neatly and immediately avoided. But that easy means of avoidance of critical problems has come to an end. Geographically speaking, we have reached the end of our frontiers; we have come to the close of a very important era in American life. From this point on, America must face realistically many of the problems that were lightly sidestepped in the past, as well as the new problems created by the passing of our geographical frontiers and the tremendous changes taking place in our population.

From less than three million people at the time of the Revolution, our estimated population for 1958 has risen to over 170 million. America has passed from sparsely settled rural communities to thickly populated areas with a majority of the people living in urban centers. In 1790 approximately five per cent of the people were urban dwellers. By 1958 the urban population exceeded 70 per cent.

The major growth of our urban population has taken place within the past century. Nowhere in the world have cities grown so rapidly. Most large cities of today were either villages or very small centers of population 100 years ago. Cities like Cleveland and Detroit were little villages in 1820, with populations of 606 and 1,422 respectively; in 1850 they were small cities of 17,034 and 21,019. Los Angeles, which now boasts a population of more than three million, was a straggling little community of 1,610 people in 1850.

This pronounced trend toward urbanization of population has spawned many serious problems. The early settlers did not dream of the almost fantastic growth of our cities or foresee the possible effects of modern technological development upon the future life and organization of cities. Consequently, urban centers now face the problem of costly corrections for the familiar conditions of narrow streets, traffic congestion, blighted areas, physical and health hazards, inadequate recreational and educational facilities, and general lack of coordination of civic activities, which have resulted from haphazard governmental, business, industrial, and residential development.

The difficulties incident to a rapid growth of population such as has been experienced in America may be replaced in the not too distant future by the problems created by a static population. Authorities on population have long predicted a slowing down of our population growth to the point where it would remain approximately stable or decline slightly. Before World War II it was predicted that shortly after 1960 the population of the United States would begin to level off and that it would reach a static condition around 1970 or 1980. Authorities now believe a static condition will not be reached before the end of the present century.[4] This means that the myriad problems of an aging society must be faced in the near future. The proportion of older people to younger will steadily increase as the birthrate falls off and medical science continues to add to the longevity. But more immediately, education is faced with the problems of expanding enrollments, need for greater physical facilities, more teachers, and better curriculum offerings to meet present population growth and needs.

In addition, our large, sprawling, somewhat chaotic metropolitan centers have provided a real challenge to effective democratic government. Our large cities generally have a reputation for corruption and mismanagement. Typical big city populations seem to find it difficult to become articulate, or even aware of conditions affecting them; this has become a matter of great concern to students of government.

Another source of concern is the diverse composition of our population. America represents a mixture of all races. Although the so-called white race is dominant, it is composed of many national elements that originally immigrated to this country. The

---

[4] For further discussion see: Warren S. Thompson, *Population Problems,* Revised. New York: McGraw-Hill Book Company, Inc., 1953; James A. Quinn, *Urban Sociology.* New York: American Book Company, 1955, Chapter 5, "Urban Population"; John Biesanz and Mavis Biesanz, *Modern Society.* Englewood Cliffs, N. J.: Prentice-Hall, Inc., 1954, Chapter 9, "From Rural to Urban Living: Our Changing Society."

majority of the population is made up of the white stock of Northern Europe; English, Irish, German, Scandinavian, French. Large blocs of our population, however, are Italian, Spanish, Greek, Central and Eastern European and Asiatic. The Negroes, some sixteen million, make up a very large part of the population in the South and have their own racial sections in the large cities. Sharply divergent stocks have not readily mixed. As a result, there are racial and cultural islands throughout our country, particularly in the East and in the cities. Racial consciousness, particularly among Negroes, and differences of social and political ideals have created tensions and given rise to real problems, the solution of which cannot long be deferred if democracy is to maintain its vitality.

2. *the challenge of change to an industrial economy*

The previous section has indicated clearly the shift in America from a rural to an urban population, the definite corollary of the shift from an agricultural to an industrial economy. In 1820, 71.8 per cent of America's labor force was employed in agricultural pursuits. This has been reduced to less than 8 per cent in 1958. The transition to industrial life with its fringe of activities now engages the major part of our labor force.

Within the past fifty years, America has moved particularly rapidly toward an industrial economy. We have moved far from the early pioneer period of great solicitude for the so-called infant industries, which claimed generous aid through protective tariffs and other special privileges so that they might compete with the strong, well-established industries of Europe. Today, nothing in Europe can compare with our mammoth industrial and business concerns. Many have become multiple billion-dollar corporations. In 1946, America had 43 billion-dollar corporations with combined assets of over 100 billion dollars. By 1956 the number of billion-dollar corporations had, through mergers and other causes, decreased to 22, with combined assets of over 150 billion dollars. In addition, there are a large number of near-billion-dollar companies. The size of these concerns is more clearly evident when it is realized that the combined assets of the billion-dollar corporations comprise more than one-fourth of the total wealth of this country.

Not only the size of the parent corporations, but also the large number of subsidiary corporations controlled by the parent corporations indicate their real size and power. For example, in 1936 one of these billion-dollar corporations, United States Steel, held control of more than 200 subsidiary corporations—some not so small. It controlled, for example, the largest pipe company in the world, the largest cement company in the world, the second-largest coal company in the world, and eighteen railroads. In 1946 the 45 largest transportation corporations owned 92 per cent of all our transportation facilities, the 40 largest public utility corporations owned more than 80 per cent of all public utility facilities, the 17 largest life insurance companies held over 81.5 per cent of the assets of all such companies, one-tenth of one per cent of all corporations owned 52 per cent of all corporate assets, less than four per cent of all manufacturing corporations earned 84 per cent of all manufacturing profits, and 1.1 per cent of all firms employing 500 or more persons accounted for 48 per cent of all such employment in the United States.[5]

During the past quarter-century and more, the government has wrestled with the problem of growing corporations and monopoly, and the public has been agitated over the good, and the evil, possibilities of giantism in business. The possibilities for either good or evil are obvious; there are plenty of case histories to illustrate both sides. It is essential that the school curriculum provide more opportunity for future generations to become familiar with the advantages and disadvantages of large corporate organizations, and with the possible means at the disposal of the

---

[5] For more detailed consideration of such facts as those given above, and their implication for our country, see *Economic Concentration and World War II*, Report of the Smaller War Plants Corporation to the Special Committee to Study Problems of American Small Business, United States Senate Document No. 206. Washington, D. C.: U. S. Government Printing Office, 1946; and *United States Versus Economic Concentration and Monopoly*, A Staff Report to the Monopoly Subcommittee of the Committee on Small Business, United States House of Representatives. Washington, D. C.: U. S. Government Printing Office, 1946.

public to insure that these colossi of business become their servants, not their masters.

It is clear that tremendous changes have been brought about by the shift from an agrarian to an industrial society. The face-to-face situation that usually characterized the employer-employee relationship before the opening of this century has given place to bargaining between the worker and employer through designated representatives of each. Naturally this involves the development of new techniques of cooperative relationships. Again, large aggregation of money in business brings with it potential corporate power with which the individual worker can no longer cope. This has led to the organization of labor into large unions with great bargaining power to offset the power of big business. When, as is true in many instances, large industries provide the major, if not the only means of employment in a community, the freedom of the worker to seek other employment is often almost nonexistent. It would mean giving up his home and seeking uncertain employment elsewhere. These and other related new conditions in working relations have led the Supreme Court to introduce the principle of a vested interest of the worker in his job. The radical change that modern industrialization has caused in the American way of life leads to almost endless problems, many of which strike deep at the roots of our ideals of democracy. Children must develop understandings and skills to meet these and more complex problems imposed by our industrial age. The school cannot evade this responsibility and challenge.

3. the challenge of change in the home

The urbanization and industrialization of our culture has had its effect upon the home. In the older agrarian culture the home was definitely at the center. The early agricultural pioneer lived a somewhat isolated life, his farm often separated from that of his neighbor by considerable distance, bad roads, and poor means of travel. Under these conditions the home was the orbit of much of his living.

Until very recently, the family was almost economically self-

contained. Much of the activities that involved the family liveli-
hood centered in or about the home. Farm activities radiated out
from the home. It was unusual for much of the farm work to be
carried on out of sight of the house. The wheat for flour, the corn
and other grains, hay and clover as fodder for the barnyard, and
garden produce provided the family with the necessities of life.
All of these were raised and converted into edible form on the
farm. Later, wheat and corn were taken to the mill of a nearby
village and the winter's supply of flour brought back. Meat and
fruit were processed in the fall and stored for winter use. Much
of the clothing was fashioned through the competent needlework
of the average housewife. In great-grandfather's day, wool from
the sheep of the farm was carded, spun into yarn, and woven into
cloth, and the hides of animals were tanned and made into leather
for various uses of the family. A man's home was indeed his
castle.

With the rise of industrial life all this has changed. One by
one the economic activities that were part of agrarian life passed
to great centers where large industrial plants could process farm
products better and more efficiently. Wheat raised on the farm
might be milled in another state, and, in turn, the flour used by
the housewife produced far from where the wheat was grown.
Today, the farmer's wife purchases various kinds of partially
cooked breakfast foods and bakery goods prepared in some large
industrial center and sold in a nearby village or city; or she may
purchase them from grocery wagons that stop at the kitchen door.

As farm life gave way to urban forms of living, many other
activities that characterized life on the farm disappeared. There
is little similarity between living conditions on the farm and in
the crowded apartment house of the modern city. For example,
living in city apartment houses creates added dependence upon
others for the major needs of heat, light, water, and transportation. This makes the average city person of today very conscious
of his interdependence with others.

Simplicity of life thus has given place to a more complex form
of existence. Dependence of the home upon many outside agen-

cies has introduced new problems often little understood by those who have gradually shifted from older modes of living to present conditions, or by the younger generation, which is quite unaware of the major lines of this transition, but is confused nonetheless by the complexities of modern life. The farmer's problem of selling the raw materials and buying the finished product on an equitable basis for the farmer, the problems of wages in relation to purchasing power, price controls, price supports, rationing, health safeguards, lockouts and strikes, and international relations, to mention a few, are now vital issues to farm or urban dwellers. Within the past few years of war and its aftermath, such problems as these have become very acute.

A further significant change in the home has grown out of the feeling of economic need for women to become gainfully employed, and the increased opportunity for them to find jobs. Many types of business and factory employment that do not require great physical strength can be done as well by women. Before the turn of the century, relatively few women worked outside the home unless it was to help with farm chores or in the field during seasonal emergencies. At the beginning of the century, three-quarters of a million married women were gainfully employed outside the home. By 1958 there were over fifteen million married women so employed. There is every reason to believe that with changing conditions and general acceptance of women in occupational activities the number of married women regularly employed outside the home will steadily increase.

New economic freedom for women presents its challenges to the status quo of the home in our cultural pattern. It has already had an apparent effect on the stability of marriage and on the institution of the family. Divorce has increased rapidly, reaching the high point in 1946 of one divorce in every 3.7 marriages, and declining slightly from that date to the present. The gradual acceptance by women of competition with men in the business world means many readjustments in the relationships of men and women that must and do profoundly affect the home as it was known by our elders.

These changes have had a tremendous influence upon the home as a social and educational institution. In many urban homes the family can scarcely be said to provide much of a unifying force as a social center. The home has been literally pulled apart by the urbanization and industrialization of our culture. The place of employment in large cities is usually at so great a distance from residential areas that many workers find it necessary to start out very early in the morning and return just in time for the evening meal. Those who follow the increasingly accelerated pace of business and professional life often are detained through the dinner period. Recently, a newspaper featured a series of interviews with wives of men prominent in business and the professions. The wife of one prominent man observed that her husband averages about one dinner at home each week. The demands of our age for extensive travel in the routine activities of business and profession further limit home contacts. The growing tendency of worker groups as well as business and professional people to live in suburban communities and commute from home to work in the city has further aggravated the trend toward disintegration of the home as a social center. Where wives and older children of the family are employed, and younger children find it necessary or convenient to have their lunches at school, the evening provides the only opportunity for social intercourse. Even this limited time has been invaded by modern industrialization of culture. Commercial entertainment has become the vogue. The motion picture, the bowling alley, the skating rink, and the ball park are typical of the array of attractions that tend to disperse the members of the average family at the only time they might have an opportunity to share experiences.

The home has declined, too, as an educational force. In the agrarian period the daughter joined with the mother in the discharge of household duties, while the boys worked side by side with the father in the field and with the chores. They thus learned needed skills and developed a point of view on many phases of life while they shared discussions in the course of the normal activities of home life. Ideals, attitudes, and values for living as well as habits of promptness, dependability, courtesy, and the ability to meet unexpected situations with confidence and resourcefulness were almost inevitable educational concomitants of this form of intimate shared living. The average urban dweller today, although he has some other advantages, finds the educational activities of the home greatly decreased. The privilege of sharing the thinking of the parents on a wide range of topics so much a part of the older agrarian home is greatly restricted. As has been pointed out, there is little opportunity for the typical urban family to be together. Further, there are few vital activities to be shared, few responsibilities to be accepted. Technological developments, and small home and apartment living, have left few responsibilities about the home for girls and boys, especially boys, to do. The accepted principle that it is one of the functions of the school to supplement the other educative agencies of our culture means that as these other agencies slough off educational tasks that once were performed by them, the challenge confronts the school to see that these tasks are not neglected.

4. *the challenge of increased crime and delinquency*

Three important factors with respect to the problem of crime and delinquency are of special interest to the school. First, for some years past, crime and delinquency in general appear to have been definitely on the increase. Criminologists recognize that the absolute figures in statistical records cannot be taken at face value. Communities vary in strictness of law enforcement, and one community over a period of years may vary its emphasis upon the suppression of certain types of offenses. Some types of behavior that today may be considered criminal or delinquent may have been tolerated, even acceptable, behavior a few years ago.

Second, as our cultural pattern changes and becomes more complex the causes and opportunities for crime and delinquency multiply rapidly. People widely separated and considerably isolated, as in the earlier agricultural era, had less provocation to unsocial behavior. The constant pressure of work left little time or incentive for conduct that might not be considered socially acceptable. Furthermore, in large, congested population areas an individual's behavior may be more easily veiled. Add to this the greater amount of leisure time modern technological development is bringing about, coupled with the increased unemployment of our age of technology, and a situation has been created that is certain to stimulate crime and delinquency.

The third aspect of this problem that presents a direct challenge to education, particularly though not exclusively, is the fact that recent data on crime and delinquency show the youthfulness of offenders. The data on arrests for crime in 1956, for example, show that 40.1 per cent were persons under the age of 15, while 45.8 per cent of arrests for major crimes were of persons under the age of 18. Over one half of the crimes against property in this period classified as larceny—theft and auto theft—were committed by youths under 21 years of age, while those under the age of 25 were responsible for two-thirds of the arrests for such crimes. For the most part these figures do not take into account the large number of children from 10 to 16 years old, estimated at almost one per cent of the near-16 million in that age group, who were brought before juvenile courts as delinquents of a less serious nature, or who were not recorded on police blotters because of their tender age.[6]

It is very easy to draw from such statistics the superficial conclusion that youth per se is becoming more vicious and lawless. Without disregarding the probability that part of the evidence of youthful crime and delinquency may be due to stricter enforcement of laws or the classification today as seriously reprehensible many types of behavior that formerly were regarded lightly or entirely ignored, the data do indicate that as a result of present standards of law enforcement and the current cultural *mores* there is a serious gap between contemporary acceptable cultural conduct standards and the behavior of youth.

It is important that society center its attack upon the cause of

---

[6] See *Uniform Crime Reports* for the United States, Annual Bulletin, Volume XXVII, No. 2, 1956. Issued by the Federal Bureau of Investigation, United States Department of Justice. Washington, D. C.: U. S. Government Printing Office, April 1957.

such overt behavior and concern itself only secondarily with the treatment of the delinquent. It is the challenge laid at the door of education to help society make the more fundamental approach to the solution of this problem. For example, to what extent do the cramped living conditions that characterize urban life today multiply personal contact problems not faced by youth of an older generation? What effect does our increasing leisure time have upon the lives of people; what bearing does this increase have on the conduct of youth? How does the shift to commercial entertainment outside the home stimulate felt needs in the face of a definite trend toward denying to youth the chance to earn legitimately the economic resources necessary to satisfy these needs? It is one thing to protect childhood and youth from economic exploitation by means of child labor laws and other devices to favor workmen with family responsibilities or trade competencies over single youth, especially in periods of oversupply of the labor market; it is quite another thing to leave the young frustrated and desperate because they find themselves hopelessly blocked in their normal right to self-expression, owing to a radically changing cultural pattern that does not sufficiently consider their economic plight. It is significant that the largest area of youthful crime involves property.[7]

5. the challenge of depletion of natural resources

Not long ago two large busloads of teachers and administrators in attendance at a curriculum workshop paused near some fields at the head of a valley in one of the midwestern states. Two state conservation officials standing by the side of the road pointed out to these educators some of the modern ways of farming to conserve the precious soil, which took 40,000 years for nature to produce to a depth of one foot. Many passing motorists betrayed

---

[7] For further detail see: Ruth S. Cavan, *Criminology,* Revised. New York: Thomas Y. Crowell Company, 1955; Negley K. Teeter and John O. Reinemann, *The Challenge of Delinquency.* Englewood Cliffs, N. J.: Prentice-Hall, Inc., 1950; Clyde B. Vedder and others, *The Juvenile Offender.* New York: Doubleday and Company, Inc., 1953; C. G. Wrenn and D. L. Harley, *Time on Their Hands.* Washington: The American Council on Education, 1941.

their bewilderment at the sight of a group of men and women standing by the side of a wheat field listening attentively to two men dressed in rough outdoor clothing. They would have been even more bewildered if they had known who these people were. Why should education and the curriculum be concerned with problems of soil conservation? Certainly it has little to do with the history, literature, mathematics, and languages that have been assumed to be the responsibility of teachers.

But these school people felt otherwise. Before the day was over they were more sure of the vital relation of education and the curriculum to conservation problems than when they began the trip. Several miles farther along the upper end of this valley, the general panorama began to indicate the gentle convergence of tableland into a more sharply defined valley in the distance. Here the workshop group stopped to study some rougher terrain that provided natural slopes and hollows to serve as water courses during rains. On this ground the farmers had planted their corn in traditional straight rows up and down the hills, inviting extensive erosion of topsoil during storms. The deep ditches that gutted the hollows and the presence of deep runways eroded along the corn rows bore mute evidence to the topsoil carried away by the rains, estimated by the conservation experts who had measured soil loss during some rains to amount to several tons per acre during a heavy downpour. Most of this loss could have been avoided by slow run-off of water through contour and strip cropping. Down in the narrow valley itself the devastating effects of malfarming in the upper valley plateau were all too evident. A place that forty years ago was a fertile valley supporting prosperous farms and villages was all but abandoned. Where fifty years ago a sparkling, clear stream, largely spring-fed, provided the pioneer settler with good trout fishing, was found a badly eroded stream bed, dry except during the rainy season when the raging torrent carrying thousands of tons of precious topsoil from the upper valley often covered the entire floor of this little valley. At one point the abandoned house of a prominent pioneer family with inches of silt over the floors was all that was left of a little village of fifteen or twenty houses, including a school where one of this workshop party had taught only 25 years before.

All this is typical of the frightening wastage or thoughtless exploitation of our natural resources—the product of millions of years. Thousands of acres of abandoned or low-fertility New England farms, the dust bowl areas of the Middle West, the depleted soil of parts of the South reveal the devastation that can be wrought on resources that took ages to create. A recent newspaper cartoon pictured a large section of fertile land with a sign reading "125,000 acres" floating down a river. The caption explained that America was losing that much topsoil each year, carried to the ocean on the floodwaters of our rivers.

Our early fathers saw little chance of serious inroads on our national forests for a thousand years. Today, our best timber land is denuded, the natural coverage for many watersheds is no longer present to save the land from terrific floods. We are also faced with dwindling stores of coal, iron ore, oil, and other natural resources. Exhaustion of the known reserves of some of them can be expected in a few short years.

A rigorous program of conservation is needed if mankind is not to imperil his future. Such men as William Vogt, in his challenging book, *Road to Survival,* have drawn the picture and warned of the urgent need to inform the public of the end results of present exploitation of our natural resources. This is a further challenge the school cannot ignore. The school curriculum must include conservation of our natural resources as one of the vital concerns of youth as well as of adults.

6. the challenge of a shrinking world

Though reams have been written to emphasize the fact that, because of modern technological development, the remotest part of the world now seems near, we are not as fully aware of the significance of this fact as we should be. No discussion of the challenge of cultural change to education can ignore the pervading influence of the fact we live in a world much smaller than that of our forefathers.

One way to grasp the more obvious aspects of this question is to visualize it in terms of elapsed time of travel and communication. Up to the middle of the last century, the time factor in bringing us nearer to other peoples of the world had changed little. During Caesar's conquests in England in the year 54 B.C., it took 14 days for a messenger traveling in the most expeditious manner to reach Rome. In 1860 it required Lord Poole, ambassador to Rome, exactly 14 days to return to England in response to an urgent summons. After the steamship began to ply the oceans, centuries-old modes of travel underwent change and within this century, since the development of the airplane, the world has really shrunk. Seventy-five years ago it required approximately 80 days to circle the globe, in 1903, 54 days, and in mid-century, approximately three days. By airplane, the remotest spot on the globe is now less than 12 hours away, and new airplanes now appearing will relegate these facts to ancient history. It is now possible to have breakfast in London, lunch in New York, and dinner in Los Angeles. Recently a feature dinner was held for which the major items on the menu had been brought in by air from the principal centers of the globe specifically for the occasion. The effects of the airplane upon our lives are still largely to be felt in the future.

The speed of the airplane has overshadowed the revolutionary effect of the railroad and automobile upon our culture. In a real sense they have fundamentally changed our mode of living within the past century; the influence of the automobile upon almost every phase of our lives will require at least another generation to be fully assessed.

The first transcontinental railroad was completed in 1869. Only 30,000 miles of track had been laid by 1860. Today, approximately 222,000 miles of track crisscross the United States, the now-familiar streamliner providing rapid transportation service between communities for passengers and the regular express freights facilitating the exchange of goods and supplies. Railroads made the industrial development of our country possible.

The automobile has supplemented and competed with the railroad. The fleets of giant auto trucks that service local and distant communities were unknown fifty years ago; passenger cars have become a vital part of our culture within this generation; motor transportation has revolutionized our modes of living. We have become a mobile people in the sense that motor travel is now part of the experience of a majority of our population. In 1957 it was estimated that over 45,000,000 automobiles would help carry people to lakes, mountains, the seashore, and other places on the Labor Day weekend. Pause by a major highway and observe the license plates of passing motorists to appreciate how extensively people from the extremes of East and West, North and South, and in-between intermingle.

Sociologically and economically, the automobile has transformed the rural community. It has made ghost towns out of little crossroads villages as business has been transferred to the larger centers. Amusement, social, and religious activities have moved from the rural to the larger town and city. It is only necessary to read books on rural life and its socio-economic problems to appreciate the transforming influence of the automobile and motorized farm equipment.

The present generation has become so used to the telegraph, telephone, and radio that it is almost impossible for those born since World War I to understand what has happened within approximately one generation. The telegraph is only a little more than a century old, but it has been superseded in many respects by the telephone and radio-phone. Most people would be startled to learn that Alexander Bell, the inventor of the telephone, died less than 50 years ago. The transformation of radio from the crystal set to the console-type that permits excellent reception even from the most remote parts of the world is definitely an achievement of this generation. The two-way radio, now standard equipment in most taxicabs, is coming into larger use. Television has developed to such a stage that it has become a matter of educational concern in many communities where youthful preoccupation with television programs has seriously affected the quality of work in the schools.

All of these advances in modes of communication and transportation offer opportunities to enrich our lives. They enable us to overcome distance and share thinking and living with others. They tend likewise to make us all very conscious of how interdependent we are. The ability to communicate with others in the most remote regions of the world, to move physically from one part of the world to another within a few hours, brings to all the realization of the actuality of the idea popularized by the late Wendell Willkie in the title of his book, *One World*. In a world of tensions such as we now experience, it makes vivid for thoughtful people the urgent, almost immediately imperative necessity of realizing the aspirations expressed in that fervent prayer of the late Franklin D. Roosevelt, read to the nation on the eve of D-day in 1944, for "a planet unvexed by war, untroubled by hunger and fear, undivided by senseless distinction of race, color, or theory." It is the challenge to education so to order its curriculum and methods as to develop in youth and adults understanding, competencies, and the will to create the kind of way of life that will utilize cultural change for the advancement of all mankind.

7. the challenge of expanding frontiers of knowledge

Recently a radio speaker made the startling statement that the world had acquired more additional knowledge within the past ten years than it would be possible for one person to master in a lifetime. Whether this statement is literally true or not, it does point up an important fact for education to consider.

It must be borne in mind that for ages past the goal of education has been the encyclopaedic acquisition of information. Many of our stunt programs such as the radio "Quiz Kids" glorify as an attainment ideal the acquisition of a tremendous array of factual information covering all phases of knowledge, past and present.

It is highly important for all to realize that cultural change and growth in knowledge have gone hand in hand, have, in fact, closely interacted. It is the old question of which came first, the chicken or the egg. There are, however, a number of indices to the rapidity with which knowledge has been amassed.

A few years ago a tercentenary celebration was held in honor of the great Moravian scholar, John Amos Comenius, whose unrealized life ambition was to compress all knowledge into an encyclopaedia to be called Pansophia, "all wisdom" or "all knowledge." Extensive though the accumulated wisdom of the ages was at that time, the project was not considered impossible. The increase of knowledge in the years since then has been greatly accelerated.

The plays of Shakespeare have long been cited for masterly use of language. It is said that a total of 15,000 words composed the vocabulary used in these plays. This, it has been assumed, was a vocabulary not equalled by that of any other writer. Although this may be true of writers of that era, vocabulary usage has increased rapidly within the past century. The vocabulary used in the state papers of the late Woodrow Wilson contained more than 25,000 words, and educated men of affairs frequently use in their writings more than double the number of words found in Wilson's state papers.

At the turn of the century the vocabulary of the average person was supposed to include about 1200-1500 words. Extensive vocabulary studies made in the 'twenties and early 'thirties placed the average word usage desirable for study at slightly over 5,000 words. Readers are familiar with the more comprehensive Thorndike and Horn 5,000-word and 10,000-word lists of most commonly used words. A study by Robert Seashore of Northwestern University in 1941 revealed a startling advance in vocabulary knowledge. He found that college students on the average knew 60,000 common words, 1,500 technical words, and 95,000 derived words. A similar study by M. J. Van Wagenen of the University of Minnesota indicates that the extensive knowledge of vocabulary found by Seashore for college students holds true as well for early adolescents. While the worth of some of the early vocabulary studies is subject to question, these studies do indicate a rapid growth in vocabulary usage and a growing awareness of the problems involved.

The rapid increase in knowledge may be observed in the expansion of the school curriculum. It has been pointed out that in 1800 the curriculum of our large universities did not equal in extensiveness the program offered today by the average high school in a city of 25,000 to 50,000 population. A study made in the second decade of this century of the extensive offerings of one of our largest universities showed that a person carrying a normal college load of studies would require 110 years to cover all the courses available. A similar study of another university, made within the past decade, stated that it would take 504 years to complete all the courses offered. School people are aware of the constant addition of courses, even of departments, to our institutions of higher learning. An alumnus returning to the teacher-training institution after an absence of a few years will be confronted by new courses dealing with ideas and problems not even contemplated in his student days.

It has been estimated that between 1700 and 1957 the number of subjects offered as basic in the elementary school increased from three to no less than 25. The high school has responded to the same pressure of expanding knowledge and reluctantly multiplied the range of possible areas of human knowledge the students might explore. In one large city in 1920 it was possible for a pupil entering high school to choose among 29 different programs of study he might wish to follow, including in all an estimated 450-500 courses. Multiple programs with a confusing array of courses confront the average boy or girl beginning high school in most large cities.

8. *the challenge of mass school enrollments*

No aspect of cultural change in America has been more significant than growth in the importance of education, as measured by increase in school attendance. The U. S. Office of Education reported a total school enrollment through grade 12 in 1956-57 of over 38 million. The Office predicts an enrollment of over 40 million by 1960, when the peak of the present influx of pupils is reached and increased birthrate has its full effect upon the schools. At the present time considerably over 98 per cent of the potential enrollment at the elementary level is now in school, and approximately 88 per cent of those at the secondary school age level are in secondary school. Within the next few years it is expected that the relation of potential elementary and secondary school population to school attendance will reach near-saturation.

To appreciate the tremendous growth in the school population it is only necessary to look at the change in school enrollment figures since 1890. At that time over 12 million children were enrolled in school. By 1940 the number enrolled in school had increased to nearly 25.5 million and in 1957 to over 38 million. The spectacular change in the school population, however, has come at the high school level. Since 1890 the secondary school population has increased nearly 4,500 per cent.

The huge increase in school enrollments means that in our society school-education has become big business. In the average local community the school has become the largest single concern of the people. Financially, education is the largest item on the tax budget and is likely to excite the most interest, as well as much voluble opposition from tax-conscious citizens. It means that the physical school plant, poor as it often is, is still the most pretentious building or set of buildings of the average American community.

The fact that the school population has grown in the past fifty years to the point where more than four-fifths of school-age adolescents are now in school creates problems not present when only the few who were preparing to enter college attended high school. A wide range of vocational interest means a need for differentiated kinds of vocational training. It has been assumed with some justification that the present student body is less homogeneous both in interests and in potential ability.

Today over one and one-quarter million teachers are at work from kindergarten through college, and there is a grave shortage of teachers. In the immediate future more than two million teachers will be required to care adequately for prospective enrollments. No other profession engages as large a number of persons as education.

Our educational emphasis has raised the educational index sharply. The average school level of those drafted for military service in 1917-18 was sixth grade. Only two decades later, the draftees for World War II had an average educational level equivalent to the tenth grade.

All of these developments suggest the profound social changes now taking place and yet to come. They suggest as well the importance placed upon education by the American people and the tremendous responsibility of education to meet the needs implicit in the radical changes now in the process of becoming.

What Are Some Implications for Education of These Cultural Changes?

As it would be unrealistic for the individual to attempt to live in the world of yesterday, it is no less unrealistic for the school not to make whatever adjustments in curriculum and related activities may be necessary to help boys and girls live successfully in a new and changing environment. At this point some of the broader implications for education of cultural change should be considered.

1. selection of curriculum materials

In the past the school has selected its curriculum materials on the assumption that life would be lived tomorrow essentially as it had been lived throughout former generations. What had proved successful as a pattern of living for our forefathers was thought to be the logical basis for successful living in the future. All that was necessary, then, was for the school to make available to youth the knowledge of the better ways of living that represented the accumulated experiences of the past. This conception of education has been generally popularized by the phrase, "the transmission of the cultural heritage." In general practice it has come to mean little more than passing on to succeeding generations the accumulated encyclopaedic information garnered throughout man's history.

Much difficulty has been encountered in the attempt to develop a curriculum based upon such a philosophy of education. The difficulty has multiplied as man's knowledge has become more extensive. It is possible that at no time have the proponents of this idea of education been in a greater state of confusion in their efforts to select curriculum materials than they are now. The expanse of knowledge, as previously pointed out, is too wide to be organized into a school curriculum. Arguments have been waged long and furiously over what should be selected for the school curriculum from our storehouse of accumulated and accumulating knowledge. Herbert Spencer, as early as the middle of the last century, raised the issue clearly in his essay, "What Knowledge Is of Most Worth?" Much educational research, particularly during the 'twenties and early 'thirties, was devoted to the question of what factual knowledge should make up the elementary and secondary school curriculum. School curricula and textbooks vary widely in their content of factual knowledge.

Another difficulty is that much so-called knowledge that was true yesterday will be incorrect or obsolete tomorrow. Many of the "facts" of science that were accepted fifty years ago, for example, are no longer accepted today. New discoveries have replaced old facts with new. Even in such an area as history, research has found many things learned by our fathers to be incorrect. A high military officer observed that the strategies of the great battles of history had little to do with the conduct of modern war. He commented that our commitment to the old concept of military strategy, which was employed as recently as World War I, along with failure to adjust to technological advances made up to the beginning of World War II almost cost the Allies victory. Under these circumstances there is decreasing confidence in a school curriculum based upon the time-honored-knowledge conception of education in a rapidly changing world that makes much that was significant yesterday inapplicable to-day.

The added fact of enrollment of practically all children in the elementary school and of most adolescents in the secondary school means a further searching study of the adequacy of the curriculum. The phenomenal growth of the secondary school population within the past half-century has led to a reappraisal of the school curriculum. Until recently, pupils in the elementary school who could not meet the curricular requirements or who lacked interest dropped out of school. Now compulsory attendance laws require all but the most abnormal cases to attend school. An older curriculum unadjusted to the needs and ability of a majority of children has had to undergo very radical changes, and is in the process of even greater change.

This older curriculum of the secondary school was transplanted directly from Europe as a college preparatory device. Before the beginning of this century, most of the pupils in high school were preparing for college through a school curriculum avowedly college-preparatory in design and based upon the ideal of quantitative knowledge. Now that a majority of our youth, with widely differentiated abilities and interests, are attending the secondary school but not planning to attend college, a new curriculum for pupils at this level is imperative.

2. development of new educational methods

The familiar teaching methods of the past were the lecture and recitation. These were appropriate to a somewhat static world and to a curriculum based upon the theory that knowledge is education. The passing on to future generations of the acquired factual knowledge of the ages was thought to be effectively and expeditiously done by the method of telling. This has been the approved method of the schools of Europe, with notable exceptions. Once it was determined what knowledge was desirable for the younger generation, this knowledge could be assembled and presented to large groups and in large doses.

In America particularly, where the number of competent lecturers was not equal to educational demands, a method known as "lesson hearing" came into vogue. The knowledge type of curriculum given boys and girls to memorize centered around compendiums of factual information collected and arranged in assorted bodies of classified knowledge. At designated intervals children were asked to "recite," that is, to repeat to the teacher what had been memorized from the assigned reading in the textbook. The more completely the learner could repeat all that he had read, the more satisfactory the educational achievement was assumed to have been. At frequent intervals oral or written examinations or both were given to check further the thoroughness with which this quantitative knowledge had been memorized. These methods were simple for the teacher to carry out and required a minimum of ability on the part of the learner.

Such methods are not appropriate to the kind of competencies children should acquire in today's world of rapid change. There has been a growing recognition that modern conditions create needs of adjustment not supplied by methods that emphasize the acquisition of subject matter of questionable validity for the present or future, or emphasize the acceptance without question of so-called knowledge because it is asserted by a lecturer to be true or it is found on the printed page. In a strange new world we need methods that place a premium on the development of critical thinking, the ability to discriminate between the truth and the fiction of yesterday, today, and tomorrow. We need methods that will enable youth efficiently to meet the many new situations now and in the future. This means the acquisition of problem-solving skills of a high order.

3. changes in the organizational pattern of the school

The nature of the adjustments that curriculum and methods must make suggests necessary modifications in the organization of the school. The familiar pattern of school organization fitted well into the older conception of education and curriculum. Subject matter "set-out-to-be-learned" could be organized into divisions such as reading, writing, geography, history, and mathematics.

The amount of each subject to be learned could be set out in neatly determined parcels to cover an average school year. It seemed logical and practical to allocate a certain amount of time each day to a given subject to be sure that no part of the "cultural heritage" deemed necessary for the pupil to master would be neglected. Since the curriculum consisted of the information brought together largely in textbooks, it was easy to develop an efficient routine for the classroom and corridors. Teachers, since they were subject specialists, taught their particular subject to succeeding groups for a class period each. This was possible because information not imparted or recited upon within a given period could as readily be covered the next day.

All of this seems out of place in the present milieu of rapid change. A new curriculum based upon problem-solving situations appears much more appropriate to the needs of contemporary youth. The learner can best develop those competencies with which to adjust satisfactorily to new situations that he meets now, and to the unknown ones that he must face in the future, as he multiplies his experiences in successfully meeting problem situations that are significant and vital to him today. To provide an experience curriculum based upon problem-situation learning is the task and the challenge of the modern school.

This new conception of the nature of the curriculum needed in our modern world cannot be grafted onto the old organizational patterns of the traditional school. Problem-situation learning does not fit conveniently into the regimented schedule with which we are familiar. More flexibility and a larger block of time is necessary for problem-solving teaching. This has long been recognized in the secondary schools by the organization of double periods, or even longer ones, for so-called laboratory instruction. Moreover, since problem situations of vital importance involve aspects of our community environment, learning activities cannot be confined exclusively to the classroom as in the past. This calls for flexibility of schedules and large blocks of time to permit groups to observe and participate in educational activities outside the classroom. Moreover, the curriculum cannot be blocked off in traditional subject areas to be taught at a given time in the day's schedule, nor can teachers be recognized as subject specialists. Problem-situation teaching cannot be fitted into the artificial, discrete divisions of the subject type of curriculum. Vital problems of life have a way of ignoring divisional subject matter lines, drawing upon data from many subject areas and upon resources not traditionally a part of the school curriculum.

Many of the implications of cultural change for the curriculum and for the reorganization of the school will be considered in more detail in later chapters, in conjunction with other factors that involve changes in modern education. It is important at this point to see only some major implications of our world of change in relation to the curriculum.

The tendency of many elementary school teachers will be to comment, "After all, we in the elementary school have been doing most of the things implied in your statement of needed modifications in the school program." To a certain extent such a reaction is justified. In our best elementary schools many needed changes are now in effect. Extensive observation, however, leads to the judgment that in the majority of elementary schools a heavy accent upon the traditional school practice is still the vogue.

It is important to recognize in the practices of our most forward-looking elementary schools many of the essential characteristics of a modern curriculum program, and the type of organizational pattern needed to implement it. It is the point of view of this book that many of the best elements in the curriculum program of some of our frontier elementary schools need mainly to be supplemented and refined to become parts of the ideal modern educational program. When this is done, the essential characteristics of such a program must be extended from the kindergarten through the secondary school.

The ideal educational program would not be too difficult to develop in the elementary school, which in general has been somewhat responsive to contemporary educational thinking. It will not involve too radical an adjustment in schools where the needs of children now take precedence in emphasis over school subjects, and where one teacher for most of the day handles a group of children from one or two grades. The necessary flexibility of program can be achieved easily under such conditions.

The problem of introducing a modern curricular program into the typical secondary school presents difficulties not faced in the average elementary school. With its long tradition of aping the college, secondary school program structure will require major adjustments in its organizational pattern. The definite commitment to highly discrete subject types of curriculum organization, emphasis upon extreme departmentalization within these subject areas, and the definite specialization within the curriculums toward college admission or vocational preparation has led to rigid, complicated time schedules that provide a multiplicity of course offerings. It has led further to extreme specialization of teachers in very limited subject-matter areas. All this has made the problem of introducing any extensive patterns of the modern curriculum into the secondary school a serious one. To effect such a change requires a major upheaval in traditional secondary school programs. More than that, by the time the secondary school is reached children have developed widened interests that must be taken into account. There is a legitimate need to recognize these growing special interests, both avocational and vocational. They involve additional program adjustments to care for educational needs common to all and for the growing differentiated needs of maturing adolescents.

The relative difficulty involved in developing a modern educational program in the secondary school by comparison with the elementary school has become the basis of some confusion of teachers at both levels. The emphasis in educational literature upon the problems incident to the introduction of the core curriculum in the secondary school has led many elementary-school people to conclude that the core curriculum is not a concern of the elementary school. This is most unfortunate, for the basic curriculum problems are the same at all school levels. These problems become more acute as they become involved in the more stratified organizational set-up of the traditional secondary school, and as the widening range of the needs of maturing adolescents is taken into account. These considerations should be kept constantly in mind as the discussion of the core curriculum continues. It is natural to give attention to those areas where most difficulty is encountered in the development of the core curriculum and in its introduction into the school. The principles and the techniques of the program, however, are essentially the same for both elementary and secondary schools.

SELECTED REFERENCES

Allen, Frederick L., *The Big Change*. New York: Harper and Brothers, 1952.

Association for Supervision and Curriculum Development, *Forces Affecting American Education*, 1953 Yearbook. Washington, D. C.: The National Education Association, 1953.

———, *Growing Up in An Anxious Age*, 1952 Yearbook. Washington, D. C.: The National Education Association, 1952.

Barnes, Harry Elmer, *Society in Transition*, Revised, 1952. Englewood Cliffs, N. J.: Prentice-Hall, Inc., 1951.

Benjamin, Harold, *The Saber-Tooth Curriculum*. New York: McGraw-Hill Book Company, 1939.

Bishop, Hillman, and Samuel Hendal, *Basic Issues of American Democracy*. New York: Appleton-Century-Crofts, Inc., 1951.

Bossing, Nelson L., *Principles of Secondary Education*, Second Edition. Englewood Cliffs, N. J.: Prentice-Hall, Inc., 1955, Chapter 6, "What Is the Nature of the Problems Facing Youth in Our Democratic Society?"

Counts, George S., *Education and American Civilization*. New York: Bureau of Publications, Teachers College, Columbia University, 1952.

Cousins, Norman, *Modern Man Is Obsolete*. New York: The Viking Press, 1945.

Drake, William E., *The American School in Transition*. Englewood Cliffs, N. J.: Prentice-Hall, Inc., 1955.

Douglass, Harl R., and others, *The High School Curriculum,* Revised. New York: The Ronald Press Company, 1956, Chapter 6, "The Curriculum and American Changing Life."

Golob, Eugene O., *The "Isms."* New York: Harper and Brothers, 1954.

Hacker, Louis M., and B. B. Kendrick, *The United States Since 1865.* New York: Appleton-Century-Crofts, Inc., 1949.

Hollingshead, A. B., *Elmstown Youth.* New York: John Wiley and Sons, Inc., 1949.

Huxley, Julian, *Man in the Modern World.* New York: Mentor Books, 1948.

Lundberg, George A., and others, *Sociology.* New York: Harper and Brothers, 1954, Chapter 18, "Social Change."

Malinowski, Bronislaw, *The Dynamics of Cultural Change.* New Haven: Yale University Press, 1952.

Ogburn, W. F., *Social Change.* New York: The Viking Press, 1950.

Ogburn, W. F., and others, *Technology and International Relations.* Chicago: University of Chicago Press, 1949.

Rugg, Harold, and William Withers, *Social Foundations of Education.* Englewood Cliffs, N. J.: Prentice-Hall, Inc., 1955, Part V, "Social and Psychological Problems in Changing America."

Stanley, W. O., *Education and Social Integration.* New York: Columbia University Press, 1953.

Stewart, George R., *American Ways of Life.* New York: Doubleday & Company, Inc., 1954.

The American Youth Commission, *Youth and the Future.* Washington, D. C.: American Council on Education, 1940.

Thompson, Warren S., *Population Problems,* Revised. New York: McGraw-Hill Book Company, Inc., 1953.

Vogt, William, *The Road to Survival.* New York: William Sloan Associates, 1948.

Washburn, C. W., *Schools Aren't What They Were.* London: William Heinemann, Ltd., 1953.

Williams, R. M., *American Society.* New York: Alfred A. Knopf, Inc., 1951.

Chapter 2

The Core Curriculum Emerges

From early colonial days the school curriculum has been a source of general interest. Until rather recently, discussion of the curriculum has been focused principally upon the question of what subjects, and how much of each, should be offered in the school program.

Curriculum change has been a major concern of both laymen and educators. Since most of our citizens of this generation have attended both the elementary and secondary schools, and have notions as to what the schools should teach, it has become something of a popular pastime for the public to criticize the school's instructional program. This form of criticism is one of the interesting phenomena of American life. An interest in the school as one of the vital agencies of our democratic society, and constructive criticism of this and other institutions of our democracy are healthy indications that democracy is at work. However, among the severest critics of the school curriculum have been the educators themselves.

31

What's Wrong with the Curriculum?

Possibly at no time in our history has the traditional school curriculum been under more intense and wide-spread criticism than now. Since the First World War not only have specific subject offerings been criticized, but also the validity of the basic concepts and structure of the time-honored curriculum has been increasingly challenged, particularly by educators. Some of the major points of dissatisfaction with the school program that the core curriculum seeks to overcome are given below.

1. There is too much emphasis on subject matter, without much relationship to the pupil's real needs, interests, or abilities. Furthermore, there is so much dependence on textbooks as the source of subject matter that only the verbally skillful pupil can succeed, and even he may achieve merely a superficial comparative success, without the engagement of any of his real interests or drives. We are still more concerned about what the boy does to the algebra problem than what the algebra problem does to the boy.

2. The conventional curriculum takes too little account of real life. The challenging economic and social issues that confront citizens daily are not sufficiently reflected in the classroom. The world about us is full of exciting useful things to study, but we set our classroom windows high enough to shut out the world and spend our time in verbal exercises.

3. The traditional school curriculum is completely inadequate to meet the needs of boys and girls who must live in a world changing as rapidly and as profoundly as is true today. The old argument that we can learn from the past how to solve the problems of the present and future has validity only in a static world. A dynamic society such as ours must have a school curriculum ever-changing and socially sensitive to meet our present and future educational needs.

4. The traditional school program is too departmentalized. Little or no relationship between subjects is established in the

pupil's thinking. He is led too often from one class to another, from one teacher to another, and therefore he has neither time nor opportunity to develop a true home-room feeling anywhere. Even in the elementary school, the pupil's day is broken up into unrelated segments such as spelling, arithmetic, and writing.

5. The classroom experiences are planned and conducted without sufficient regard for what we now know about the learning process. Much educational practice is in direct contradiction to the facts revealed by research in child growth and development.[1]

6. The pupils themselves receive little or no experience in assuming responsibilities or in making choices. The instructional procedure is decided for them by the teacher, or by the textbook or course of study. They are told what to study, when to study, how to study, and whether or not they have improved through study.

7. The class periods are often too short for extended activities that vitalize learning. For example, the day is too segmented to encourage teachers to use field trips, moving pictures, plays, or construction activities.

8. The traditional school offers little real opportunity for guidance: teachers and pupils do not become well enough acquainted. Effective guidance demands a continuous, warm, pupil-teacher relationship, which is not provided in the departmentalized school. Of even greater significance, the traditional subject-centered school has not contemplated guidance as an essential part of the curriculum or of the school's responsibility.[2]

The trend toward the core curriculum in American schools arises in general from efforts to improve these eight conditions of the traditional school curriculum. Little space in this book will be devoted to the supporting evidence for these criticisms. That evidence has already been presented by many other writers in the

---

[1] See Chapter 5 for a discussion of the nature of learning in relation to the core curriculum.

[2] Chapter 8 treats of the way in which guidance becomes an integral part of the core curriculum.

field of education.[3] This book will deal rather with the core curriculum, as one of the significant efforts currently being made to overcome these conditions.

WHAT EFFORTS ARE BEING MADE TO CORRECT THESE DIFFICULTIES?

The reader of this book is familiar with the picture of the traditional subject curriculum of the elementary and the secondary school. Reading, writing, spelling, and arithmetic form the bases of the elementary school curriculum, each subject assigned a definite period on the day's recitation schedule. Likewise, English, a science, algebra or geometry, and a history, usually make up the "musts" or "required" subjects of the high school curriculum, with Latin or French, bookkeeping, typing, home economics, among other subjects, constituting the "elective" privileges of the student. Each subject is assigned a definite period on the daily program, and unlike the conventional type of elementary school where each teacher teaches all subjects, each high school subject is taught by a teacher who is a specialist in that particular subject.

The criticisms of the traditional school program previously mentioned have led many to consider changes more in harmony with the newer developments in educational thinking. The National Commission on the Reorganization of Secondary Education, for example, published a report in 1918 that contained the following paragraph:

---

[3] See for example J. Paul Leonard, *Developing the Secondary School Curriculum,* Revised. New York: Rinehart and Company, Inc., 1953, Chapters 1-4; J. Galen Saylor and William M. Alexander, *Curriculum Planning.* New York: Rinehart and Company, Inc., 1954, Parts 1-2; Harold Alberty, *Reorganizing the High School Curriculum,* Revised. New York: The Macmillan Company, 1953, Chapters 1-4; Harold Rugg and William Withers, *Social Foundations of Education,* Englewood Cliffs, N. J.: Prentice-Hall, Inc., 1955, Parts 2 and 3; National Society for the Study of Education, *Adapting the Secondary School Program to the Needs of Youth,* Fifty-second Yearbook, 1953. Chicago: University of Chicago Press, 1953, Part I; Association for Supervision and Curriculum Development, *What Shall the High Schools Teach?* 1956 Yearbook. Washington, D. C.: The National Education Association, 1956.

Secondary education should be determined by the needs of the society to be served, the character of the individuals to be educated, and the knowledge of educational theory and practice available. These factors are by no means static. Society is always in process of development; the character of the secondary school population undergoes modification; and the sciences upon which educational theory and practices depend constantly furnish new information. Secondary education, however, like any other established agency of society, is conservative and tends to resist modification. Failure to make adjustments when the need arises leads to the necessity for extensive reorganization at irregular intervals. The evidence is strong that such a comprehensive reorganization is imperative at the present time.[4]

This statement is noteworthy for its early recognition of the changing responsibility of secondary education, and for its reference to the slow tempo at which secondary schools usually change to meet new conditions and challenges. The *Cardinal Principles* report from which the paragraph was quoted went on to propose seven basic objectives to which all high school subjects should contribute if they were to be retained. The now famous seven objectives proposed were health, command of the fundamental processes, worthy home membership, vocation, civic education, worthy use of leisure, and ethical character.[5]

How Did the Schools Initiate Curriculum Changes?

In response to the challenges of its new function, the secondary school has gradually broadened its program of subject offerings, especially since 1920. It has added music and dramatics, practical arts, and vocational subjects such as agriculture, homemaking, and commercial courses. It has made at least an initial concession to the problems of civic education in such courses as problems of

---

[4] Commission on the Reorganization of Secondary Education, *Cardinal Principles of Secondary Education*, Bulletin No. 35. Washington, D. C.: Bureau of Education, 1918, p. 7.

[5] This statement of objectives was later officially accepted as the objectives of the elementary division of our schools. Hence, these objectives should be considered the objectives accepted in the early 'twenties for both elementary and secondary education.

democracy, citizenship, and consumer science. The secondary school has also evidenced some recognition of the personal-social interests and problems of youth by its considerable extension of extracurricular activities—athletics, social activities, music, dramatics, debate, and hobby-interest organizations. Pupil participation has made some inroads in this extracurricular area, in the form of an at least nominal student council. An expanded physical education program has been developed in response to pressures arising from our two national experiences with the selective military draft.

Most of these changes were initiated in our secondary schools during the first three decades of this century. By 1930 the typical American high school had introduced some, if not all of the above modifications of its elective program of studies and of its extracurricular offerings. Yet the depression years offered much convincing evidence that such changes were not enough. Young people were dropping out of high school in alarming numbers. Without the lure of employment to explain the phenomenon, it was difficult for high school educators to dismiss lightly the fact that over half of those who enrolled in school in the kindergarten had dropped out before the end of the twelfth grade.[6] Roving bands of unemployed and uprooted youth alarmed the nation. The organization of the National Youth Administration and the Civilian Conservation Corps to serve youth of high school age was evidence to many educators of the basic failure of the secondary school to meet the needs of youth.

Meanwhile, the better elementary schools had been experimenting for many years with methods that went far beyond the addition of new courses described above. Among these basic changes in elementary school teaching might be mentioned the project method, which involved the learning-by-doing concept, and the problem method, which emphasized the educative value of actual problem-solving in the classroom, as opposed to rote

---

[6] *The Improvement of Public Education in Michigan.* Lansing, Michigan: Michigan Public Education Study Commission, 1944, page 13. For additional data covering this period see *Biennial Survey of Education in the United States* from 1930 to 1950.

learning of answers. Elementary schools had also passed through the "activity" movement in which child activity was emphasized as a major form of education, and many of them had reached the stage of philosophy now known as the "experience curriculum." Under this concept, activities are regarded as educative when they (1) stem from real purposes in the learner, (2) are geared to his present problems and interests, (3) derive their sequence from the learner's normal growth and development, and (4) are interpreted, analyzed, or intellectualized as an aid to the possible redirection of the learner's purposes.[7] Thus the better elementary schools were deriving the learning experiences from actual planning by pupils and teachers, and organizing these activities into a sequence of experience-centered, lifelike units in contrast to the use of textbooks and courses of study as the determining factors in planning the curriculum. In the experience curriculum, most of the learning activities grew out of the group's study of some actual problem or area of interest that was real to the pupils. They were learning to read and write and figure through this unit study. They were also learning to plan together, to evaluate their experiences, and to get along increasingly well with their peers. They were learning to seek information in relation to their problems and to relate the information to their own needs.

It need scarcely be said that this unit approach represented a radically different organization and use of subject matter. Instead of the subject matter being planned in advance, it was arrived at and selected by teacher-pupil planning. Instead of its being an end in itself, subject matter became a means to the solution of a problem or to the gratification of a need. Instead of having the curriculum organized by subjects, it was built up around units of life experience.

---

[7] For a better understanding of the way in which the newer educational ideas were fermenting in the elementary schools, particularly in the early decades of this century, read: *The Dewey School* by K. C. Mayhew and A. C. Edwards, 1936; *The Activity School* by G. G. Schoenchen, 1940; *The Activity Concept* by Lois Mossman, 1938; *The Activity Movement*, Part II, Thirty-third Yearbook, National Society for the Study of Education, 1934.

These developments in the elementary schools represented a distinct departure from typical secondary school teaching in 1930. A sharp cleavage developed between the philosophy and procedures in the elementary and secondary schools. The success of the elementary schools with the experience curriculum and the unit method presented a new challenge to progressive educators in the secondary schools.

basic studies undertaken

Under these conditions it is not surprising that a keen interest developed during the 'thirties in a basic study of the purposes and program of the secondary school. This interest resulted in the organization of a number of carefully planned regional and national studies. In 1932, the Progressive Education Association Commission on the Relation of School and College launched an eight-year experimental study involving thirty member schools, which were freed from the conventional patterns of college preparation by a signed agreement with the colleges. These schools were given encouragement and assistance in reorganizing their programs, modifying subject content and curriculum structures, and introducing new types of pupil experience.

The various reports of the Eight Year Study constituted a milestone in professional writings on the secondary school and made one of the most significant contributions toward the improvement of secondary education to date.[8]

In 1933 the Cooperative Study of Secondary School Standards was initiated under the auspices of the National Association of Officers of Regional Associations. This study resulted in the development of the well-known Evaluative Criteria, and the widespread application of this instrument since 1940 to the evaluation of the effectiveness of secondary schools throughout the

---

[8] Wilford M. Aikin, *The Story of the Eight Year Study.* New York: Harper and Brothers, 1942; H. H. Giles, S. P. McCutchen, and A. N. Zechiel, *Exploring the Curriculum.* New York: Harper and Brothers, 1942; E. R. Smith, and others, *Appraising and Recording Student Progress.* New York: Harper and Brothers, 1942; *Thirty Schools Tell Their Story.* New York: The Progressive Education Association, 1942; Dean Chamberlin, and others, *Did They Succeed in College?* New York: Harper and Brothers, 1942.

nation.[9] The recent revision of the Policies and Criteria of the North Central Association is one of the many results of the Cooperative Study.

In the fall of 1935 the Board of Regents for the state of New York began a comprehensive two-year inquiry, of which one major division was secondary education, into the character and cost of public education in that state. The report of the Regents' inquiry, published in 1938, contained an appraisal of the current program and recommendations of practical steps by which the State Department of Education might improve the work of the secondary schools.[10]

The state of California launched a five-year study in 1935 in which ten member schools were encouraged and assisted in the redefinition of activities and experiences.[11]

The American Youth Commission was created in 1935 by the American Council on Education for the purpose of conducting a five-year study of the care and education of American youth. Their published report sheds valuable light upon the problems and needs of youth of high school age, and highlights the current ineffectiveness of the secondary school.[12]

Other studies of secondary education launched during the 1930's were the United States Office of Education Committee on Youth Problems (1934), the Southern Association Commission on Curricular Studies and Research (1935), the plan for Curriculum Reorganization in Secondary Schools of Ohio (1938), the National Association of Secondary School Principals Study of the Adjustment of Secondary Youth to Post-School Occupational Life (1939), the Florida Program for the Improvement of Schools

---

[9] *Evaluative Criteria.* Washington: The Cooperative Study of Secondary School Standards, Revised, 1950. See also *How to Evaluate a Secondary School.* Washington: The Cooperative Study of Secondary School Standards, 1939.

[10] Francis T. Spaulding, *High School and Life,* The New York Regents Inquiry. New York: McGraw-Hill Book Co., 1938.

[11] Information about the California Study is contained in the California State Department of Education Bulletin, *Programs of the Cooperative Secondary Schools in California,* Bulletin 3. Sacramento, California: The Department of Education, 1939.

[12] Howard M. Bell, *Youth Tell Their Story.* Washington, D. C.: The American Youth Commission, American Council on Education, 1938.

(1938), the Michigan Study of the Secondary School Curriculum (1938), and several state surveys of secondary education that were launched in the late 1930's. This decade saw also the organization of the Educational Policies Commission, whose reports have had a profound effect upon reorganization trends in secondary schools.[13]

How Have Colleges Influenced Curriculum Change?

The thirty schools of the Eight-Year Study began their investigation of how to meet the needs of their students, fortified by a contractual agreement with the three hundred colleges and universities that their graduates entered. During a five-year period, this agreement permitted the more able, recommended students to enter college without presenting the usual sequences of required subjects.

Such an agreement was considered an important psychological aid to curriculum development. As long as schools had to make provision for certain required subjects in patterns established by the colleges, it was difficult to prevent this college preparatory function from establishing the school's total curriculum. Although only about 14 per cent of the high school graduates entered college at that time, a great many more enrolled in the college preparatory program. Indeed, in the smaller schools there was no other program available to students.

Many teachers and administrators in the high schools had difficulty thinking objectively about the total program of the school as long as they could shift to the colleges the blame for the teaching methods and subject requirements of the secondary school. Under the new agreement, a genuine stimulus toward evaluation and planning resulted.

In spite of its obvious advantages, the agreement was regarded with some suspicion and fear, even by many high school teachers.

---

[13] Especially, *The Purposes of Education in American Democracy,* 1938; and *Education for All American Youth,* Revised, 1952. Washington, D. C.: The Educational Policies Commission, National Education Association.

The assumption still persisted that college success must be based on certain tried and true patterns of high school preparatory subjects. Accordingly, the Commission on the Relation of School and College of the Progressive Education Association set out to discover whether the graduates of these thirty schools succeeded in college as well as those who entered with the conventional entrance requirements. An intensive study was made of 1,475 matched pairs of graduates, one of each pair from an experimental and one from a conventional high school. Careful analysis of the study revealed that the graduates of the thirty experimental schools did somewhat better than their comparison group, whether judged by college standards, by fellow-students, or by the subjects themselves. A special study of the graduates of the six most experimental schools revealed a marked superiority over the students with whom they were paired in grade point averages, achievement ratings, academic honors, intellectual curiosity, scientific thinking, and in all qualities of good citizenship. In the words of the investigators, the study revealed that "the more experimental the school, the greater degree of success in college." [14]

One highly significant outcome of this investigation was its validation of the belief that there is no one pattern of subject preparation for college which is superior to any other pattern. On this point the report of the study was most emphatic:

If the proof of the pudding lies in these groups, and a good part of it does, then it follows that the colleges got from these most experimental schools a higher proportion of sound, effective college material than they did from the more conventional schools in similar environments. If colleges want students of sound scholarship with vital interests, students who have developed effective and objective habits of thinking, and who yet maintain a healthy orientation toward their fellows, then they will encourage the already obvious trend away from restrictions which tend to inhibit departures or deviations from the conventional curriculum patterns. [15]

---

[14] Dean Chamberlin, and others, *Did They Succeed in College?* p. 209.
[15] Chamberlin, *Did They Succeed in College?* pp. 174-175.

On the foundation of this confirmation many curriculum improvements, including the core curriculum, have been erected since 1940.

The Michigan Secondary School Curriculum Study began its work with fifty-five member schools in 1938, protected by an agreement similar to that obtaining in the Eight Year Study. The agreement stated, in short, that graduates of the fifty-five member schools were to be admitted to Michigan colleges and universities during the period 1940-50 in accordance with the regular admission standards of the colleges, but without reference to the pattern of subjects they had pursued. The agreement further provided that these candidates were to be recommended by the schools from among the more able members of the graduating classes.

The Michigan Study Agreement provided protection and stimulation for a rather widespread program of curricular experiments during the period 1940-50. One of the most widely applied among the innovations developed in the member schools was the core curriculum. As the Study drew toward its end, a new College-Secondary School Agreement was drafted and extended to all accredited high schools in Michigan. This new agreement differed in certain significant ways from those of the Eight Year Study and the Michigan Secondary School Curriculum Study. It was worded as follows:

> The college agrees to disregard the pattern of subjects pursued in considering for admission graduates of selected accredited high schools, provided they are recommended by the school from among the more able students in the graduating class.

WHAT CURRICULUM PATTERNS HAVE EVOLVED?

Within recent years we have witnessed many efforts to modify the older pattern of the curriculum. Several patterns have appeared within the framework of the subject curriculum. At least three of these can be identified.

1. *correlation*

As might be expected the first cautious attempts to modify the rigid and highly isolated pattern of the subject curriculum were an effort to maintain the separateness of one subject from other subjects but to show some interrelation between certain subjects. For example, a teacher of United States history whose class was studying early New England colonization might arrange with the geography teacher who had in her class many or most of the pupils also in the history class to study the geography of the New England and the Atlantic seaboard areas. Or, the teacher of literature who had in her class many of the pupils from the history class would direct the reading of her group to such works as *Evangeline, Leatherstocking Tales,* and similar literary accounts of life in this pioneer period.[16]

2. *fusion*

Many educators were dissatisfied with the cautious and not too effective attempts at correlation. It was difficult to get subject matter specialists to plan and work together; and at best there was still rigidity in the lines of demarcating subjects. Fusion represents a more radical effort to interrelate subjects. It is an attempt to merge two or three subjects by combining the content of these subjects into one. Instead of attempting to correlate United States history and geography these would be combined into one subject with blocks of subject matter from each course placed in juxtaposition where the natural relationship between the blocks of subject matter became obvious.

With the coming of a better understanding of the learning process, a more complete fusion of the content of two or more subjects was attempted, centered around the use of problems as the unifying or fusing agent. A teacher of science decided that the best understanding of the principles involved in high school

---

[16] For early attempts to develop correlation with English as the base, see Ruth M. Weeks, editor, *A Correlated Curriculum,* Report of the National Council of Teachers of English. New York: Appleton-Century-Crofts, 1936.

courses in chemistry and physics could be more completely achieved through a fusion course made up of problems illustrative of the principles in both subjects. He realized, as modern educators do, that many vital problem situations in life which would involve principles of physics would also involve some principles of chemistry, and most likely principles from other sciences as well. The following problems suggest the approach of this combined physics-chemistry course: "What's wrong with this photograph?" "What should one look for in buying an automobile?" "How can comfort be increased by air conditioning?"

3. *broad fields*

This is generally considered an expanded form of the idea of fusion. When we pass beyond the attempt to bring together the content of two or three subjects into one unified course, and recombine many subjects into one broad course, this is known as the *broad fields* approach. This approach is still based upon the concept of subjects composing the school curriculum, but in an enlarged pattern of subject content grouping. An example of the *broad fields* approach may be given in the attempt that was made to combine the subjects of science into two broad areas. The first area brought together the content of physics, chemistry, geology, astronomy, and physical geography and this area was called the Natural Science course. Another area called the Life Science course combined the content of courses in zoology, botany, biology, and physiology.

There are many examples of attempts to develop *broad fields* curriculum patterns. One of the earliest of these was suggested by the Curriculum Committee of the North Central Association of Colleges and Secondary Schools. Four fields of living were suggested as areas into which the usual subjects of curriculum could be organized.[17]

---

[17] Lewis W. Webb, and others, *High School Curriculum Reorganization*. Ann Arbor: North Central Association of Colleges and Secondary Schools, 1933; Lewis W. Webb, "Ten Years of Curriculum Planning by the North Central Association," *Curriculum Journal*, 8:23-238, October 1937.

(1) Health and physical fitness
(2) Leisure time
(3) Vocational activities
(4) Social relationships

A second pattern of the broad fields approach more typical of those generally attempted is:

(1) Language arts
(2) Social studies
(3) Science and mathematics
(4) Health and physical education
(5) Fine arts and music

Another type of the broad fields approach that paved the way for the core curriculum in many secondary schools has been known as the "unified studies" course. In such a program, these broad subject areas were fused together into a more or less integrated approach, with a longer time provision than the conventional single period, and with either the single master teacher trained in these areas or a committee of subject specialists working in close cooperation. The most common combination for this purpose was that of English and social studies, but experiments were also undertaken in the unification of mathematics and science, home economics and shop, and many others. Many schools have undertaken the unified studies plan as the initial step away from a subject curriculum in the direction of the core curriculum.[18]

---

[18] For a more comprehensive discussion of the problems of correlation, fusion, and the broad fields approaches to curriculum organization, see L. T. Hopkins, and others, *Integration—Its Meaning and Application*. New York: Appleton-Century-Crofts, 1937, pp. 197-301; J. Minor Gwynn, *Curriculum Principles and Social Trends,* Revised. New York: The Macmillan Company, 1950, pp. 430-435; American Association of School Administrators, *American School Curriculum,* Thirty-first Yearbook. Washington, D. C.: The National Education Association, 1953, Chapter 3; J. Galen Saylor and William M. Alexander, *Curriculum Planning.* New York: Rinehart and Company, Inc., 1954, Chapters 8-9; Vernon E. Anderson, *Principles and Procedures of Curriculum Improvement.* New York: The Ronald Press Company, 1956, Chapter 12.

SELECTED REFERENCES

Aikin, Wilford M., *The Story of the Eight Year Study*. New York: Harper and Brothers, 1942, Chapters I and VI.

Alberty, Harold, *Reorganizing the High School Curriculum*, Revised. New York: The Macmillan Company, 1953, Chapters V and VI.

Alexander, William, and J. Galen Saylor, *Secondary Education*. New York: Rinehart and Company, 1950, Chapter III.

American Association of School Administrators, *American School Curriculum*, Thirty-first Yearbook. Washington, D. C.: The National Education Association, 1953, Chapter III.

Anderson, Vernon E., *Principles and Procedures of Curriculum Improvement*. New York: The Ronald Press Company, 1956, Chapters XII-XIII.

Benedict, Agnes, *Dare Our Secondary Schools Face the Atomic Age?* New York: Hinds, Hayden, and Eldridge, 1947.

Bossing, Nelson L., *Principles of Secondary Education*, Second Edition. Englewood Cliffs, N. J.: Prentice-Hall, Inc., 1955, Chapter XII.

Corey, Stephen, and others, *General Education in the American High School*. Chicago: Scott, Foresman and Company, 1942, Chapter III.

Douglass, Harl R., Editor, *The High School Curriculum*, Revised. New York: The Ronald Press, 1956, Chapter XII.

Dressel, Paul L., and Lewis B. Mayhew, *General Education: Explorations in Evaluation*. Washington: American Council on Education, 1954.

Gwynn, J. Minor, *Curriculum Principles and Social Trends*, Revised. New York: The Macmillan Company, 1950, Chapter XIII.

Krug, Edward A., *Curriculum Planning*. New York: Harper and Brothers, 1957, Chapter IV.

Leonard, J. Paul, *Developing the Secondary School Curriculum*, Revised. New York: Rinehart and Company, 1953, Chapters XI and XIII.

Lurry, Lucile L., and Elsie J. Alberty, *Developing a High School Core Program*. New York: The Macmillan Company, 1957.

Mossman, Lois C., *The Activity Concept*. New York: The Macmillan Company, 1938.

National Society for the Study of Education, *The Activity Movement.* Bloomington, Ind.: The Public School Publishing Company, 1934, Part II.

———, *General Education,* The Fifty-first Yearbook. Chicago: The University of Chicago Press, 1952, Part I.

Pierce, Paul, *Developing a High School Curriculum.* New York: The American Book Company, 1950, Chapter III.

Rice, T. D., and R. C. Faunce, *The Michigan Secondary Study.* Lansing, Michigan: The State Department of Public Instruction, 1945.

Romine, Stephen A., *Building the High School Curriculum.* New York: The Ronald Press Company, 1954, Chapters II-III.

Schoenchen, Gustav G., *The Activity School.* New York: Longmans, Green and Company, 1940.

Spears, Harold, *The High School For Today.* New York: The American Book Company, 1950, Chapter III.

Waskin, Leon S., "The Michigan Secondary School-College Agreement," *Bulletin,* National Association of Secondary School Principals, January 1949, pp. 49-64.

Wright, Grace S., *Core Curriculum Development Problems and Practices,* Bulletin 1952, No. 5. Washington, D. C.: U. S. Office of Education.

Chapter 3

The Core Curriculum Defined

Three major types of curriculum patterns that have been developed since approximately 1925 were described in the previous chapter, in an effort to bring the organization of the subject curriculum into greater conformity with the changing conceptions of learning and of the curriculum.

The more radical innovations of the *fusion* and *broad fields* attempts at curriculum reorganization did, to a limited degree, meet some of the requirements of developing thought concerning the nature of learning and of the curriculum. The use of the problem as a basis of interrelating the subject-matter content from two or more subjects in part met the problem-solving requirements of the modern conception of learning. There was a definite breaking down of the sharper lines of subject departmentalization, and a hesitating approach to real-life interests where the problems concerned meaningful life situations. Too, there has been a tendency in the *fusion* and *broad fields* approaches to utilize a two-period block of time, thus permitting a better acquaintance of student with student and teacher with student.

The serious limitations of these efforts at curriculum adjustment to meet the criticisms of the traditional school program have been all too obvious. The curriculum still remained subject-dominated, with the emphasis upon the coverage of specific quantities of subject matter without due regard to the pupils' interest and understanding. A high degree of inflexibility in the curriculum has persisted with a prescribed content dictated by the teacher or subject specialists in the form of textbooks and courses of study. Possibilities for genuine, cooperative teacher-pupil planning do not fit well into this form of curriculum organization. With the primary emphasis upon the mastery of subject matter as the *summum bonum* of education, guidance was not regarded as having a real function in the school or the classroom.

Two major developments in educational thinking within the past three decades, particularly, have done much to give form to the *core* idea. The first of these has been the growing emphasis upon what has become known as *general education*. There appears to be quite general agreement among educators that the term *general education* refers to that part of the educational program designed to meet the needs of all pupils, in contradistinction to the education provided to meet each pupil's special needs.

On the other hand, there has been a wide divergence of judgment as to what the nature and pattern of this *general education* should be. Many writers hold to the point of view that *general education* should represent a definite pattern of subjects required of all pupils. Others would accept a minimal-essentials body of subject matter content presented in some pattern of possible broad fields organization, while still others would accept a common body of type-problem-learning experiences to which all pupils should be exposed as the meaning and form of *general education*. This latter concept of general education has conformed most closely to the modern *core* idea.

Beginning about 1935, programs of general education in varied forms were experimentally undertaken in many schools through-out the nation. Programs were developed in laboratory schools such as the West Virginia University Demonstration School, the

Ohio State University School, the University of Minnesota School, the University of Chicago High School, Lincoln School of Teachers College, Columbia University, and the P. K. Yonge Laboratory School of the University of Florida. The various versions of the core curriculum were also increasingly to be found in large and small high schools across the nation, beginning about 1935. Among the better known programs were those at Wells High School, Chicago, Illinois; the high schools of Denver, Colorado; the New School at Evanston Township High School, Illinois; the Central and Daniel Webster High Schools of Tulsa, Oklahoma; the New Trier Township High School of Winnetka, Illinois; the Long Beach, California, high schools; the junior high schools of Los Angeles, California; the McKinley High School of Honolulu, Hawaii; and the Theodore Roosevelt High School of Des Moines, Iowa.

Within recent years a completely different conception of the curriculum has been coming into general acceptance by educational leaders. Instead of thinking of the curriculum as consisting of the subjects taught in the school, educational leaders now conceive of the curriculum as composed of the learning experiences which children have in the school. One of the most generally accepted definitions of the experience curriculum is stated as follows: *The curriculum consists of all the experiences the learner has under the direction of the school.*[1] In order to emphasize the full significance of the difference between the traditional and the new conceptions of the curriculum, others have defined the curriculum as consisting of all the experiences which the learner has, irrespective of their character or when or where these experiences take place.[2] A still more recent definition of the curriculum emphasizes the centrality of the experience nature of

---

[1] See Hollis L. Caswell and Doak S. Campbell, *Curriculum Development.* New York: American Book Company, 1935, p. 69; Edward A. Krug, *Curriculum Planning.* New York: Harper and Brothers, 1950, p. 4; William R. Ragan, *Modern Elementary Curriculum.* New York: The Dryden Press, Inc., 1953, p. 3.

[2] See L. Thomas Hopkins, *Interaction: The Democratic Process.* Boston: D. C. Heath and Company, 1941, p. 30.

the curriculum but calls attention also to the total environmental matrix in which pupil experiences take place:

In this book the curriculum is defined in terms of the quality of pupil experiences. It is conceived of as the whole of the interacting forces of the total environment provided for pupils by the school and the pupil's experiences in that environment.[3]

Considerable attention is here given to the experience curriculum concept because it represents a fundamental break with the traditional subject matter conception of the curriculum, and because the experience curriculum is considered basic to our interpretation of the core curriculum. Following the definition of the curriculum given above, Anderson makes this trenchant observation with respect to the nature of the curriculum and its radical differentiation from the subject curriculum concept:

To guide these experiences, the school must furnish a fertile learning environment; the teachers, the pupils, other adults in the school, the physical plant, the equipment, the learning materials, the course content, and the procedures used are all important factors interacting in the total environment. Changing the curriculum, then, involves changing these interacting forces. . . . If we accept the modern concept of curriculum, we must be willing to pay the consequences. Perhaps the price is too great, for when curriculum change is considered from this point of view, a great deal more is at stake than if we think of curriculum change as involving a change on paper. It means changing ourselves, our relations with others, our values and our ways of working: the most important factors in the total environment of the pupil.[4]

After pointing out the subject versus the experience extremes of curriculum concepts, Beauchamp summarizes his discussion in these words, "In this chapter it has been pointed out that there are two basic and opposed curriculum types, each with different

---

[3] Vernon E. Anderson, *Principles and Procedures of Curriculum Improvement.* New York: The Ronald Press Company, 1956, p. 9. See also Harold G. Shane and E. T. McSwain, *Evaluation and the Elementary Curriculum.* New York: Henry Holt and Company, Inc., 1951, p. 128.

[4] Anderson, *Principles and Procedures of Curriculum Improvement,* pp. 9, 10, and 12.

assumptions and different characteristics." [5] Krug maintains this same point of view in these words:

The course of study offering may be organized primarily either in terms of the logical patterns of human knowledge or in terms of some conception of the needs and problems of children and youth and of society. . . . But the organization of the course of study must choose one basic underlying principle or the other. It is a rare instance of an either-or proposition.[6]

Pioneers in the use of the experience curriculum were fully aware of the fundamental differences underlying the conceptions of the experience versus the subject curriculum. Whereas the traditional curriculum, conceived of as consisting of subject-matter, was organized on the basis of patterns or a collection of subjects so familiar to all, the experience curriculum concept necessitates a new basis of organization. Since learning experiences are possible only in the milieu or matrix of life activities, the experience curriculum is organized around some form of broad areas of life activities.

An early example of this form of curriculum development, the fundamental basis of which has been generally followed with some modifications, was that of the Mississippi state curriculum reorganization plan adopted in 1939. Instead of a pattern of subjects Mississippi considered the basis of the experience curriculum to involve the totality of life's activities which it labelled the "Major Areas of Human Activities." These areas of human activities it was thought could be grouped into nine divisions as follows:

1. Protecting life and health
2. Making a home
3. Conserving and improving material conditions
4. Cooperating in social and civic action
5. Getting a living
6. Securing an education
7. Expressing religious impulses

---

[5] George A. Beauchamp, *Planning the Elementary School Curriculum*. New York: Allyn and Bacon, Inc., 1956, p. 37.

[6] Krug, *Curriculum Planning*, pp. 85-86.

8. Expressing esthetic impulses
9. Engaging in recreation[7]

No two school systems or curriculum writers have classified the areas of human activities identically. These area groupings have varied from the low of three listed under what Stratemeyer calls Persistent Life Situations to sixteen broad social functions which make up the scope of the curriculum as used by the Long Beach, California schools.[8]

However, the basic relationships of the area groupings thus far proposed are obvious upon comparison of the several lists. This is as should be expected particularly at a pioneering stage in the development of a radically new curriculum idea.

What Is Core?

There have been some interesting patterns of organization of the experience curriculum by those who have tried to innovate the core curriculum concept. However, there has been a general unanimity evident in these organizational schemes that give recognition to two broadly differentiated types of personal-social competencies of citizens needed within our society. First, those general competencies which all must have in order to live most effectively within our democratic way of life; and second, those specialized and varied types of competencies necessitated by a highly complex social structure, which a flexible curriculum should provide for in terms of the special interests and aptitudes of individuals.

---

[7] *Mississippi Program for the Improvement of Instruction: Curriculum Reorganization in Secondary Schools, Grades 7-12,* Bulletin No. 7. Jackson, Mississippi: State Department of Education, 1939, p. 28. An extended discussion of the list used by Mississippi is to be found in O. I. Frederick and Lucille Farquear, "Areas of Human Activity," *Journal of Educational Research,* 30:672-79, May 1937. Among the earlier efforts to develop a basis for the organization of the experience curriculum the reader will find it of interest to study the programs developed by the Virginia State Department of Education in 1934, the Santa Barbara, California, schools in 1940, the Wells High School in Chicago, 1942, among others recorded in the literature on education.

[8] Florence B. Stratemeyer, and others, *Developing a Curriculum for Modern Living.* New York: Bureau of Publications, Teachers College, Columbia University, Revised, 1957, pp. 149-150. See Long Beach Public Schools, Office of Curriculum Development, for descriptive material published in December, 1954.

The organization of the experience curriculum into two major divisions to care for the general and the special needs of the learner, though radically different in concept and plan, parallels roughly the patterns of "required" and "elective" divisions of the traditional subject curriculum. It is a recognition that society needs citizens with both common and differentiated competencies and that the school must provide for these in its educational plan.

what is the meaning of core?

This organization of the experience curriculum to provide for the common and special needs of youth provides the basis for our present conception of core. *In modern education the term core has come to be applied to that part of the experience curriculum which is concerned with those types of experiences thought necessary for all learners in order to develop certain behavior competencies considered necessary for effective living in our democratic society.*

Caswell, who pioneered in attempting to set up a modified form of the core curriculum in Virginia, defines core as:

A continuous, carefully planned series of experiences which are based on significant personal and social problems and which involve learnings of common concern to all youth.[9]

Pierce, who spent many years in the development of the *core* curriculum in a high school of which he was principal, has written a stimulating book that describes the core plan he and his staff developed, and also provides a clear statement of his conception of core, "The core program consists of the activities of living necessary for *all* as worthy members of our social order." [10] As another authority defines it:

---

[9] Hollis L. Caswell, and others, *The American High School,* Eighth Yearbook of the John Dewey Society. New York: Harper and Brothers, 1946, p. 143.

[10] Paul R. Pierce, *Developing a High School Curriculum.* New York: American Book Company, 1942, p. 129.

The "core," then, as we are using the term, refers to that part of the curriculum which takes as its major job the development of personal and social responsibility and competency needed by all youth to serve the needs of a democratic society.[11]

Another definition of core that emphasizes its fundamental nature is that of Anderson:

The core curriculum is a way of organizing some of the important common learnings in the high school curriculum, using a problem-solving approach as its procedure, having social and personal problems significant to youth as its content, and the development of the behaviors needed in a democratic society as its purpose. This represents a fundamental reorganization of the curriculum of the secondary school, rather than just a combination of the traditional subject-matter.[12]

In 1944 the Educational Policies Commission, in *Education for All American Youth,* a book of epoch-making significance for secondary education, popularized the core concept through a curriculum pattern called *common learnings.* The experience conception of learning and of the curriculum were accepted as basic in the plan. Then those experiences which all youth should have in order to become competent citizens are organized into a curriculum pattern the same as core. A few quotations from this book will make clear the similarity of the concepts:[13]

What does this title, "Common Learnings," mean? It means that this course consists of learning experiences which *everyone* needs to have, regardless of what occupation he may expect to follow or where he may happen to live. . . .

"Common Learnings" . . . extends through the three years of high school and the two years of community institute. It meets for two periods daily, in grades ten, eleven, and twelve, and for one period daily in grades thirteen and fourteen. It is required of all students . . .

---

[11] J. Paul Leonard, *Developing the Secondary School Curriculum,* Revised. New York: Rinehart and Company, 1953, pp. 396-397.

[12] Anderson, *Principles and Procedures of Curriculum Improvement,* pp. 316-317.

[13] Educational Policies Commission, *Education For All American Youth.* Washington, D. C.: The National Education Association, 1944, pp. 248-252. See also the 1952 Revised Edition, pp. 237-241; the point of view remains unchanged.

Here is a course designed to provide most of the learning experiences which, it is believed, all young people should have in common in order to live happily and usefully during the years of youth and grow into the full responsibilities of adult life. It is not intended to provide education in vocational skills and knowledge; in mathematics, the sciences, foreign languages, or other subjects required for vocational purposes or for advanced study; or in avocational and intellectual fields which students may elect because of personal interest . . .

Briefly stated, the distinctive purposes of the course in "Common Learnings" are to help all youth grow in six areas:

1. Civic understanding and competence
2. Understanding of the operation of the economic system and of the human relations involved therein
3. Family relationships
4. Intelligent action as consumers
5. Appreciation of beauty
6. Proficiency in the use of language

To these should be added certain other purposes, which are not distinctive of this course alone, but which are looked upon as common aims for every course and teacher in the American city schools. Chief among these are the purposes to help youth grow:

1. In ability to think rationally and in respect for truth arrived at by rational processes
2. In respect for other persons and ability to work cooperatively with others
3. In insight into ethical values and principles
4. In ability to use their time efficiently and to budget it wisely
5. In ability to plan their own affairs, as individuals and as groups, and to carry out their plans efficiently

Prominent writers in the curriculum field appear to be in close agreement on the basic meaning of *core*. It is accepted as a phase of the experience curriculum concept and relates to that part of this curriculum concept that is concerned with the development of those common competencies which it is thought all citizens should have to live successfully within a democratic society.

what is the meaning of "core program"
and "core curriculum"?

There has been a widespread tendency to use the terms *core, core program,* and *core curriculum* interchangeably. Failure to recognize the fundamental nature of core as a pervasive form of organization of the experience type curriculum has led to some ill advised practices in schools professing to use core, and to serious danger of a poorly balanced, fragmentary, and inadequate set of learning experiences for pupils.

Many schools which claim to be using the core idea have in fact nothing but a number of independent groups of pupils and teachers meeting for a two or more hour block of time. Each class is left to determine what it shall study without consultation or group planning between teachers as to what should constitute the common competencies that should be sought, or the extent to which each teacher is contributing to the realization of balanced learning results.

Obviously such a large and vital part of the total curriculum as would be required by the definition of core above could not be left to chance. Continuous and careful planning of all phases of the school activities related to core are essential to insure that all the competencies for which the core is responsible are satisfactorily developed. This over-all planning for core is more important for the success of core than in the case of the subject matter curriculum. *The core program, then, refers to the total organizational activities of that part of the school curriculum devoted to the determination of the personal and social competencies needed by all, and the procedures, materials, and facilities by which the school assures the adequacy of the learning experiences essential to the development of these competencies.*

It is unfortunate that the failure of those who have not understood the real meaning of core and the need for careful coordinated planning of the core curriculum has led to three widespread false impressions: (1) that the core curriculum requires little or no organization and staff coordination; (2) that teachers and pupils in each class follow willy-nilly the impulses of the moment in what they study with little regard for the educational significance of what they do; and (3) that pupils in core classes do not achieve the essential competencies they need.

Another source of grave difficulty associated with the organization of the curriculum on the core basis is the failure to see the wholeness of the core idea in the curriculum. This has arisen in part from the failure to see core as an organizational form of the total experience curriculum. Many school people, and even some curriculum writers who profess to accept the concept of experience learning and the experience curriculum, apply sound learning principles to the core program but beyond that fall back upon a traditional subject curriculum organization for the division of the curriculum devoted to the development of the special competencies.

It is highly important to see the wholeness of the curriculum and to recognize that the learning processes applicable to achieving the core competencies apply equally to the development of the special interest competencies. There cannot be two opposing theories of learning and of the curriculum successfully in operation at the same time. This basic unity in the experience learning and the curriculum concept is recognized in the term *core curriculum* as applied to an organizational form of the experience curriculum. To point up sharply the basic relationship and difference between the "core program" and the "core curriculum" the *core curriculum refers to a pattern of the experience curriculum organized into a closely integrated and interrelated whole, in which one division, the core program, is devoted to the development of the common competencies needed by all, and the other division emphasizes the development of special competencies based upon the recognition of individual differences in interests, aptitudes, and capacities; the entire curriculum utilizing consistently the same basic principles of learning, teaching methods, and problem organization.*[14]

---

[14] For a further discussion of the concept of "core program" and "core curriculum" see Nelson L. Bossing, *Principles of Secondary Education*, Second Edition. Englewood Cliffs, N. J.: Prentice-Hall, Inc., 1955, pp. 401-412. Also by the same author, "What Is Core?" *School Review*, April 1955, pp. 206-213.

what are some characteristics of core?

Several writers have given lists of characteristics of core that reveal the essential nature of the core curriculum idea. These provide an excellent summary statement of significant aspects of the core curriculum. The list presented below by the authors may serve better to summarize the discussion of the preceding pages. These major characteristics are:

1. The core idea is based upon the fundamental psychological principle that learning involves change in behavior brought about through experience. Thus the heart of the curriculum consists of those types of learning experiences most likely to produce desirable behavioral change.

2. The core is organized around the types of problems of personal and social concern common to all youth in our democratic society.

3. The core seeks to draw upon a wide range of informational sources, materials, and appropriate activities necessary to the solution of these vital problems of personal and social concern. Whatever in the total environment will contribute to the solution of these problems is considered "grist for the mill" by the alert, discerning teacher. It involves a complete disregard of existing subject-matter lines or subject-matter emphases.

4. The core emphasizes the utilization of genuine problem-solving procedures and techniques in the solution of personal and social problem situations.

5. The core involves and provides for a wide range of co-operative curriculum planning by teachers. The core-curriculum activities must be seen and planned for as a whole, and by all teachers as a group as well as individually. In the core, teachers do not function as prima donnas within their own pre-empted areas but work as part of a professional team, contributing their general and special skills to the common goal of helping boys and girls develop in maximal degree the competencies needed for successful living.

6. The core involves joint planning by pupils and teachers for the solution of vital problems.

7. The core makes individual and group guidance an integral part of teaching, the core teacher accepting as his basic responsibility many of the major functions now assumed by guidance specialists and counselors in traditionally organized schools with a subject-matter, compartmentalized curriculum. In the core idea, teaching and guidance become largely synonymous terms.

8. The core idea involves a recognition of the over-all organization of the curriculum into two highly integrated and interrelated divisions, namely, (a) the core program devoted to the types of problems common to all youth and the common competencies all must possess to function successfully in our democratic society, and (b) the section of the curriculum devoted to the development of the special concerns of pupils, in which individual interests, aptitudes, and abilities are explored and opportunity is provided for development of the requisite understandings and skills for each. Both divisions of the curriculum are based upon the same principles of learning, teaching methods, and problem organization.

9. Administratively important to the success of the core idea is the provision of large blocks of time in the day's schedule to facilitate the maximum use of problem-solving processes and the use of community resources.

10. Administratively important to the success of the guidance function of the core is the need to provide for longer spans of association between core teachers and pupils in order that teachers may know the pupils better—their environmental backgrounds, their interests, abilities, and learning development. Some schools are experimenting by allowing teachers to remain as advisers to a group for two or more years.[15]

---

[15] Nelson L. Bossing, "What Is Core?" pp. 212-213. Essentially the same list is to be found in Bossing, *Principles of Secondary Education,* Second Edition, pp. 409-410. See a similar list in Leonard, *Developing the Secondary School Curriculum,* Revised, pp. 397-400. Also J. Galen Saylor and William M. Alexander, *Curriculum Planning.* Rinehart and Company, 1954, pp. 310-313. For a statement of what the core is not, see Harold Alberty, "A Sound Core Program," *National Education Association Journal,* 45: 20-22, January 1956.

WHAT ARE THE ADVANTAGES OF CORE?

Some of the advantages claimed for core are based on the educational principles that appear to inhere in the core concept; others evolve partially out of the experiences of those who have experimented with core. While many of these advantages are considered elsewhere in this book, some of the principal ones are briefly enumerated here:

1. The core is in harmony with the best we know about the nature of learning. Learning is recognized as an active process; it involves goal-seeking arising out of the felt needs of the learner, and the experiences that take place in this goal-seeking activity result in the achieving of increased power to overcome other problem situations. The core utilizes the best principles of experience-learning.

2. The core centers around vital problems of personal and social concern to the learner. Such problems are likely to have much more educational significance than subject-matter-to-be-learned, which is often without challenge to him because he does not or cannot see any relevance of these materials to his felt needs. Core unifies the learning experiences of pupils around real problems.

3. The core, with its problem-centered emphasis through experience learning, provides a superior opportunity for pupils to learn such essential social skills as cooperative planning and working together. The natural problems that arise in a group-inspired undertaking require understandable personal-group skills of give and take compromise in devising ways of achieving group goals; the individual must often subject his own immediate desires to that of group decision, accepting cheerfully as his part of a cooperative task that which the group determines as it parcels out necessary tasks for each in the total undertaking.

4. The core makes possible greater attention to the individual differences of children. The core, based on the principle of experience learning, recognizes that no two individuals have had

the same experiential background; therefore each approaches new situations differently in understanding, attitudes, and acquired competencies. The core teacher realizes clearly that each pupil must be regarded individually, and in some measure must be treated differently from others in the class. The natural flexibility characteristic of the core curriculum, plus the tendency to utilize larger blocks of time for core classes, provides greater freedom for the teacher to give real attention to the peculiar needs of each pupil.

5. The use of the multiple period now commonly associated with the core organization, combined with the emphasis upon personal-social problems as basic in the core, provides an excellent opportunity for the teacher to exercise the guidance function now accepted as the central activity of teaching. Whereas the conventional school plan uses single class periods, with each teacher daily having 180 to over 200 pupils in her classes, the multiple period normally limits the daily pupil load of the core teacher to 70 or less. Under these circumstances it is possible for each teacher to know more intimately the pupils in her classes, and their family environmental backgrounds. The teacher thus favored can personalize her work and can carry on the guidance function of teaching more effectively.

6. The lifelike activities and purposeful atmosphere of the core curriculum are most conducive to the serious motivation of pupils, and thus to a lessened concern of the school with disciplinary problems. It is a basic principle of education that motivation is necessary for real learning. And motivation can be present only when the pupil feels some need so intensely that he is ready to engage in definite goal-seeking to satisfy that need. When the pupil sees meaning in what he is doing in relation to his needs or desires he is likely to give himself wholeheartedly to the task in hand. It is also well understood that overt behavior problems arise in situations where the demands upon the pupil are teacher-imposed without the learner seeing any relationship between the task at hand and his personal or social needs. It has generally been the experience of core teachers that where genuine problems

of a personal or social nature are made the heart of the curriculum, serious purposeful activity on the part of the pupil takes place and a wholesome social atmosphere in the classroom and school is in evidence.

7. The core curriculum provides for a natural integration of school, home, and community living. In core it is recognized that experience learning cannot be restricted to the schoolroom or to the school itself. The quality of the experiences the pupil has in the home and the community may implement or directly counteract the kind of behavior patterns the school is trying to develop. Therefore, those committed to the core idea are concerned that the learning activities of the school be closely identified with the total living activities of the pupil outside of school. This requires the closest cooperation of school, home, and community to insure consistency in the learning experiences of the pupil.

8. The core concept makes the so-called extracurricular activities a natural, integral part of the curriculum. The newer conceptions of learning have forced upon the schools committed to the subject curriculum the necessity of making some provision for so-called extracurricular activities in the school program. Obviously they cannot be treated as are the traditional subjects of the curriculum. Consequently, they have been set apart for special treatment as a somewhat artificial adjunct to the regular curriculum. In the core concept all learning experiences are to be considered as educationally significant, and, therefore, so-called extracurricular experiences are to be handled as any other potentially educative experience.

9. In the core concept teachers take on a new status. Under the subject curriculum concept teachers were essentially drill masters. Certain quantities of knowledges and intellectual skills were to be learned by the pupil, and the teachers' task was to see that pupils learned (memorized) these bodies of knowledge. Teaching procedures became largely those of the imposition of learning tasks upon pupil. The core teacher, instead, becomes a guide to meaningful learning in the personal-social areas of concern to the pupil. The core teacher is not expected to be a

walking compendium of encyclopaedic information, but rather is expected to be a careful student of the nature of the pupil and the learning process, adept in human relations, and able to stimulate and guide the pupil in the development of skills of problem solving, and of acquiring those personal-social skills that will enable him more effectively to solve his problems of social adjustment and successful participation as a member of our democratic society.

10. The core curriculum provides the theoretical bases favorable to the establishment of rapport and cooperative efforts within the school staff. Core teachers do not consider themselves "prima donnas" with vested interests as specialists in specific subject matter areas, as has been so characteristic of teachers of the subject curriculum. They look upon their task as a cooperative-coordinating one to insure both adequacy and balance in the educative experiences of pupils. They recognize the pervasive nature of learning experiences, and that these experiences cannot be fenced in by any scheme of discrete compartmentalization as has been the assumption in the subject curriculum. Likewise, the nature of the educational task is seen to involve the cooperative efforts of teachers and the administrative staff to coordinate all aspects of the school in order to insure the best possible learning situations.

WHY THE CONFUSIONS ABOUT CORE?

It would be unrealistic, indeed, to assume that the concept of the core curriculum developed in this book is universally accepted. It is only necessary to read the numerous articles pertaining to core or some textbook discussions of core, or visit a number of schools that lay claim to an exemplification of the core in their curriculum practices, to become aware of the confusions that exist as to the meaning of the core concept.

The use of such terms as "correlated courses," "unified studies," "fused course," "general education," "multiple period," "block of time," or "combined English-social living course," as synonyms of "core" serves to highlight this confusion. Few contemporary educational terms are more widely discussed or more generally misunderstood and misused.

It is difficult, for example, to understand how the meaning long associated with the word "fusion" has come to be so widely accepted as synonymous with "core." The words "correlation" and "fusion" became familiar to educators more than a quarter of a century ago through the vigorous discussion of the concepts underlying them. Even in those days the word "core" was never used in juxtaposition with the terms "correlation" or "fusion," or with the ideas these terms represented.

Referring to the frequent confusion of the terms "correlation," "fusion," and "broad fields" with core, Krug points out that these curriculum patterns are based "on the organization-of-a-knowledge approach" and that those who have superficially confused these curriculum patterns with core have been concerned "with the thickness of the slice rather than with the nature of the cake. . . . Many a fusion class has gone by the name 'core curriculum,' to the intense bewilderment of teachers, curriculum workers, administrators, youth, and the lay public." [16]

The fact that fusion, unified studies courses, and similar deviations from the older single subject curriculum pattern have usually involved the use of a double class period and the use of a single teacher apparently has led to a superficial identification of such courses with core. In an extended study of so-called core practices, the Office of Education found that the overwhelming majority of schools that claimed to have core programs in fact did so on the basis of combinations of two or more subjects, taught by a single teacher, and usually allotted a two or three hour block of time.[17]

A second reason that may account in part for this confusion in the meaning of core arises from the failure of many to understand the fundamental differences in the conceptions of learning

---

[16] Krug, Curriculum Planning, p. 91.

[17] See Grace S. Wright, Core Curriculum in Public High Schools: An Inquiry into Practices, 1949, Bulletin 1950, No. 5. Washington, D. C.: U. S. Office of Education, p. 13.

that differentiate the subject curriculum from the core curriculum. The subject curriculum has been based on the centuries-old theory of learning that conceived of the brain as a sort of a non-leakable container in which could be stored much of the world's accumulated knowledge. The school curriculum has consisted of selected portions of this accumulated knowledge organized into subjects, the content of which was to be stored in the pupil's mind for possible future use. On the other hand, the core curriculum is based upon the theory that learning consists essentially in the modification of the behavior patterns of the learner which results from his learning experiences.[18]

A third possible reason for some aspects of this confusion about the meaning of core may result from the fact that historically the word "core" has undergone a change in meaning. It is a difficulty that has plagued other phases of education besides, and arises from the persistent attempt to infuse new meaning into old terms—proverbially "to pour new wine into old bottles."

There was a time when the limited school curriculum was taught *in toto* to all pupils. As the accumulation of knowledge began to increase rapidly within the past century, it became a problem for the schools to decide what increments of knowledge should be taught. As schools struggled to keep abreast of the rising tide of knowledge more subjects were added to the curriculum. Many schools found their expanding curriculums to include scores of subjects, often as many as two hundred or more.

It became obvious that during his normal span of school years each pupil could study only a small number of the subjects offered. Educators began to ask whether there were some subjects of greater value than others. This led to the designation of some subjects regarded as important for all pupils to study as "required" subjects, and of others which pupils might choose to study, as "electives." At times the "required" subjects have been called the "core" subjects. For many, "core" and "required" became

---

[18] This conception of learning and the curriculum has been considered previously and is dealt with in more detail in Chapter 5.

interchangeable terms applied to a preferred group of subjects in the traditional subject-matter curriculum.

A fourth possible source of confusion in the use of the term "core" may arise from the need of a long transition period in order to make a complete changeover from the subject curriculum to the core curriculum. Such a radical curriculum change may require a number of years to accomplish. Unless teachers and administrators are thoroughly grounded in the educational principles that underlie these sharply divergent curriculum concepts, they may easily mistake stages in the transition from the old to the new as in essence the full achievement of the core curriculum.

At this point it cannot be too strongly emphasized that the development of a core curriculum is a long term process. It requires a slow transition from long accepted curriculum thinking and practices by intermediate stages to the goal of a true core. Most teachers find it hard to shift at once to the radical changes in thinking and procedures demanded in true core teaching. As is pointed out in Chapter 13, most teachers and schools find it desirable to begin with a double period class but with little immediate change in class procedures, cautiously changing to some form of a unified studies approach, and gradually emerging into an experience learning classroom situation with primary attention focused upon the personal and social problems of pupils.

What Is the Future of Core?

what is the growth of the core idea in theory and practice?

Studies of the growing interest in the core idea are limited and fragmentary. The theoretical interest in core has been developing rapidly. Within the past fifteen years most general texts on the curriculum and those on the secondary school curriculum have included some consideration of the core curriculum. The past half dozen years have witnessed larger sections of such texts devoted to a discussion of the core idea; and, what is of greater significance, a greater maturity of thinking is evidenced on this subject and a growing unanimity as to the basic conception of the core curriculum. Even the recent books more specifically devoted to the elementary school curriculum are devoting more space to a consideration of core.

The plethora of articles now appearing in educational journals and even in journals of general public interest, attests a growing interest in this subject. Published materials on the core have become so numerous that, beginning in 1953, *The Educational Index* has included a separate classification, "Core Program," under the general heading, "Curriculum," the former listing more than thirty titles the first year it was employed.

Several status studies have been made to discover the extent of the introduction of the core idea into school practice. The most extensive study made in this field was made by the Office of Education in 1949, followed by a more limited but more intensive study reported from that office in 1952. Wright found that approximately 3.5 per cent of all public secondary schools claimed some form of the core organization.[19] It was significant that 11.3 per cent of schools enrolling over 500 pupils indicated the presence of core in their schools as against only two per cent of the schools with enrollments under 500 pupils. A total of 1119 core classes were reported.

The fragmented and elemental nature of the practices called core by these schools is revealed in the fact that combinations of English and social studies courses accounted for 72.7 per cent of core classes; and English and social studies in combination with one or more other subjects, 19.2 per cent; thus a total of 91.9 per cent of so-called core classes presented a "unified studies" or "fused" approach to curriculum change. This study indicates that in 1949 the vast majority of schools claiming core had taken but the first cautious step in the direction of a real core curriculum.

---

[19] See Grace S. Wright, *Core Curriculum in Public High Schools op cit.,* and *Core Curriculum Development Problems and Practices,* Bulletin 1952, No. 5. Washington, D. C.: U. S. Office of Education. The Office of Education is completing another study probably to be published in 1958.

In 1956 the National Association of Secondary School Principals reported a study of the place of core in public junior high schools. There were 1150 replies to questionnaires sent to 1250 junior high schools. The use of the block of time, with two or more periods combined, was found in 57.3 per cent of the reporting junior high schools.[20]

Bossing in 1956 attempted a brief study to discover the prevalence of some form of so-called core in the senior high schools or the upper four grades, 9-12, of the public secondary schools. One thousand such schools in the United States were sampled by questionnaire. Contrasted with Wright's 1949 study for "undivided and junior-senior high schools" where she found 6.4 per cent of the schools reported core classes, Bossing, in 1956, found 9.3 per cent; for "regular high schools" Wright reported 1.4 per cent against 5.8 per cent reported by Bossing; and in the "senior high school" Wright reported 3.5 per cent using core in contrast with 6.6 per cent reported by Bossing. This would suggest a significant increase in so-called core classes in the upper grades of the secondary school within a span of a half dozen years.

Of considerable significance were the findings of Wright that 91.9 per cent of the so-called cores consisted of combinations of English-social studies, or these in further combination with one or more additional subjects. In Bossing's study 50 per cent of the schools reported core courses representing large blocks of subject matter, evidently some form of unified studies organization, and 63.6 per cent reported core courses organized around some form of personal-social problems approach. Both types of organization were reported in several schools. This is an encouraging advance in the direction of the real core emphasis upon personal-social problems as the basis of core curriculum organization. On the question of future interest in expanding the core approach, 17 per cent of those schools in the grade bracket 9-12 reported that they

---

[20] Data from the N.A.S.S.P. on the place of core in the 1250 junior high schools reported in February 1956, at Chicago. For a further study of core development in the junior high school see Leonard V. Koos, *Junior High School Trends*. New York: Harper and Brothers, 1955, Chapters 4-5.

contemplated the future introduction of core courses into their schools, while 10.1 per cent of the schools including grades 10-12 had such plans.

There are other well authenticated indices of a growing interest in the core curriculum idea. Among these has been the establishment of a national organization, growing rapidly since its inauguration in 1952, called The National Conference on Core Teaching. The Association for Supervision and Curriculum Development, one of the major national educational groups, has set up one of its permanent commissions devoted to problems of the core curriculum. Other major educational organizations concerned with the curriculum are giving increased attention in the programs of their national meetings to the core curriculum. Within the past few years many states have set up regular annual state core conferences and in some parts of the country regional core conferences are now being held annually.

Educational institutions are rapidly becoming conscious of the need to prepare teachers and administrators for their parts in developing the core curriculum in the schools. In 1946 the first teacher training program for the preparation of core teachers was established in a major university. Now possibly twenty or more institutions of higher learning have set up definite teacher training programs for core teachers. Each year other institutions are establishing such programs. In 1953 Wright reported a study made of courses offered on the core curriculum by institutions of higher learning. She found that of 85 responses to her questionnaire ". . . at least 30 institutions (25 universities and 5 teachers' colleges) in 21 States and the District of Columbia provided a total of 46 courses which dealt entirely or in large with the core program." [21]

what will be the future development of core?

It is clear that the trend towards some form of the core curriculum is steadily gathering momentum. The big question now is

---

[21] Grace S. Wright, "Core Curriculum Offerings for Teachers," *School Life*, 36:6-7, October 1953.

what will be the future organizational form of the core curriculum? Many critics of core complain that there is no clear core curriculum pattern in evidence; almost anything that deviates from the traditional subject pattern of the curriculum is labelled core. Others who accept the philosophical and psychological basis for core still do not see how to spell out an implementation of the ideas which they approve.

Yet those who have given most thought to the concept of core can identify the developing strands of a theoretically consistent, over-all pattern. It is encouraging to note the growing consensus on the part of curriculum workers as to what the major characteristics of such a curriculum should be. It is even more encouraging to observe the practical efforts at curriculum building in many communities. These places are steadily emerging with organizational features clearly giving expression to the recognized characteristics of a good core curriculum.

We may expect within the next decade or two to see some general patterns of the core curriculum take on clearer definition as curriculum workers give imaginative leadership to the implementation of the core idea. The probabilities are that there will be several patterns of the core curriculum emerging; diverging in form at many lesser points to reflect both the varying educational needs of different communities and the creative genius of imaginative leadership, but similar in their over-all basis patterns.

This is as it should be. Too little is yet known to build programs rigidly. Concerning the broad aspects of learning and the nature of the learner there appears to be a general consensus based upon a respectable and growing body of research. To the over-confident, however, it may not be out of place to offer the comment of an eminent psychologist that "There are no laws of learning which can be taught with confidence." [22] Likewise, even though we may agree on the over-all nature of the principles of education involved, much practical research and much experi-

---

[22] Ernest R. Hilgard, *Theories of Learning*, Revised. New York: Appleton-Century-Crofts, Inc., 1956, p. 457.

72   THE CORE CURRICULUM DEFINED

mentation needs to be done on the operational aspects of the core curriculum.

SELECTED REFERENCES

A Primer for Common Learnings. Minneapolis: Minneapolis Public Schools, 1948.

Alberty, Harold, *Reorganizing the High School Curriculum,* Revised. New York: The Macmillan Company, 1953, Part II, "Determining the Design of the Curriculum."

American Association of School Administrators, *American School Curriculum,* Thirty-first Yearbook. Washington, D. C.: The National Education Association, 1953, Chapter 3, "Organizing the Curriculum."

Association for Supervision and Curriculum Development, *Preparation of Core Teachers for Secondary Schools.* Washington, D. C.: The National Education Association, 1955.

Anderson, Vernon E., *Principles and Procedures of Curriculum Improvement.* New York: The Ronald Press Company, 1956, Part IV, "Some Problems of Organizing and Planning the Curriculum for the School."

Beauchamp, George A., *Planning the Elementary School Curriculum.* New York: Allyn and Bacon, Inc., 1956, Chapter 2, "Conceptions of the Curriculum."

Birkmaier, Emma M., "Core Curriculum: A Promising Pattern for the Education of Adolescents," *The School Review,* 63:330-333, September 1955.

Bossing, Nelson L., "What Is Core?" *The School Review,* 63:206-213, April 1955.

———, "Development of the Core Curriculum in the Senior High School," *School Review,* 64:224-226, May 1956.

———, *Principles of Secondary Education,* Second Edition. Englewood Cliffs, N. J.: Prentice-Hall, Inc., 1955, Chapter 13, "How Can the Core Curriculum Be Developed?"

———, "The Core and Common Learnings Curriculum," in R. H. Beck, Editor, *The Three R's Plus.* Minneapolis: University of Minnesota Press, 1956.

Cramer, Roscoe V., "How Effective Is the Core Curriculum in the Junior High School?" *Bulletin,* National Association of Secondary School Principals, 38:172-179, April 1954.

Douglass, Harl R., and others, *The High School Curriculum,* Revised. New York: The Ronald Press Company, 1956, Chapter 14, "The Core Curriculum."

Educational Policies Commission, *Education for All American Youth: A Further Look,* Revised. Washington, D. C.: The National Education Association, 1952, Chapters 7 and 8, "Schools for Youth in American City."

Fair, Jean, "The Comparative Effectiveness of a Core and a Conventional Curriculum in Developing Social Concern," *The School Review,* 62: 274-282, May 1954.

Harvill, Harris, "Eight Advantages of the Core Organization," *Social Education,* 18:4-6, and 32, January 1954.

Koos, Leonard V., *Junior High School Trends.* New York: Harper and Brothers, 1955, Chapter 4, "Organization of the Curriculum," and Chapter 5, "Retreat from Departmentalization."

Krug, Edward A., *Curriculum Planning.* New York: Harper and Brothers, 1950, Chapter 3, "Relating Educational Purposes to the All-School Program." See also Revised Edition, 1957.

Leonard, J. Paul, *Developing the Secondary School Curriculum,* Revised. New York: Rinehart and Company, Inc., 1953, Chapter 14, "Developing the Core Curriculum."

Lurry, Lucile L., and Elsie J. Alberty, *Developing a High School Core Program.* New York: The Macmillan Company, 1957.

MacConnell, C. M., and others, *New Schools for a New Culture,* Revised. New York: Harper and Brothers, 1953.

Mudd, Dorothy, *A Core Program Grows.* Bel Air, Maryland: Board of Education of Harford County, 1949.

Noar, Gertrude, *Freedom to Live and Learn.* Philadelphia: Franklin Publishing and Supply Company, 1948.

—, *The Junior High School—Today and Tomorrow.* Englewood Cliffs, N. J.: Prentice-Hall, Inc., 1953, Part III, "Modern Curriculum Content and Techniques."

Pierce, Paul R., *Developing a High-School Curriculum*. New York: American Book Company, 1942.

Ragan, William B., *Modern Elementary Curriculum*. New York: The Dryden Press, Inc., 1953, Chapter 3, "Organizing Learning Experiences."

Romine, Stephen A., *Building the High School Curriculum*. New York: The Ronald Press Company, 1954, Chapter 12, "Building the Core Curriculum."

Saylor, J. Galen, and William M. Alexander, *Curriculum Planning*. New York: Rinehart and Company, Inc., 1954, Chapter 10, "The Core Curriculum Plan."

Wright, Grace S., *Core Curriculum in Public High Schools: An Inquiry into Practices, 1949*. Bulletin 1950, No. 5. Washington, D. C.: U. S. Office of Education.

————, *Core Curriculum Development Problems and Practices*, Bulletin 1952, No. 5. Washington, D. C.: U. S. Office of Education.

————, *The Core Program Abstracts of Unpublished Research: 1946-1955*. Washington, D. C.: U. S. Office of Education, 1956.

Chapter 4

The Philosophy and Purposes of the Core Curriculum

Why are we interested in the core curriculum? What advantages does it have over the other forms of curricular organization and teaching procedure? This is the type of question that thoughtful teachers and administrators raise, or should raise, as they are asked to adopt radically new approaches in education. Failure to understand fully the meaning and purpose of the core curriculum in many schools where it has been adopted has led to confusion, dissatisfaction, and unfortunate classroom results for teachers attempting to introduce it. Furthermore, inability of the school personnel to explain intelligently to anxious parents and public the purpose and merits of the core curriculum has led to its being considered a new educational fad, and to a demand that the school get back to the "old-time fundamentals."

Unfortunately, there has been a tendency in educational circles to frown upon a too critical concern for the why of things, too much of a tendency to jump on the bandwagon of educational innovations and set out with only vague notions of what they are all about. This is only a part of the general pattern of thinking that has characterized the "go-getter" mood of our older generation. Action was their chief concern and ideal; they were impatient with too much consideration of the larger significance of the action. The prevailing attitude of a few years ago in educational circles toward the value of philosophy to educational practices is typified by the reaction of a professor who was depreciating the emphasis upon courses in philosophy in the proposed study program of a student. He said, "I am vitally concerned that your training in technique should function one hundred per cent."

It is the position of the authors that the core curriculum involves a fundamental educational point of view vital to our American democracy and represents a radical departure from older traditional educational practices. It is important that teachers and administrators understand the real significance of the core curriculum and appreciate its broader implications for our democratic way of life.

How Are Philosophy and Purpose Related to Behavior?

When we speak of a democratic way of life, we are, of course, referring to a pattern of individual and group behavior. Such a pattern of behavior, it is recognized, grows out of acceptance of a point of view as to the way life should be lived. It is clear, then, that the relationship of the individual's outlook on life to the values that he regards as standards for the guidance of his conduct is crucially important. This has been expressed in a homely but pointed way by the late G. K. Chesterton: "We think that for a landlady considering a lodger, it is important to know his income, but still more important to know his philosophy. We think that for a general about to fight an enemy, it is important to know the enemy's numbers, but still more important to know the enemy's philosophy." As Chesterton implies, the major concern of the landlady should not be the lodger's ability to pay, important as that is, but the sense of obligation the lodger feels to pay and to pay promptly. The latter is not related so much to his ability to pay as it is to the general outlook on life that he accepts as the standard for his conduct. Does he believe the world owes him a living without any obligation on his part, and that he is justified in getting it any way he can? Or does he accept as a guiding principle of his life the idea that he is obligated to pay in some equitable manner for the satisfactions he enjoys? To what extent does he maintain a high sense of personal responsibility to others as a matter of common justice? Does he believe firmly that in the long run greater happiness and more genuine satisfaction will come to him who practices the maxim, "Do unto others as you would have them do unto you"? All would probably agree that the lodger who believes the world owes him a living, or who is a thoroughgoing individualist, would be a poor risk for the landlady, even if he is able to pay. The lodger of modest means but with a high sense of personal responsibility and social obligation would be a much safer risk.

This is only to recognize that man's behavior is basically controlled by his purposes, his goals, his values—in other words, his philosophy of living. His behavior at times may appear to be confused, even aimless, giving little evidence of direction, but it is never without purpose. Sometimes the purpose or goal of his immediate behavior may not be too clearly envisioned by the individual himself. The reasons for this should be clearly understood by the teacher. By the time he has reached maturity, in the first place, the typical individual has developed broad patterns of behavior consistent with a basic philosophy of life. Major specific behavior action is the result of more or less deliberate reflection and conscious decision by the individual, and therefore the intent of such behavior conforms in general to the broad purpose or standard of conduct accepted by him. The specific behavior reactions to minor, almost incidental, situations are likely to be somewhat automatic habit reactions, and tend to fit into the general pattern of major but consciously determined behavior action. People differ, of course, in degree of sharpness of the outlines in the conscious pattern. The more clearly one has refined the implications of his philosophy of life the more likely that there will be a general consistency between his behavior and his philosophy.

In the second place, biologists and psychologists agree that the behavior of the biological organism is always purposive, even from birth. They suggest that all behavior of the infant is biologically purposive; that within the organism itself are implanted the basic springs to action that have for their object the satisfaction of those needs that result in the normal growth and development of the organism—in short, its survival. The behavior of the infant, although biologically purposive, may not be intelligently directed. It feels pain, and as a result there are bodily movements of a random sort, not very discriminatingly or directionally made by adult standards, but biologically induced for the specific purpose of protecting the organism from injury. Very early, the infant begins superficially to understand cause and effect relations. He feels hunger and responds biologically by restless movements and by crying. He soon learns that crying brings attention, food, and relief from the discomfort of hunger. His behavior thereafter becomes more consciously purposive and more efficiently directed.

In an effort to indicate the dynamic nature of these biological springs to action in relation to human needs, an early writer tried to classify them into what he called basic "wishes." He identified four major categories: (1) the desire for security, (2) the desire for recognition, (3) the desire for response, and (4) the desire for new experience.[1] Contemporary writers, in discussing these recognized basic purposive urges of the organism, generally refer to them as "drives." It is important here only to be aware of the persistent nature of these biological pur-

---

[1] W. I. Thomas, *The Unadjusted Girl*. Boston: Little, Brown and Company, 1923, Chapter I.

posive urges, or drives, and of their significance for individual and group behavior.[2]

How Are Philosophy and Purpose Related to Education?

Few would question that philosophy and purpose are in some way related to education, although many would not be sure how, and a few would minimize the importance in education of philosophy as they understand it. Before this question can be answered it is necessary to examine what is meant by education.

When we examine educational concepts past and present, we find them very divergent. Some are based on older notions of the meaning of learning, for in all phases of cultural change, many cling to the old in the midst of the new. It is important that those who read this book understand clearly the conception of education that is here accepted as basic and that underlies our consideration of the core curriculum. For this purpose, *the function of education is conceived to be the adjustment of man to his environment, including man's adaptation to and reconstruction of his environment, to the end that the most enduring satisfactions may accrue to the individual and to society.*

The careful reader must be impressed at once with the fact that philosophy and purpose are essentially involved in such an idea of education. The conception expressed in *adjustment* is twofold. As the individual looks out on his world he finds that to live at all, he must conform to many conditions as he finds them. He recognizes in his environment many physical elements dangerous to comfort and life. He early learns to make adaptations to fire lest he get burned. He seeks shelter from both heat and cold, whether for comfort or for protection

---

[2] For fuller discussion of the dynamic nature of purpose, needs, and drives in the human organism see Gardner Murphy, *Personality*. New York: Harper and Brothers, 1947, Chapters V, VI, XII; L. F. Shaffer and E. J. Shoben, Jr., *The Psychology of Adjustment*. Boston: Houghton Mifflin Company, 1956, Part I; H. C. Lindgren, *Educational Psychology in the Classroom*. New York: John Wiley & Sons, Inc., 1956, Chapter 2.

against sunstroke, frostbite, or freezing to death. He laboriously takes a long way around to reach a desired spot rather than to take the easy, direct way of jumping from a dangerously high cliff. Because of the danger to health he remains sheltered during inclement weather; this often involves interruption of anticipated activities and consequent disappointment. In his relations with other individuals he again discovers that many adaptations are necessary. Unlike Robinson Crusoe on his island, he faces many restraints upon his impulses as he comes in contact with others. Through bitter experience, perhaps, he discovers the meaning of the social concept of "mine" and "thine." He discovers further that the group has evolved an exasperating set of rather inflexible "rules of the road" (conventions and mores), accepted and enforced by it with unpleasant physical or social consequences for those openly unwilling to conform.

In all of these typical situations the normal reactions of a totally untrained person would be to resist conformity. He would chafe particularly against the social restrictions placed upon his freedom to act on normal impulses. If he can be brought to accept the limiting conditions of his environment as a desirable type of adaptation for his own good and that of the group, he and the group will experience general satisfaction. On the other hand, failure to accept his environment and to try to make some satisfactory adaptation to it must lead to discontent, moroseness, frustrations, and the probable development of serious antisocial attitudes and conduct. Under strong emotion this could lead to grave mental maladjustments. To achieve a sense of personal satisfaction, therefore, the individual must begin early in life to develop toward his world a wholesome point of view that includes acceptance of desirable and necessary adaptation to existing conditions—to develop, in short, a philosophy of living.

The definition of education given above clearly indicates that one of its goals is desirable adaptation of the individual to his environment. Education must help the child from the cradle on to learn to accept willingly the adaptations to immutable environmental situations.

The second aspect of adjustment envisaged by this definition of education involves the reconstruction of the environment. Man has not been content to accept his world as he has found it. It is a mark of man's uniqueness that he has undertaken so many radical changes in his environment in order to multiply his comforts and satisfactions.

It may be argued that not all of his efforts to modify his surroundings have resulted in the benefits anticipated. It cannot be questioned, however, that he has immeasurably enriched his life in physical comforts. A retrospective view of life in the cave-dwelling age compared with life today indicates how profoundly man has reconstructed his environment so that it might better contribute to his satisfactions. The cold, dark, clammy cave and the lean-to with its damp, earthen floor and poorly thatched roof and walls are far cries from the spacious, well-ventilated, dry, mechanically heated, brightly illuminated dwellings that typify modern man. Contrast the laborious snail's-pace travel of primitive man as he moved from place to place on foot or by crude canoe with the relative speed, ease, and comfort with which modern man travels the world in air-conditioned automobiles, and luxurious streamliners, steamships, and stratocruisers. Reflect on the tremendous changes in our environment that have resulted from technological development—massive factories, skyscrapers of steel and concrete, labor-saving power machinery of every kind, irrigation projects, hydroelectric power plants, telephones, telegraph, radio-television, sound movies and technicolor, and a thousand and one electrical gadgets.

All these efforts of man to increase his comforts and satisfactions by changing the physical aspects of his world have in turn forced him to reconstruct his social life. Primitive man lived in a very simple type of social organization. He possessed little; and, like many of the American Indians, when he wanted to change his abode he could pack his few possessions on his back or on his pony and seek a more attractive location elsewhere. Organized on a family and clan or tribal basis, his numbers were few and his social organization was simple.

With the development of fixed, immovable properties and extensive and complicated production machinery, man found his numbers increased, and of necessity a more complex social organization was required. Man became more interdependent. Consequently, he has constantly sought ways of reconstructing his social pattern so that it would facilitate rather than hinder the achievement of the greatest possible degree of happiness. The more extensively man has tried to make his physical environment serve him, the more inadequate he has found the rules and conventions of his social organization to be. A new pattern was required; the old had become obsolete or needed some modification.

As a result man has been forced to give increasing attention to his goals in life. It has been necessary for him to examine more carefully and more consistently his particular social organizational structure in terms of his purposes for himself and for his group. In our complex world the individual is forced to think beyond his family, his community, even his country, to the peoples of the world, if he and they are to attain the greatest happiness and the most complete satisfaction to which they aspire. He must realize how vitally important it is for all, himself included, to develop a philosophy of life consistent with the nature of a changing world, so that intelligent judgment will be exercised as to what adaptions and what reconstructions should take place in our physical and social environment. It is equally important that each citizen develop a well-defined, consistent point of view as to the desirable ways and means of obtaining the kind of adjustment desired.

Assisting man to develop a point of view toward life and its goals, in short, a philosophy of life, has always been a recognized part of the responsibility of education. From primitive times to the present the social group has looked upon education as a device by which oncoming generations were led to acquire certain ways of thinking about life, certain ideals or values for living in harmony with the group. Since children lived within the family circle from babyhood, they were expected to be well indoctrinated in certain ways of thinking and doing. It was the responsibility of the family to insure that its children accepted in rudimentary form the ideals exemplified in the thinking and practices of the family, which in turn were supposed to reflect the pattern of thinking of the group.

As he reached adolescence, early man passed through initiatory rites conducted by the tribal elders. The purpose of these rites was the further induction of the child into the pattern of thinking of the group. It was an additional insurance that the child would understand the goals and values of life, and the approved ways for their attainment. As life became more complex, and more prolonged and systematic education of children seemed increasingly necessary, the school came into existence to supplant the initiatory rite ceremonies. The function of education through the school has been clearly accepted because of its antecedents. A well-known principle of education has it that *the school is one of the agencies of society for the continuation and re-creation of itself.* Every modern society has set up some form of official agency to which it entrusts the education of its children. When a society sets up such an institution, it naturally expects this school to accept as its major task the indoctrination of those under its care in the general ideals of the culture. It is expected that when a youth passes from the school into the active adult life of society, his philosophy of life, his purposes, his goals, his accepted values for living, will have been intensified and deepened in meaning to a point beyond that at which they were received in the home and from other community sources, but will be in full harmony with the philosophy of the society that supports the school. Further implications of the relationship between philosophy and education in a democratic form of society will be considered later in the chapter.

It is one thing to suggest that education through the school is concerned with the philosophy and purposes held by the pupil; it is quite another to think of education as a process by which philosophy and purpose become operative in the life of the individual. Earlier in this chapter we discussed education's role in relating philosophy and purpose to behavior. It is important also to consider education in its second major aspect, namely, as a process.

Neither the teacher nor society will be satisfied if the person produced by our educational program can glibly recite desirable goals and purposes but ignores them in his behavior. It used to be considered an exhibition of perfect educational achievement when the learner could verbally demonstrate his acquisition of many precepts of the good life as an act of memorization. Extensive researches have shown little relationship between behavior and such verbal demonstrations. It is now recognized that while behavior is closely related to genuinely understood and accepted philosophy and purposes of living, the mere ability to recite lofty precepts is no guarantee that they are understood or fully accepted. There is still much truth to the old adage, "Reputation is what you are thought to be, character is what you are."

We have experienced, therefore, a definite shift from emphasis upon education as the acquisition of quantitative information and the consequent stress upon the improvement of the processes of memorization to a recognition that desirable change in manner of living of the individual is the acid test of the effectiveness of education. This has meant emphasizing the process of helping boys and girls to develop ways of living successfully within their environment. It represents, then, recognition of the importance of philosophy and purpose in education, but recognizes their vital significance to the individual and society only to the extent that they appear in the daily behavior pattern of the learner.

How Is Education Related to Democracy?

It has been noted that society has always looked upon the institutional phase of education as its primary agency to insure its perpetuation. This is as true of our democratic form of society as of any other. There is a uniqueness in the relation of education to democracy, however, that grows out of the very uniqueness of democracy itself.

Democracy can be thought of basically as a philosophy that permeates every aspect of living. One characteristic of democracy is the emphasis it places upon the worth and importance of the individual in the social group. Each individual is regarded as a unique personality who should have the right and be encouraged to develop in a maximum degree his own peculiar powers. Consequently, emphasis is placed upon the right and necessity of each individual to determine his own values. This importance of the individual in our society has never been understood by those in whose culture the individual is of relatively little worth. During World War II the Japanese were frequently astounded at the risks taken by Americans to rescue a man lost at sea or isolated from his unit. It has been equally difficult for the Westerner, committed in his thinking to the supreme worth and dignity of the individual, to understand the apparent unimportance, sometimes the almost cold disregard, in which the East holds human life.

The democratic philosophy of life has also placed great emphasis upon the equality of man. Every man is the peer of every other. Caste in any form is contrary to this principle. The early pioneer prided himself on being the equal of his neighbor and was contemptuous of any vestigial holdover from Old World social thinking. Such holdovers occasionally did crop up, however. There were those who could not forget their ancestral status. This was manifest in caste-conscious old Boston, ". . . where the Lowells talk to Cabots and the Cabots talk only to God." Although America is not free in social practice from some negation of the ideal of equality, the principle is resolutely held as a cornerstone of our democracy. This has far-reaching significance for the democratic way of life.[3] It means not only that in basic relationships no man is superior to another in human right, but also that all carry equal responsibility for the solution of major problems that confront the group. The old ideas of the divine right of kings are broadened in the democratic slogan, "every man a king."

Another important idea inherent in democracy, an idea that derives in part from the belief in the equality of man, is that group action is dependent upon group decision. No one has preferential right to decide matters of group interest; therefore, the decision of the majority is accepted as the basis of policy-making and of judgments that involve the interests of the group. This places a tremendous premium upon the judgment of every member of the group. The action of the group can be only as intelligent and valid as the average level of wisdom of all. It is very important that each individual be highly capable and fully informed on all matters that require group decision. Ethical and moral equality among men does not guarantee that men will be equally informed, or trained to render equally valid judgments. It is the responsibility of the group to raise individual competency to the highest possible level through education. One of the crucial problems of the democratic way of life in our contemporary society is to know what types of policy decisions should be made by the group and what types of technical procedural decisions should be delegated to an individual or to a small group who possess specialized competency in a specific area.

One of the very unique aspects of the concept of democracy is that its expression as a way of life changes with time. It is a recognized principle that we learn through experience. As we

---

[3] The task of education in this regard is clearly pointed in the revelation of the extent to which caste exists *sub rosa* in American life today, as reported in such studies as A. B. Hollingshead, *Elmtown's Youth.* New York: John Wiley and Sons, 1949; W. L. Warner, and others, *Democracy in Jonesville.* New York: Harper and Brothers, 1949; W. L. Warner, and others, *Social Class in America.* Chicago: Science Research Associates, 1949.

examine a new idea, we discover new meanings not at first apparent. As we test the idea in practice and further reflect upon it in the light of our experiences, it tends to take on still other new and enriched significance. In the crucible of experience, ideas and ideals are subject to adaptation or change in many of their characteristics. This has been well expressed in the statement that in the very nature of an ideal, it can never be attained. As we approach an ideal, it appears to recede and change. This simply means that as our practices tend to approach conformity with the implications of the ideal as we originally understood it, it takes on new facets of meaning and its realization appears to demand additional changes not before visualized.

Democracy is a dynamic concept and a continually evolving one. Its major outlines are much different today from those visualized by our grandfathers, and the characteristics that will be accepted as the democratic ideal of our grandchildren will be as equally different from ours. Unlike Hitler, who boasted of setting up a pattern of life that would remain unchanged for a thousand years, we know that change is inevitable. In its very essence, democracy is adventurous, it is experimental, and its genius lies in the fact that interpretation of the values it seeks is always subject to the majority judgment of the group.

The history of democratic society in America abundantly illustrates democracy as a dynamic concept. The ideas and ideals that prompted the Mayflower pilgrims to seek asylum in a new world did not imply setting up a new form of government on a foreign shore. Had such a sequence of events been clearly foreseen by them as a logical consequence of their coming to America, it is probable the Plymouth settlement would not have been. They were loyal subjects; the idea of a war of separation would have been most repugnant to them. They came seeking freedom to worship according to their conscience, a freedom denied them in their homeland, but it did not occur to them that their right of freedom of worship implied an equal right for others of different beliefs. They would not have understood or accepted the concept of religious freedom practiced in America in the middle of the twentieth century. Our forefathers, who proclaimed the noble idea that "all men are created equal," would have been horrified, would have denied emphatically that these words even remotely implied the equal rights of women to the franchise, granted them in the Nineteenth Amendment. Yet today we look upon these and scores of other practices in our democracy as the logical expression of the ideals proclaimed, but not fully understood, by the founding fathers. We may well expect a further development of these basic ideas and ideals as changing conditions and future experience indicate their fuller implications.

Some aspects of the democratic way of life become more sharply defined as the concept of democracy is viewed in relation to government. It is customary to think broadly of two types of government, authoritarian and democratic. The former is based upon the idea that authority to control the governed is vested in a single individual or in a small group with virtually unfettered power. This form of government is frequently characterized as autocratic. For the purposes of this discussion autocracy and authoritarianism when applied to government may be considered synonymous terms. Political democracy, on the other hand, carries the philosophy of the democratic way of life into the framework and conduct of government. In its simpler form the town hall of colonial days exemplifies the expression in government of the democratic ideal. Here, the citizens of the community gathered to discuss issues of local government concern, to initiate and pass upon laws or regulations thought to be for the general good, and to elect from among their peers officials to whom they delegated for a stated period of time, subject to good behavior, responsibility for carrying out the laws enacted. Abraham Lincoln defined the simplicity of democracy in its basic governmental ideal in the famous words: "Government of the people, by the people, and for the people."

It is clear, then, that the success of democracy rests in no small measure upon the critical thinking of every citizen, whereas unquestioning acceptance of the mandates of those in power is the ideal of authoritarian governments. Amid rapidly changing conditions to which new and untried adjustments must be made, democracy depends upon the skill of its members to meet problem situations, whereas the skill desired of those in autocratic society is simply that of following directions.

The function of education in a democracy, therefore, is radically different from its function in an authoritarian society. In the latter type of society a premium is placed upon docility and ability to follow orders without question. Consequently, education in an autocracy is concerned almost exclusively with ways and means of developing greater skills of adaptation and conformity in the subject. Democracy, on the contrary, recognizes the need for skill in adaptation, but places its emphasis upon the ability to meet new situations adventurously, critically, and constructively, so that by cooperative effort changing conditions can be turned to man's advantage.

WHAT IS THE RELATIONSHIP OF DEMOCRACY TO THE CURRICULUM?

Much of our school curriculum was not developed to meet the needs of a democratic society. The program of the eight-year elementary school of the Middle West and West appears to have been patterned originally after the Volksschule (Common School) of Germany. The purpose of this school was to educate children in the adaptive skills required in an autocracy. Through the powerful influence exerted by this European school and the prevailing school practices of the early nineteenth century, the kind of education offered American children was based largely on the adaptive principle better suited to the needs of an authoritarian society. The curriculum and methods of both elementary and secondary schools were based on the general assumption that a more or less static condition existed in our culture. The assignment of a factual kind of material largely glorifying the past, the method of the recitation, and the regimented conduct of the school all tended to produce the docile, uncritical acceptance by the learner of what was told him in books or by the teacher. Thus, the curriculum and procedures of the early school, essentially didactic in nature, were excellently suited to produce the meek yes-man of an authoritarian society.

A democracy demands a curriculum of a radically different type from that of an autocracy. The school curriculum must provide materials and situations that will enable the child to develop the competencies needed to live successfully within a democratic society. Inasmuch as responsibility for the kind of society in which the learner will live devolves upon him, it is necessary that the curriculum provide him an adequate understanding of the nature of his culture, its changing character, and its ideals and purposes. The curriculum also must provide him with an appreciation of those aspects of his culture to which adaptation is desirable and with the means by which he can develop the necessary adaptive skills. A unique characteristic of democracy lies in the imperative necessity that every citizen be able to participate cooperatively in the reconstruction of the pattern of life of his culture. It is essential that the curriculum of the school provide the opportunity to develop the creative competencies needed by the individual as an individual and as a member of a pioneering cooperative group.

How Are Philosophy and Purpose Related to the Core Idea?

In recent years there have been many experimental innovations in patterns of the school curriculum in an effort to discover more effective ways of implementing democratic philosophy. Within these curriculum patterns there have been many points of similarity suggestive of a growing awareness of the kind of school curriculum needed in a democracy. The core curriculum embodies the better features of all of these patterns and appears to offer the greatest promise of meeting the needs of education for democratic living.

It has been said that living involves problems and that life without them would be difficult to conceive. In some types of society, problems for the individual are supposed to be reduced to a minimum, but not in a democracy. Under the democratic way of life, it is assumed that final recourse for the solution of all problems confronted in the process of living must be to the individual. Therefore, the ability to solve problems intelligently and expeditiously is a basic necessity for successful living in a democratic society. This the core curriculum has clearly recognized. Doing away with the time-honored subjects, the curriculum consists of problem situations accepted by the members of the group as of vital concern to them and to society. An effort is made over a long period of time to involve the pupils in a wide range of problems of personal and societal significance so that each pupil will develop the ability to confront every problem situation calmly and critically. In these problem situations, the pupil learns how to go to the heart of the problem to solve it.

Many problems that are vital to the pupil arise out of some failure to appreciate the nature of his culture or the changes he sees occurring within it. To insure that he understands the kind of world he lives in, extensive use is made of current problems arising in the local community, or those of national or international importance. Not long ago, in a school with the core curriculum, several class groups were observed studying strikes and labor unions. The pupils evinced eager interest in these issues and wanted to know how they affected their homes and themselves. Five or six weeks before, a transportation strike ended that for some time had paralyzed transportation in that community. These problem situations of immediate interest to the pupils provided excellent opportunity to explain many facets of our culture under the stress of adjustment to changing conditions of community living.

Understanding the culture and learning the basic skills of

problem solving necessary for effective participation in the democratic way of life cannot be satisfactorily achieved within the four walls of a classroom, or within a program rigidly segmented into 20-minute, 30-minute, or 50-minute units of time. Life is not lived that way. An appreciation of the working of society often can best be understood by direct contact. Problem solving is educationally most effective when done in a vital situation. Modern education, therefore, emphasizes the need of our citizens to have personal experiences with institutions, living conditions, and processes essential to our way of life wherever possible. The set-up of the core curriculum gives special emphasis to this need. In order that pupils may have the fullest freedom to observe first-hand and to participate in community efforts to solve its problems, the core curriculum has provided great flexibility in its schedules. Many elementary schools are organized on a full-day basis with one teacher and a flexible program. In the secondary school, large blocks of time varying from two hours to half-days provide opportunities to encounter more lifelike situations for problem solving, as well as community visitation and participation. One core-type secondary school has set up a half-day block of time with one teacher and has provided added flexibility for community activities by arranging alternation of schedules. For example, Group A, meeting Monday morning, would meet on Tuesday afternoon, while Group B, meeting in the afternoon on Monday, would meet Tuesday morning. By this device, the largest possible use of community resources is available to pupils for visitation or participation.

Democracy places great stress upon the worth of the individual in his own right and as a member of society. Since the success of democracy rests upon the contributory abilities of each member toward the total well-being of the group, the development of each individual with his special aptitudes is of major importance. The core curriculum provides for maximum development of the individual's capacities. A technique of group activity provides that each pupil shall participate in that phase of the problem-solving situation in which his special aptitudes can be developed, not neglecting, of course, the development of all his capacities in maximum degree. To guide and stimulate the interests of the individual pupil in all phases of his total learning activities so that his general *and* special capacities are developed is one of the major responsibilities of the core teacher. In order to do this well, the teacher must have the opportunity, not possible in the traditional program, to know the pupil intimately, his interests, abilities, achievements, home and community background, and must have time for personal consideration of his problems. The core curriculum assumes the guidance function as an essential responsibility of the teacher in any educational program designed to prepare boys and girls for rich, effective living in a democratic society.

Setting up the program in large blocks of time provides each teacher with a small number of pupils whom he can come to know intimately. This is particularly important in the secondary school, where under the traditional curriculum, with teachers for each subject meeting different classes at 40- to 50-minute intervals, an average teacher meets 150 to 200 or more pupils during the day with no chance to know individuals well or to confer with them. With blocks of time ranging from two hours to a half-day, the core teacher in the secondary school may be responsible for 50 to 70 pupils instead of the traditional 150 to 200.

Many elementary schools have divided the typical six-year period into two units enabling a teacher to remain three years with the same small group of pupils. Some authorities advocate that teachers follow their groups through the entire elementary school period. Secondary schools under the core curriculum must prolong the time a teacher spends with a group. Many schools keep the teacher with the core group for one year. Some are experimenting with keeping teachers with their core groups for the three years of the junior high school and using another teacher who picks up the group in the senior high school for a three-year period. These devices characterize the efforts in the core curriculum to provide opportunities for the close personal contact of teacher with pupil, so necessary for effective guidance of the pupil in the development of his capacities and for aiding him in his personal adjustments.

The specific task of the core curriculum, then, is to see that the common competencies needed by all citizens to function effectively in a democratic society are achieved; by the very nature of its purposes it assumes that the development of special interests and vocational competencies, which is also a part of its function, is the responsibility of the rest of the school curriculum.

Democracy is in essence a uniquely cooperative form of living. To achieve a high level of cooperative living, certain individual-group skills are essential. Working together involves the ability to communicate readily with one another. Over and above the ability to speak, read, and write is complete exchange of ideas. It is necessary that word symbols used have the same meaning to all, an exceedingly difficult thing to achieve because meaning is the result of the experience each brings to the interpretation of given word symbols. Another difficult task is how to say what you want to say, in such a way and at such a time as is most appropriate or effective in group interchange. Often the tone of voice betrays the overtones of disbelief, closed mind, sarcasm, and the like, and creates a similar normal reaction in others.

How to carry on an interchange of ideas with the assurance that all angles of the question have been explored, and that those with special experience or competency in the subject have been heard; how to evaluate essentials in the discussion; how to develop a thought intelligently—these are just a few of the considerations that enter into the ability to exchange ideas effectively. How to plan together to reach common goals once decided upon and to share tasks cooperatively is a *sine qua non* of democratic living. Today research and the development of techniques of group dynamics can provide helpful aid in cooperative living.

The old curriculum did not make much provision for this necessary form of education. The core curriculum is designed to make this kind of education a reality. With the emphasis upon problem solving in lifelike situations exemplifying the democratic process, and the provision of large blocks of flexible time, with the informality of group life encouraged in the core curriculum, a natural environment is created for developing effectively, through actual experience, the skills needed for cooperative group living in a democracy.

These are but a few of the ways in which the core curriculum definitely relates to the larger aspects of the philosophy and purposes of democratic living. It is interesting and may prove most profitable to compare the foregoing discussion with the purposes of the core curriculum as viewed by teachers and educational leaders.

Forty-five core teachers in eight Michigan high schools recently listed and then rated their purposes for the core curriculum in the following order:

1. More effective guidance

    1-1 To provide better guidance
    1-2 To know pupils better through reduced pupil load
    1-3 To meet pupils' needs better
    1-4 To develop closer teacher-pupil contact
    1-5 To know pupils' needs
    1-6 To give pupils opportunities to develop potential abilities and be freed from domination
    1-7 To combine guidance and curriculum
    1-8 To lay basis for counseling
    1-9 To improve mental health
    1-10 To adapt work to level of pupil
    1-11 To provide security for pupil

2. Synthesis or correlation of experiences and learnings

    2-1 To correlate learning experiences
    2-2 To make learning real and meaningful
    2-3 To strive for well-rounded individual
    2-4 To provide more well-rounded coverage
    2-5 To teach via whole concepts

3. Greater flexibility and adaptability

    3-1 To provide more flexible program
    3-2 To secure developmental, dynamic program
    3-3 To avoid mechanical time breaks
    3-4 To provide time for creative activities
    3-5 To adjust program of non-college student
    3-6 To break from formal patterns

4. Practical application of theory

    4-1 To apply theory to practice
    4-2 To apply theory in community and in life
    4-3 To develop better consumers
    4-4 To adjust education to changed conditions of living

5. Democratic processes

    5-1 To teach democracy
    5-2 To develop good citizens
    5-3 To provide more effective pattern for exchange of ideas
    5-4 To teach assumption of responsibility

6. Professional growth of teacher

    6-1 To provide in-service growth
    6-2 It's more fun to teach core; it is a rewarding professional experience.

Some interesting emphases appear in these statements. The guidance theme evidently assumes a major emphasis in the thinking of these core teachers. In their response to the question of their purposes, such items as knowing pupils better through a reduced daily load, meeting pupils' needs more effectively, understanding their needs, and developing closer contact by working with fewer pupils are the most significant.

The synthesis of pupil experiences appears to be a close second in these teachers' purposes. The remaining purposes (flexibility, practical application of theory, democratic processes, professional growth of teachers), were rated as important by fewer teachers.

The following purpose-statement for the core curriculum

emerged from six weeks of summer study by a group in the 1938 Ann Arbor Workshop of the Michigan Secondary School Curriculum study:

The core course is an attempted means of enabling the child and the teacher to see life and live it in school, home, and community as a unifying experience. The subject matter for such a course is based on the expressed and implied needs of the individual. In satisfying these fundamental needs it is felt that the core curriculum:

1. Makes school life more democratic by offering opportunities to:
   a. Practice democratic living by giving pupils an active part in shaping their society
   b. Create situations in which students may develop a sense of responsibility toward themselves and toward the group for:
      (1) The satisfactory completion of their own work
      (2) The execution of mutually laid plans

2. Integrates the entire individual in terms of his immediate and future needs and interests by offering opportunities for:

   a. An education which concerns itself with the behavior and growth of the child
   b. Experiences through which the child may develop as a social being
   c. Guidance toward wholesome personal satisfaction
   d. Development of the ability to use leisure time profitably
   e. Development of mental, social, and physical health
   f. Experiences which will lead to continuous growth throughout life.[4]

It may be of interest to compare these statements of purpose for a core curriculum with at least one other statement that has wielded a wide influence in secondary education. In *Education for All American Youth,* the Educational Policies Commission sets forth the following purposes for a "Common Learnings" core course in American city schools:[5]

---

[4] *Source Materials for the Development of Core Courses,* Michigan Secondary Curriculum Study. Lansing, Michigan: The State Department of Public Instruction, 1938, pp. 3-4.

[5] Educational Policies Commission, *Education for All American Youth,* Revised. Washington, D. C.: The National Education Association, 1952, pp. 225-226.

Under the proposed comprehensive course students can better understand the relations between the different things which they are learning. . . .

Within the broad areas planned for the year, classes can begin their work in any year with the problems and purposes of which students are most keenly aware at the time. . . .

The proposed course would permit the adaptation of learning experiences in some fields to changing interests and outlooks as students become more mature. . . .

Greater flexibility in use of time would be possible, and with it types of learning experiences that were impracticable under the system of single period courses. . . .

Most important of all, each teacher in the proposed course would have fewer different pupils and more time to work with and observe each pupil in a wide variety of situations. Therefore, the teachers of "Common Learnings" would serve also as counselors to their students. . . .

It is probably not profitable to quote additional statements on this matter of the purpose of the core curriculum. The statements that we have quoted agree substantially that the core curriculum is designed to achieve better group and individual guidance, to help the pupil develop an all-important understanding of the democratic way of life, and develop skills in living democratically through experience, to give him an opportunity to assume some responsibility and choice in the learning process, and to provide a flexible time block in which a rich learning experience can take place.

SELECTED REFERENCES

Alberty, Harold, *Reorganizing the High School Curriculum,* Revised. New York: The Macmillan Company, 1953, Chapter 2, "The American High School: Its Philosophy and Purposes."

Benjamin, Harold, *The Saber-Tooth Curriculum.* New York: McGraw-Hill Book Company, 1939.

Bossing, Nelson L., *Principles of Secondary Education,* Second Edition. Englewood Cliffs, N. J.: Prentice-Hall, Inc., 1955, Part III, "Present Task of American Education."

Commager, Henry S., *Living Ideas in America*. New York: Harper and Brothers, 1951.

Counts, George S., *Education and American Civilization*. New York: Bureau of Publications, Teachers College, Columbia University, 1952, Part V.

Cremin, L. E., and M. L. Borrowman, *Public Schools in Our Democracy*. New York: The Macmillan Company, 1956.

Douglass, Harl R., Editor, *The High School Curriculum*, Revised. New York: The Ronald Press Company, 1956, Chapter 3, "The Nature and Function of the Curriculum," and Chapter 5, "The Curriculum in An Industrial Democracy."

Drake, William E., *The American School In Transition*. Englewood Cliffs, N. J.: Prentice-Hall, Inc., 1955, Part IV, "Modern Tendencies in Education."

Educational Policies Commission, *Education for All American Youth: A Further Look*. Washington: National Education Association, 1952.

———, *Purposes of Education in American Democracy*. Washington: National Education Association, 1938.

Edwards, N., and H. G. Richey, *The School in the American Social Order*. Boston: Houghton Mifflin Company, 1947.

General Education in a Free Society, Harvard Committee Report. Cambridge: Harvard University Press, 1945, Chapter 2, "Theory of General Education."

Hall, Calvin S., and Gardner Lindzey, *Theories of Personality*. New York: John Wiley and Sons, Inc., 1957, Chapter 14, "Personality Theory in Perspective."

Krug, Edward A., *Curriculum Planning*. New York: Harper and Brothers, 1957, Chapter 3, "The Bases of Educational Objectives."

Leonard, J. Paul, *Developing the Secondary School Curriculum*, Revised. New York: Rinehart and Company, Inc., 1953, Chapter 3, "The Determinants of the Curriculum."

Mead, Margaret, *The School in American Culture*. Cambridge: Harvard University Press, 1951.

National Society for the Study of Education, *General Education*, Part I, The Fifty-first Yearbook. Chicago: The University of Chicago

Press, 1952, Chapter 2, "The Philosophical Foundations of General Education," and Chapter 16, "The Design and Operation of Programs of General Education."

Newlon, J. H., *Education for Democracy in Our Time*. New York: McGraw-Hill Book Company, Inc., 1939.

Roming, Stephen A., *Building the High School Curriculum*. New York: The Ronald Press Company, 1954, Part II, "Curriculum Foundations."

Rugg, Harold, and William Withers, *Social Foundations of Education*. Englewood Cliffs, N. J.: Prentice-Hall, Inc., 1955, Part VI, "The Nature of Culture," and Part VII, "A Cultural Approach to Education."

Saylor, J. Galen, and W. M. Alexander, *Curriculum Planning*. New York: Rinehart and Company, Inc., 1954, Part 2, "What Major Factors Must Be Considered in Curriculum Planning?"

Warner, W. Lloyd, and others, *Who Shall Be Educated?* New York: Harper and Brothers, 1944.

Willing, Matthew, *Schools and Our Democratic Society*. New York: Harper and Brothers, 1951.

Chapter 5

The Learning Process and the Core Curriculum

Much that is important for our consideration of learning in relation to the core curriculum has been brought to light within the past quarter of a century. Indeed, most of what we know about learning in general has been acquired only within this generation. Our forefathers were long on speculation about the way people learned, but short on facts—that is, on experimental evidence to support their theories. Although many research studies are now available on various phases of learning, the educator must accept what we know, even today, with some tentativeness; much is still not known, and some things believed to be true today may in the future need to be modified or even rejected. But there are some phases of learning for which the research evidence now appears conclusive enough to warrant confidence in the validity of the general conclusions reached.

Educational practices prior to the turn of the century were based upon erroneous ideas of how learning took place. These

101

ideas were based mostly upon pure conjecture, often upon cause and effect reasoning drawn from superficial practical observation. It may seem difficult fully to appreciate how older curriculum practices, venerable but unscientific, could come to be accepted so completely by such a large section of the public and by some older educators. Such an appreciation, however, will make possible a better understanding of the need for radical changes in the curriculum and in general educational practices, as the implications for education of present knowledge of the learning process become clear.

It is the purpose of this chapter to consider very briefly and in non-technical language some of the major aspects of the psychology of learning that bear upon curriculum changes, and more particularly upon the development of the core curriculum. In a limited discussion of this kind, it is not possible to consider many interesting and, to the specialist, important items of detail in connection with the major aspects of learning, nor does it seem desirable, for our purposes.

How Are Theories of Learning Related to the Core Curriculum?

There are many theories of learning, and many books have been written to expound them.[1] We may classify them into three somewhat broad categories. The first and oldest is popularly known as the *mind reservoir* or *mind storage* theory of learning. For many centuries the mind was thought of as a reservoir or vessel in which unlimited information or knowledge could be stored.[2] It was assumed that this information or knowledge could at any future time be drawn upon as needed, through recall. The seat of the mind, of course, was thought to be the brain. There was no satisfactory explanation as to

---

[1] A recent book of this type is Ernest R. Hilgard, *Theories of Learning,* Revised. New York: Appleton-Century-Crofts, Inc., 1956.

[2] Technically, a distinction does exist between the terms *information* and *knowledge* in educational parlance. The words have come to be interchangeable in popular usage, as they will be in this non-technical discussion.

how this stored-up knowledge was arranged to be always on tap so that when a situation demanding any data arose, the appropriate machinery would be set in motion to bring it immediately to recall. It was believed simply that the relevancy of this information to a given need would in some way set in motion the right springs of selective recall.

It follows from such a theory that learning in its essence became the simple process of memorizing. The goal of education became the storage in the mind of large quantities of information; and the proper curriculum, in turn, was thought to consist of large blocks of information brought together and made available to the learner for commitment to memory, in other words, for storage in the mind.

The familiar subject-matter curriculum thus finds its origin in this older theory of learning. As knowledge became more extensive an effort was made to give it some semblance of organization for convenience of instruction. Gradually, the broad patterns of subject divisions came into being. For example, those items of information that involved number relations came to be classified together as arithmetic. Long strides had been made toward classification of knowledge into subject-matter divisions by the early fifth century, A.D., when writers distinguished the *seven liberal arts,* with two divisions: The *trivium,* consisting of grammar, rhetoric, and dialectic (logic); and the *quadrivium,* consisting of arithmetic, geometry, astronomy, and music. These subjects were arranged in some sequential order for pupil learning. This general idea of a subject-matter type of curriculum has come down to us from antiquity. As knowledge increased at a rapidly accelerating pace, it began to be further subdivided and classified.

Some of the contemporary difficulties due to the tremendous increase in knowledge have been acutely felt in the schools. Many problems have arisen because of the use of a curriculum based upon quantitative subject matter. There is the problem of selecting what subject matter to teach. Then too, with the intensive subdivision classification that has taken place, many knowledge items have had a way of refusing to stay classified solely in one subject.

It seems strange that this theory of learning could have held almost complete sway for so many centuries, and even stranger that it could still be so firmly entrenched. But there was a deceptively simple logic to the idea of subject-matter organization of curriculum based upon the mind storage theory. And since critical thinking associated with observation was not the vogue until recently, there was little stimulus to doubt.

Many forces within the past three centuries have combined to create a boldly inquisitive spirit. Finally, questions began to be raised about the validity of this theory of learning. The simple matter of forgetting, subjected to critical study, revealed that the mind, instead of being a good storage tank, showed a surprising tendency to leak; that, in fact, it could much better be likened to a sieve. Factual material with little or no meaning, such as lists of numbers or nonsense syllables, was forgotten one day after memorization to the extent of 60 per cent; after thirty days, approximately 80 per cent was forgotten. On the average, approximately 50 per cent of facts learned and not used are forgotten within six months to a year, and after two years forgetting may amount to 80 per cent. After the initial period of forgetting, the loss continues in decreasing ratio. Many factors affect the rate of forgetting and retention. These studies, although not the only basis for rejection of the mind storage theory of learning, left little room for continued belief in a theory of learning so thoroughly discredited by experimental evidence.[3]

The theory of *mental discipline* or *faculty psychology* began to assume more general importance as the mind storage theory lost status. This theory of learning centered around the belief that the mind had many functions—reasoning, memory, judg-

---

[3] For a summary discussion of the research evidence on forgetting and retention, see Howard L. Kingsley and Ralph Garry, *The Nature and Conditions of Learning,* Revised. Englewood Cliffs, N. J.: Prentice-Hall, Inc., 1957, Chapter 12; and B. R. Bugelski, *The Psychology of Learning.* New York: Henry Holt and Company, 1956, Chapter 12.

ment, discrimination, imagination, and so on. Learning consisted of the exercise of these various functions. As memory was used this faculty was strengthened and improved. If reasoning was carried on extensively then the general power of reasoning would be greatly increased. In this conception of learning, each function was a unit and its development was thought to be general. For example, reason was a general ability and would function equally well in any situation where reasoning was required. A person would be able to reason equally well in matters of philosophy, politics, business, or love and romance. As one proponent of this new theory of learning asserted: "No means are known whereby the faculties of the mind can be developed but by exercising them. By potent spell of the magic word Exercise, is evoked all human power." In order to explain what went on in this form of learning, frequent reference to the exercise of the "muscles" of the mind became popular. It was recognized that the mind did not have muscles, but the comparison did convey something of what was believed to take place in the strengthening of the mental functions. This exercise, it was assumed, had permanent effects on the mind, so that after exercise it increased in relative future effectiveness. While the mind operated as a unit, its parts were distinct, compartmentalized, and localized in the brain.

For education and the curriculum, it is obvious that the theories of mind storage and mental discipline are leagues apart; indeed, they have virtually nothing in common. Stored-up knowledge is beside the point in the mental discipline theory. The acquisition of large quantities of factual knowledge is misplaced educational emphasis. Some facts are needed to carry on the ordinary pursuits of life but this is incidental to the principal concern with mind training. This mental training is achieved by purely mental exercises.

Since mind-training could not be carried on in a vacuum and was considered a mental exercise, subject matter was recognized as a natural medium for the training of the mental functions. But now the purpose and criterion for the selection of the subject matter of the curriculum changed radically. Subject matter became important as an instrument, not an end in itself. It had value in relationship to the mental function it was to be used to develop; as Mr. Dooley commented, "It don't matter now what you study, just so it is hard and ain't liked." For the development of the power to reason it was necessary to scan all the divisions of subject matter and select the ones that appeared most likely to stress reasoning. Mathematics was considered one of the naturals for this purpose. It became one of the prized and emphasized subjects of the school curriculum. No need was felt to defend algebra, geometry, and arithmetic, even in aspects that had no demonstrable value for practical use in life as information, their educational curricular value resting entirely on their qualities for developing the faculty of reason. By the same token, Greek and Latin held honored positions in the school curriculum, not because of any practical worth but because they were thought to be excellent media for the exercise of the mental faculties of discrimination and judgment, and had some claim to value as a stimulus to the functions of imagination and memory. This writer still has vivid memories of the repeated emphasis of his Latin and Greek instructors in the secondary school on the worth of these subjects as mind developers.

The theories of mind storage and mental discipline long shared honored acceptance among educators. Often, among the less discerning educational workers, both theories simultaneously were held in equal, if confused, reverence. There are still many who attempt to defend in the same breath both of these divergent old theories of learning.

The awakening spirit of questioning brought this theory of learning under investigation as it had the mind storage theory. Under the searchlight of objective inquiry this theory too was found to lack a factual basis for support. The studies of such men as James, Thorndike, Lashley, and Koffka have made the mental discipline theory of learning no longer tenable. The rejection of this theory does not imply that there is no transfer of training in learning. Some attention to the nature and extent of transfer will be given in connection with the third theory of learning to be discussed.

The theory of learning that is coming into general acceptance today may be stated simply as *learning through experience*. As a process, it means that *learning is the changing or modification of behavior through experience*. If learning is to be looked upon as the end-product, then it may be defined as *the changes in behavior that result from experience*. According to this theory of learning, our concern is with changing behavior patterns of the learner and how changes in behavior patterns are achieved. This conception of learning through experience has been described in these words:

Learning may be defined as the progressive change in behavior which is associated, on the one hand, with successive presentations of a situation, and on the other, with repeated efforts of the individual to reach to it effectively. Learning may also be thought of as the acquisition of ways of satisfying motives or of attaining goals.[4]

This conception of learning deserves careful study. It is revolutionary in its implications, particularly by comparison with the two previous theories of learning. At first glance the emphasis upon behavior in this theory may not appear to be significant. All learning theories have been based upon the assumption that learning would affect behavior at least indirectly. Otherwise, why learning? The storage of masses of knowledge was assumed to be for the purpose of enabling the person intelligently to determine how he would act. The training of the faculty of reason, for example, was expected to help the individual to guide his behavior by the dictates of his superior powers of reasoning. However, learning itself was directly concerned with mental development processes within the brain.

---

[4] From Arthur I. Gates, and others, *Educational Psychology*, Revised. New York: The Macmillan Company, 1942, p. 299. Also see L. L. Cronbach, *Educational Psychology*. New York: Harcourt, Brace and Company, 1954, Chapter 3; W. C. Morse and G. M. Wingo, *Psychology and Teaching*. Chicago: Scott, Foresman and Company, 1955, Chapter 8.

In this theory of learning through experience, learning *is* change in behavior. Attention is focused upon what *changes* take place in the *behavior* of the individual as the acid test of whether learning has occurred. No change in behavior, no learning. It may be relevant at this point to note that behavior involves the whole learner, not just his brain. His brain, his nervous system, his muscles, his bones, his organic system—all are involved in behavior. The major aspects of one type of behavior change may require obvious change in some form of physical coordination, such as playing the piano or throwing a baseball; or it may concern a change in attitudes, such as respect for other races, interest in good music. But unless the changes in attitudes express themselves in some form of appropriate observable change in behavior, they are presumed not to exist.

The family had moved into a new community, and the opening day of school brought little Alice face to face with a strange new situation. In her former home she had lived near enough to school so that she could return home for lunch. Furthermore, eating facilities at the little school she attended had been very poor. In her new home she lived some distance from school, and since this school had an excellent cafeteria lunchroom, it was thought desirable that Alice should eat at school. At noon the teacher in Alice's room suggested that all those who were going to eat in the lunchroom should line up and go as a group. Alice had never been to a cafeteria before and was quite bewildered as she came into the lunchroom and saw the array of different kinds of salads, fruits, and cookies in small dishes on the counter, and behind a section of the counter women standing by large kettles of hot soups, meats, and vegetables. The tables where pupils ate were bare, not like the luncheon table at home. Fortunately for Alice, she was near the middle of the line, which gave her time to observe what those ahead of her did. She noticed that each took a tray, napkin, knife, fork, and spoon as they moved along the serving counter. She saw some children served soup or meat and vegetables by the women behind the counter, while others passed on to select a salad, a dessert, and a bottle of milk. Hungry and not quite certain what to do, Alice came to the cashier's desk with a tray full of appetizing food. Here she discovered that her lunch took practically all the money she had planned to use for lunch, paper, pencils, and some other school supplies. While she was eating, she discovered that the price of each dish was posted on a big blackboard near the serving counter, so that the pupils in line could have time to select carefully what they wanted to eat and could afford to pay for. Alice found too that her eyes were bigger than her stomach. She resolved that the next day she would choose her food more carefully and stay within her lunch allowance.

Alice had faced a typical new situation similar to that faced by many new pupils, similar to countless situations we all face from time to time. Alice had reacted to this situation in a reasonably intelligent manner. The next time she would do better, and after a short time she would become quite efficient in the selection of a satisfying, nutritious meal at low cost.

Alice had had an *experience*. Everyone recognizes in the cafeteria episode all the factors involved in confronting a problem situation, attempting to understand it, and trying to control and adjust behavior in order satisfactorily to meet the requirements imposed by the situation. An experience, then, represents all the activities progressively involved in the efforts of a person to adjust successfully to a new problem-situation. Learning is the change in the pattern of behavior that occurs as a result of such an experience. Unless such experiences take place, there can be no learning.

There are some very important facets of learning in the experience of Alice. The problem-situation Alice confronted grew out of a definite desire on her part for food to satisfy her hunger at the noon hour. Her desire for food was strong enough to express itself in a definite resolve to seek food. The realization of this purpose became her immediate goal as she got into line with the other pupils to go to the cafeteria. She recognized this as an important step in the final achievement of her purpose.

Having definite purposes is a *sine qua non* of learning. Had

Alice not been hungry, or had she not identified these hunger pangs with the fact that food would relieve her hunger, she would not have consciously desired food, and consequently no effort would have been put forth to secure food. Getting to the cafeteria would not have been a goal to be reached. In other words, she would not have confronted a problem-situation because there would have been no problem involved.

In this connection, it is important to understand three things. First, problem-situations arise only when a sufficiently intense desire or need is identified with a goal that, if reached, will satisfy that desire or need. Second, such goal-seeking involves action. Activity is necessary in learning. One authority has defined learning as "activity under tension toward a goal." Third, problem-situations are of necessity individual. It may happen that similar clearly identified and understood desires arise in a number of individuals almost simultaneously. But still they are personal and identified by the individual as related to his personal needs or desires. In our example, some perceived that these desires were related to goals that could be achieved by going to the lunchroom, others by going home for lunch. John Dewey has repeatedly emphasized that learning can take place only in relation to goals clearly perceived and desired.

The concept of learning as change of behavior through experience, as implied by the definition and by the experience of Alice, means that the medium of learning is essentially problem solving. That purposes and goals are essential in learning implies something to be attained that is much desired but cannot be reached until difficulties in the way have been resolved. Alice faced a situation bristling with problems for her tender years. How to secure from the women behind the counter the food desired, how to make a selection that would satisfy her appetite fully and that would contain the balanced diet she had been taught at home was important, how to stay within her lunch allowance and get the most for her money, these were complex and perplexing elements in a situation that required real problem-solving activity and competency. Alice had learned some ways of behaving appropriate to the solution of this problem in previous problem-situations. She could walk to the cafeteria, she had developed behavior patterns of observing, of seeing cause and effect relations, which helped her to grapple with newer problem aspects of this situation.

Another important aspect of this kind of learning is that successful learning implies the development of a satisfactory working, behaving relationship in the situation confronted. For example, a person has a desire to play an instrument, say, the piano. It is necessary to get in position before the instrument, but that is not as simple a matter as may be supposed. Watch the virtuoso as he goes through all the motions of getting seated in just the correct position before the piano. Adjusting the chair to the right distance from the keys and the pedals is a matter of precision. Then there is the matter of adjusting his body in proper relation to the chair and the instrument, his hands at the right height above the keys. As everyone who has attempted to play the piano knows, the problem of adjustment has just begun. How to translate the notes and symbols on the music sheet to the appropriate keys for the fractional amount of time needed begins the real adjustment difficulties for the aspiring musician. When he is able to bring the behavior of his hands and fingers into such harmonious relationship with the situation that as the eye sees F sharp on the music score the fingers deftly, almost automatically, strike that key, a high degree of adjustment skill has been achieved, and a glow of satisfaction replaces the early anxiety and frustration that existed before the achievement of behavior adjustment appropriate to the needs of the situation. In every experience, then, the degree to which behavior patterns are brought into appropriate relationship with the situation so that the difficulties are resolved marks the extent to which successful learning has taken place.

Inherent in this form of learning, to which allusion has already been made, is the gradual change in the behavior pattern of activities that results from successful efforts to resolve a new situation. Seldom, if ever, is satisfactory behavior adjustment in a new situation achieved in one effort. As implied in the definition, repeated efforts are necessary to achieve success in learning. It required long hours for the piano player to reach a point in his playing where almost automatically the right key was struck as he read the score. Alice did not resolve her cafeteria situation satisfactorily the first or second trip. Every time she tried to make a satisfactory behavior adjustment to her situation she studied her successes and failures, and the reasons for them. Each new effort involved approaching her problem from the vantage point of a new level of behavior effectiveness, until finally, after a week or ten days, she felt satisfaction and confidence that she would select the most wholesome and tasty food, and within a price range admitted by her lunch allowance.

Possibly no facet of the theory of experience learning has been more misunderstood than the need for repeated effort to develop efficient, appropriate behavior patterns by which to resolve problem-situations. Many have felt that time-honored drill or practice no longer was necessary in experience learning. It is true that drill as it was understood and conducted in the old learning theories is no longer accepted. How familiar to oldsters is the type of instruction that used to be given when they were children in school, a type not altogether unknown in classrooms today. The teacher would assign a spelling list to the class with the words, "Now study these until you can spell all the words," or an arithmetic teacher would assign a section of the multiplication tables and say to the class, "Study these tables until you know them." What did either teacher mean? Generally, it was meant that the pupils should continue to spell the word list or repeat the multiplication tables until they could do so without a mistake. Each repetition was presumably made in exactly the same way from the first to the last drill. The pupil finally arrived, but exactly how he got there he could not tell. He would face his next assignment in the same blundering way.

The new theory of learning rejects this sort of drill, but not the idea of repeated efforts at behavior adjustment. After each studied effort to make the behavior changes needed in a situation, some change in the total behavior pattern of the individual nearer to that demanded by the situation does occur. The next effort will bring further desirable modifications in the total behavior pattern, and so on with each effort until such satisfactory changes in the behavior pattern of the learner have been made that he can successfully cope with the situation. But this will be efficiently realized only as the learner takes stock of his achievements after each major effort and adjusts his manner of reacting to the changing conditions that each new effort requires of him. Alice started out each lunch time with more effective ways of behaving that brought her each day nearer her goal. Special effort was made each day to continue successful parts of her behavior and to substitute correct behavior for those parts of her total behavior pattern that she recognized as unsuccessful. There was a definite plan to begin the second effort at the point of progress made after critical appraisal of gains and failures made in the first effort, with a consciously modified plan of attack outlined to reach the goal. This process was continued until attainment of the goal crowned successive efforts.

Not blind repetition, but a critical, modified plan of attack upon the problem with each successive effort is the approved way in experience learning. It is for this reason that many who accept the concept of experience learning have hesitated to use the word "drill," which suggests to many just blind, haphazard repetition. Unfortunately, the absence of such emphasis upon drill has often led to the hasty conclusion that repetition of effort to achieve a goal was frowned upon by the advocates of the new learning.

It is well to repeat here, at the risk of overemphasis, that the modification of behavior in the direction of effective attainment of goals is a matter of progressive or gradual change in that behavior made as a result of successive criticized efforts to reach desired goals. The teacher, whether dealing with aspects of learning often thought of as involving simple skills, numbers, spelling, reading, typing, music—or those traditionally thought to involve reasoning skills—mathematics, literature, social science

—should keep constantly in mind that whether the learning be considered relatively simple or complex, necessary modification in behavior patterns is made gradually and as the result of successive efforts critically appraised and involving several or many similar experiences.

An important aspect of the concept of learning through experience is that experiences are always taking place during the waking hours. Experiences are always involved in the over-all interaction of the learner and his environment in his attempt to make some adequate adjustment to a problem situation. No two experiences are identical, since no two situations are precisely the same. Total behavior patterns are changed in some degree by every experience, however imperceptible these changes may be.

Therefore, adjustment to a given situation, although the situation may appear not to have changed, requires a somewhat different approach. These peculiar characteristics or qualities of experience have far-reaching implications for education and the curriculum.

The experience learning concept clearly does not fit into the traditional subject-matter curriculum. This older form of subject-matter curriculum served well the mind storage and mental discipline theories of learning. It consisted of masses of information handily collected and organized to be put before the pupil to be memorized, or to tease the mental faculties and thereby strengthen them. The new theory of learning is concerned directly with change in behavior and requires a curriculum appropriate to its needs. We are concerned with the experiences children have through which learning—appropriate change in behavior—takes place. Experience involves all that happens to the individual as he reacts to a situation. The curriculum of the child based upon this idea of learning may be defined as follows: *The curriculum consists of all the experiences that the child has irrespective of their character or when or where they take place.* Experiences outside of school are often much more significant in the education of the child than those within the school. The above conception of the curriculum does not lend itself to practical use in the school. The school has access to the pupil for but a part of his active day. The school, while it should be aware of what is going on in the total life of the child, is not solely responsible for his education. It must consider a functional curriculum for that part of the day allotted to it, influencing as far as possible the total pattern of experiences the child has. The more limited definition of the curriculum for the school usually accepted may be stated: *The school curriculum consists of all the experiences the child has under the guidance of the school.*

Such a conception of the curriculum represents a fundamental and irreconcilable cleavage from the traditional subject-matter notion of curriculum. It was possible to control the traditional curriculum by controlling the materials of the curriculum. These were textbooks or activities of the teacher, and therefore could be controlled at the will of the teacher. It was possible to leave off and pick up again at will at a given point in the subject-matter curriculum. Since information-to-be-learned constituted the curriculum, it could be selected and organized in advance for long periods of time, sometimes as far ahead as the school life of the child.

Not so the experience curriculum. Here the continuous nature of experience makes the formation of a cut and dried curriculum impossible. Even the day-by-day needs of the child cannot be determined with precision, much less the specific needs covering a sequence of years. There must be great flexibility in the modern curriculum. The content of the experience curriculum is concerned with the organization of problem situations and the materials related thereto in such a way as to provide the learner with the type of experiences most likely to involve the behavior changes desired.

A curriculum pattern such as this cannot well be blocked out within the subject-matter school program. Problem situations need longer, more flexible blocks of time in which the pupil can come to grips with them. Even more important, the behavior changes anticipated in the experience curriculum will be of value only to the extent that they help the learner to make satisfactory adjustments to the requirements of a democratic way of living. Opportunities both in the school and in the community are essential for the necessary experiences that will develop the attitudes and skills of democratic living. All these are best provided in the curriculum organization involved in the core pattern, with its flexible organization, emphasis upon problem-solving situations pertinent to democratic living, and a close teacher-pupil relationship that makes possible maximum personal and group guidance in learning.

How Are Individual Differences Related to the Core Curriculum?

Recent knowledge of the extent and character of individual differences has had a profound effect upon education and the curriculum. Before the turn of the century, little was known about the way individuals differed in capacity, ability, or interests. In fact, only within very recent decades have the subtle nuances of these differences been known. The fact that people were in some way different, of course, has been recognized for ages. But the dunce cap did not mean to an older generation what it symbolizes for us. To them, it meant mostly laziness and disinclination to learn. Otherwise, making an exhibition of the individual by placing a dunce cap on his head and placing him on a special stool in front of the class or in a corner had no meaning. It was done to shame the pupil into industriousness on the assumption that he could learn as well as other members of the class if he wanted to.

In the decades just before 1900, a number of studies began to throw light on this important subject. One of the first major publications dealing with many phases of individual differences appeared in 1914, when Thorndike published his notable volume, *Mental Work and Fatigue and Individual Differences and Their Causes*. This summary of important studies, and the published work of other men, forced educators to take into account types of individual differences not previously recognized.[5]

Individual differences are now understood to be quite varied and complex. We now know that differences between individuals include much more than varying degrees of mental ability. Differences in special aptitudes, interests, and emotional and social variations are now recognized as important, as the school tries to meet the needs of individuals. One individual has a special flair for music, another shows unusual talent in art; one pupil appears to be calm, almost phlegmatic in his reactions, another is nervous, high-strung, easily excitable; that pupil now speaking to the class is popular, has a knack for getting along with others and getting them to do things, while that pupil over near the window is timid, seldom speaks in class, and seems to have no leadership ability. These are some forms of observable differences easily recognized by every teacher, although all too frequently nothing is done to adjust the curriculum or instructional procedures to fit the needs here evident.

There are other forms of more complex differences that our lockstep school organizational system and traditionally uniform types of curriculum do not meet. It is well known now that individual differences in ability vary widely in any given class. For example, a typical fifth grade class of 32 pupils was found to vary in chronological age from 9 years, 10 months to 11 years, six months, and on the basis of an intelligence test, to have a range of I. Q.'s from 79 to 143. According to the results of a nationally known achievement test, the class showed a spread from fourth grade to sixth grade in arithmetic, third grade to tenth grade in science, second grade to ninth grade in spelling, fourth grade to eleventh grade in geography, and second grade to eleventh grade in reading. Studies show that in the typical sixth grade class you can expect a variation in accomplishment

---

[5] For more recent discussions on individual differences, see Anne Anastasi and J. P. Foley, Jr., *Differential Psychology,* Revised. New York: The Macmillan Company, 1949; L. E. Tyler, *The Psychology of Human Differences,* Revised. New York: Appleton-Century-Crofts, 1956; and K. Eells, and others, *Intelligence and Cultural Differences.* Chicago: University of Chicago Press, 1951.

in the traditional curriculum of six to nine years. A test of basic skills given by a teacher to her fourth grade class of 36 pupils revealed these interesting differences in a large class.[6]

Tests	Grade Spread
Reading Comprehension	5 years 8 months
Reading Vocabulary	6 " 5 "
Map Reading	3 " 2 "
Use of References	8 " 5 "
Use of Index	7 " 6 "
Use of Dictionary	7 " 0 "
Punctuation	4 " 0 "
Capitalization	4 " 2 "
Correct Usage	8 " 2 "
Spelling	7 " 1 "

Startling as these indications of wide differences in achievement are, the problem of a wide range of achievement differences within one pupil is even more startling. The same achievement test given the fifth graders was given the sixth grade in May, in anticipation of its transfer in the fall to the junior high school. The spread in the achievement record of one pupil is not unlike the differences that existed in the achievements of the rest of the class. In spelling and general composition, this pupil stood at the fourth grade level, in arithmetic, sixth grade, in geography, eighth grade, in literature, science, and social studies, above the junior high school achievement norms.

It is obvious that traditional grade classification and grade level curriculums are wholly unrealistic and unadjusted to the educational needs of children with such wide variation in capability and achievement. It is equally clear that the traditional uniform curriculum with subject-matter emphasis does not meet the needs of young people with a wide range of individual differences, nonacademic in nature. It is vitally important in a democracy that the social and emotional differences of pupils be given equal

---

[6] Adapted from data in *A Guide for Better Instruction in Minnesota Schools,* Curriculum Bulletin No. 1. St. Paul, Minn.: State Department of Education, 1946, p. 128.

consideration with other forms of individual differences. The core curriculum with its emphasis upon a program type of flexible organization provides the best milieu for the development of each individual in keeping with his individual needs. In the core curriculum, with its emphasis upon individual as well as group needs, the pupil can develop his peculiar interests without neglecting the balance needed in the development of all the competencies necessary for success in a democratic society. The effort in the core curriculum to provide continuity of teacher guidance of the pupil's learning through keeping the teacher and group together over a period of years further facilitates attention to pupil differences through more intimate acquaintance of the teacher with each pupil. The fact that the core curriculum is definitely organized to care for the common needs of all accentuates the special-interest function of the rest of the curriculum to provide for individual differences outside the core program in avocational and vocational areas, but in full harmony with all that we know about the complex nature of differences both among and within individuals.

How Is Motivation Related to the Core Curriculum?

Motivation is an integral and emphasized part of the theory of learning through experience. In the definition of learning, goal-seeking and purpose were recognized as the springboards of action. Problem-situations grow out of the presence of a felt need or desire clearly perceived in relation to a goal that would satisfy that need or desire. When the clearly perceived need or desire is strong enough, the individual proposes to do something about it. This is called *motivation*. Since one usually is stirred to action not only by the inner urges, needs, or desires of the organism, but also by recognition of the object or goal that will satisfy the need or relieve the tension when attained, motivation is generally thought of in this larger context or relationship.

Motivation is of supreme importance in learning; without it

learning does not take place. The teacher should be fully conscious of this fact in all educational planning. The wise teacher understands the springs to motivation and creates learning situations that capitalize upon these natural drives. Who has not seen the listless, indifferent pupil suddenly galvanized into alertness when he was able to relate his school work to personal desire or need? It is always a stimulating experience to see boys and girls in the early elementary school years eagerly working with crayon, scissors, and paste, as they cut out heart-shaped forms, color them, and properly inscribe them as precious valentines to mother and father. About five o'clock one evening a visitor was standing outside a high school in conversation with the science instructor, when he chanced to look up at the window of the science room. Lights were burning brightly. Thinking they had been left on accidentally by the instructor, he called attention to the lights. The instructor commented, "That is a real example of motivation. Fred, you know, plans to go into engineering and wants to take advanced courses in physics in college, so he asked if he could work on some special problems after school. He has been using all his spare time during school hours on work in physics and frequently stays after school." When Fred entered college, he was permitted to skip freshman physics and enter advanced courses.

These examples suggest the importance of real purposes and goals in motivation. They give direction to the pupil's activities and tend to focus all his energy upon the attainment of the goal in question. Visitors to schools where an intelligent core curriculum is in operation usually marvel at the genuine interest and eagerness displayed by the pupils. Class activities appear to be focused and energized beyond anything found in the typical subject-matter classroom. Pupils are working on problems that are clearly understood in relation to important goals. Motivation has thus released energy for and provided direction to their activities, which they see as meaningful and necessary in resolving their problem-situations. As these pupils carry on the different phases of their work, the visitor is further impressed with the fact that the pupils appear quite indifferent to the presence of strangers in the classroom and to other normal occurrences that tend to be serious distractions in traditional classes. They seem to go forward with their activities with conscious purposiveness and a minimum of lost motion. An important characteristic of motivation is that as it focuses attention upon the goals to be achieved in any activity, it also tends to select and channel these activities in a purposeful direction. The learner tends to select those particular items for attention that contribute to his purposes and ignore those that do not appear to do so.

These particular characteristics of motivation become much clearer and their importance more evident in relation to so-called school discipline. There are two sharply divergent conceptions of the meaning of discipline. To those who believe in the authoritarian form of society, it means the will and ability to adapt to the rules laid down by someone in authority. It is not important that the person who does the adapting understands why. The important information needed by the one obeying is how. The words of the famous poem, *The Charge of the Light Brigade,* "Theirs not to reason why, theirs but to do and die," express the idea and ideal of discipline of an authoritarian type. In fact, too much knowledge of the why may lead to critical thinking, so it is frowned upon. Japanese autocracy, before and during World War II, set up what are called "thought controls" to discourage thinking lest it lead to questioning of mandates handed down, and to consequent disobedience. Severe penalties were established for any indication of doubt as to the rightness of the rules laid down by the authorities. Fear becomes the motivation of behavior in this type of society and with this concept of discipline.

The subject type of curriculum is inherently suited to the development of individuals motivated to accept authority. The transmission-of-the-cultural-heritage idea is essentially authoritarian in basic concept. It rests upon the authority of wisdom accumulated and passed on to future generations to direct the adaptation of behavior. Conformity without questioning the wisdom garnered from the past is the very essence of this idea of education. The school that holds the philosophy of the subject-matter curriculum, therefore, places a premium upon ready, un-questioning obedience to regulations. Good discipline in the traditional school is measured by the degree to which pupils without questioning give ready acceptance and conformity to the established program of the school.

A concept of discipline now generally accepted in American educational circles, but not extensively practiced, holds good discipline to consist in the extent to which boys and girls understand what kind of behavior results in the greatest good for all, and consciously endeavor to control their own behavior in conformity with these standards of conduct. In the school conducted in harmony with this idea of discipline, conduct controls would not be motivated by fear of violating the dictation of authority, but by a conscious desire to behave in certain ways because this would most probably result in the greater satisfaction of basic needs and desires. This concept of discipline is now recognized as in harmony with the democratic ideal of living, indeed, as essential to it. Some have defined discipline as synonymous with education for democratic living. As one writer insists: "Discipline means preparing boys and girls for life in a democratic society."

The core curriculum is inherently unsuited to the disciplinary ideal of authoritarianism, but is in full harmony with the ideal of democracy. Its organization around problems creates skills in critical thinking, and its emphasis upon the method of cooperative teacher-pupil planning and attack upon problem situations gives practical experience and training in democratic group processes. It is the democratic way of life in day-by-day practice in school life.

An observer was visiting a junior high school organized on the basis of the core curriculum. He was impressed with the excellent spirit of the classes visited. The pupils were alert, interested in what they were doing, and the general atmosphere of the classroom was conducive to wholesome group work of the kind in progress in the classes visited. Frequently the teachers would pause in what they were doing to explain the activities of groups clustered around various tables, and indicate the central problem of the class. It did not seem to matter to the class that the teacher might be talking at length to the observer and the school principal; the groups had purposes to be realized and evidently had well in mind the general procedures they proposed to follow. All were intent upon their work. No behavior that might be classified as distracting was noticed. As the observer and the principal passed through corridors of this large school, the observer commented: "I see no indication here of corridor monitors." The principal replied, "No, I would not have them around. We maintain our school morale on a different basis. But I could show you schools where they think it is even necessary to have policemen around."

A noted educational leader reported a visit to two senior high schools of about equal size in another large city, both located in poorer sections of the city, and both attended by youth of mixed races. Of the two, the traditional school had once been a famous school serving an aristocratic district, but the community had been taken over by mixed racial groups. The visitor found many windows broken and stuffed with cardboard, corridors and class-rooms dirty and defaced, and a state of general confusion through-out. Several policemen were present within and without the building. They were regarded as necessary to maintain sufficient order for schoolwork to continue. The other school, located in a tenement district of much lower economic status but organized on the core curriculum basis, presented a definite contrast. No windows were broken, there was a fine lawn planted by the students and cared for by them, the corridors were clean, the atmosphere of the school and classrooms was orderly and business-like, and the students were alert, studious, and courteous.

How can such drastic differences in schools be explained? The answer is to be found in the quality of motivation present in these schools. In the school where unsocial behavior of a very serious character was present, the curriculum was organized upon a traditional subject-matter basis. Compulsory attendance laws forced the students to attend this school and to study subjects for which they saw no relation to recognized needs and desires.

To the student, the content of the subjects studied bore no observable relation to the world he lived in, and at no point helped him consciously to solve the vital personal, social, and economic problems that vexed and worried him. Consequently, the students rebelled at the idea of doing something that held no promise of satisfying their needs. Frustrated because they were compelled to do things in which they saw no value, these students engaged in a form of behavior that struck blindly out against forces that seemed to deny them the right to pursue activities consistent with their purposes and goals in life. Only force, or the fear of consequences more unpleasant than satisfying the demands of the school with as little effort as possible, kept these students in school, studying in desultory fashion. Any semblance of socially acceptable or conforming behavior is secured in this school largely under adult authority supported by visible evidence of force. Motivation is through compulsion and fear.

On the other hand, in the school where the core curriculum is operative, an entirely different type of pupil behavior is present. The reason is obvious to observers, and inherent in the core curriculum. Here the curriculum consists of problem-situations that are vital to the learner and are so recognized by him. Under the guidance of the teacher, the pupils and teacher together explore the problems, personal and social, that they face or are likely to face in the future as they try to live successfully within their culture. They have together decided upon some of the behavior competencies needed if they are to grapple with the kind of problem-situation they know they must be able to solve. In other words, they have explored their needs and desires in a preliminary way and related them to objectives or goals that, when attained, will bring satisfaction. The school curriculum is understood. It exists only to help them become able to realize cherished desires by reaching well-understood and accepted goals. Teachers are there to help them develop efficiently the ways of doing the things they want above all else to be able to do.

Teachers are not taskmasters who force them to do useless, non-sensical things, but friends upon whom they rely as older, experienced persons to advise and help them. The school is a privileged place in which they learn how to achieve their purposes in life much better than anywhere else. They think of the school as a place where they learn to live happily in group life, to make and hold friends, to develop qualities of leadership, to become respected citizens and homemakers, to acquire the skills needed for business success. Here, motivation is through awareness of the vital relationship of the school program to the realization of purposes and goals in life.

To ask which type of curriculum program, as exemplified by these rather extreme examples, best serves the democratic way of life seems superfluous. Democratic living requires intelligent participation, skill in the art of group study and learning, in critically modifying and setting up rules of the road for the direction and control of social behavior, and personal readiness to adjust behavior accordingly. This can be achieved only in a school environment in which pupils learn by practice how to live together democratically. Only in such an environment can pupils discover the rational basis of personal and social values that provides the motivation for such living and learning. If "the proof of the pudding is in the eating," then the schools organized on the basis of the core curriculum provide the type of motivation and learning that meets best the needs of our democratic society.

SELECTED REFERENCES

Alberty, Harold, *Reorganizing the High School Curriculum,* Revised. New York: The Macmillan Company, 1953, Chapter 3, "Democratic Values and Learning."

American Educational Research Association, "The Educational Program: Adolescence," *Review of Educational Research,* Vol. 24, February, 1954. Washington, D. C.: The National Education Association.

———, "The Educational Program: Later Adolescence," *Review of Educational Research,* Vol. 24, October, 1954. Washington, D. C.: The National Education Association.

Association for Supervision and Curriculum Development, *Creating a Good Environment for Learning,* 1954 Yearbook. Washington: National Education Association, 1954.

Ausubel, David P., *Theory and Problems of Adolescent Development.* New York: Grune and Stratton, 1954.

Bernard, Harold W., *Toward Better Personal Adjustment,* Revised. New York: McGraw-Hill Book Company, Inc., 1957.

Bossing, Nelson L., *Principles of Secondary Education,* Second Edition. Englewood Cliffs, N. J.: Prentice-Hall, Inc., 1955, Chapter 4, "What Is the Nature of the Secondary School Pupil?"

Bugelski, B. R., *The Psychology of Learning.* New York: Henry Holt and Company, 1956.

Cantor, Nathaniel, *The Teaching-Learning Process.* New York: The Dryden Press, 1953.

Cole, Luella, *Psychology of Adolescence,* Revised. New York: Rinehart and Company, Inc., 1954.

Cruze, W. W., *Adolescent Psychology and Development.* New York: The Ronald Press Company, 1953.

Estes, W. K., and others, *Modern Learning Theory.* New York: Appleton-Century-Crofts, Inc., 1954.

Frank, Lawrence K., *Individual Development.* Garden City: Doubleday and Company, 1955.

———, and others, *Personality Development in Adolescent Girls.* New Orleans: Louisiana State University School of Medicine, 1953.

Gallagher, J. R., *Understanding Your Son's Adolescence.* Boston: Little, Brown and Company, 1951.

Gates, A. I., and others, *Educational Psychology,* Revised. New York: The Macmillan Company, 1948.

Gesell, Arnold, Frances L. Ilg, and Louise B. Ames, *Youth: The Years from Ten to Sixteen.* New York: Harper and Brothers, 1956.

Helping Children Live and Learn. Washington, D. C.: Association for Childhood Education International, 1952.

Hilgard, Ernest R., *Theories of Learning*, Revised. New York: Appleton-Century-Crofts, Inc., 1956.

Hoskins, R. G., *Endocrinology*, Revised. New York: W. W. Norton and Company, 1950.

Jenkins, Gladys G., and others, *Guidebook for Teen-Agers*. Chicago: Scott, Foresman and Company, 1955.

Kingsley, H. L., and Ralph Garry, *The Nature and Conditions of Learning*. Englewood Cliffs, N. J.: Prentice-Hall, Inc., 1957.

Kuhlen, R. G., *Psychology of Adolescent Development*. New York: Harper and Brothers, 1952.

Landis, Paul H., *Understanding Teen-Agers*. New York: Appleton-Century-Crofts, Inc., 1955.

Lindgren, Henry C., *Educational Psychology in the Classroom*. New York: John Wiley and Sons, Inc., 1956.

Martin, W. E., and C. B. Stendler, *Child Development: The Process of Growing Up in Society*. New York: Harcourt, Brace, and Company, 1953.

Menninger, William C., and others, *How To Be A Successful Teen-Ager*. New York: Sterling Company, 1955.

Morse, W. C., and G. M. Wingo, *Psychology and Teaching*. Chicago: Scott, Foresman and Company, 1955.

Remmers, H. H., and others, *Introduction to Educational Psychology*. New York: Harper and Brothers, 1954, Chapter 9, "What Are the Influencing Factors and Functions of Learning?" and Chapter 10, "How and Why We Learn."

Saylor, J. Galen, and W. M. Alexander, *Curriculum Planning*. New York: Rinehart and Company, Inc., 1954, Chapter 5, "The Pupil As a Factor in Curriculum Planning."

Schaffer, L. F., and E. J. Shoben, *The Psychology of Adjustment*, Revised. Boston: Houghton Mifflin Company, 1956.

Smithies, Elsie M., *Case Studies of Normal Adolescent Girls*. New York: Appleton-Century-Crofts Company, Inc., 1933.

Stolz, Herbert R., *Somatic Development of Adolescent Boys*. New York: The Macmillan Company, 1955.

Trager, Helen G., and Marian R. Yarrow, *They Learn What They Live*. New York: Harper and Brothers, 1952.

Chapter 6

The Core Class in Action

What actually goes on in a core class? How does a class "get ready" for the process of group problem solving? How do students select a problem for study? After they have selected a problem, how do they organize themselves to attack it? What is the role of the teacher in such planning?

Such questions as these are asked every time teachers consider the process of teacher-pupil planning. They are highly important questions, for without some understanding of the actual process of group problem solving, teachers are quite likely to make some mistakes which may defeat or delay the process instead of facilitating it. Perhaps even worse, some teachers have become convinced by their initial errors that they cannot direct the process of teacher-pupil planning and as a result they have sometimes abandoned their efforts toward it.

In many cases, the mistakes which teachers make are the result of certain false assumptions. Let us look at a few of these mistaken beliefs which can defeat our efforts to plan with students.

SOME FALSE ASSUMPTIONS

1. *All teachers can be categorized as either authoritarian or democratic in their methods.* Classroom democracy, like democracy generally, is a goal toward which people grow as they live and work together. Its absolute achievement cannot be "granted" at one fell swoop. It must be earned and learned.

2. *A teacher who falls back upon authoritarian methods should feel guilty.* On the contrary, every effective teacher has found it necessary on occasion to assume a firmly parental role when students have revealed that they cannot as yet supply their own controls and choices of alternatives.

3. *All adolescents are equally ready for teacher-pupil planning.* Not only do individuals within a class vary widely in their emotional "readiness" for planning, but also certain classes differ sharply from other classes in this regard.

4. *Readiness for planning depends on the age-level of students.* We hear such comments as "only the older senior high-school students are mature enough for such freedom." We also hear that "only in junior high school or elementary schools do teachers dare permit students to help select the areas they will study." Actually, the experiences they have had in planning and their own feelings about it are more important criteria of readiness than the ages of students. Children and youth of all ages, including the kindergarten year, have engaged successfully in group planning and evaluation.

5. *It takes years of conditioning to prepare students for teacher-pupil planning.* On the contrary, many groups have overcome their initial handicaps and moved into effective group planning almost immediately, or after a week of orientation and try-out. Other groups may require a longer period.

6. *The teacher is only an observer, or at most an equal participant in the teacher-pupil planning process.* This assumption ignores a number of dynamic roles played by the democratic teacher. Analysis of these roles will be included in Chapter 8. At this point it may be sufficient to state that the aim of a good core teacher should be to operate in such a way as to help students learn, gradually but surely, to handle their own controls and to develop skills in making wise choices of subject matter and procedures. Such a teacher will eventually "graduate" from the roles of disciplinarian and decider into those of resource person and counselor.

Meanwhile, even the successful core teacher will, on occasion, find it necessary to assume the helm when the vessel is dangerously off its course and the crew is temporarily demoralized.

The kindergarten class was finally in their little chairs in a circle. Delays had resulted when Effie had to tell Miss Shafer about her birthday party next Saturday, John wanted to know when it was his turn to ring the bell, and Sue had presented Miss Shafer with a dusty cluster of green grapes. Now Miss Shafer stood at the front board and printed a schedule for today's activities as the class made suggestions about what they should do first, then next. No serious disagreements arose about the plans, but Mary and Kate criticized Calvin at one point for leaving the blocks scattered around during clean-up time yesterday. Miss Shafer asked Calvin if he would like to show everybody that he could put away the blocks by assuming this responsibility today. Fourteen children made suggestions about activities. Consensus was indicated by a frequent showing of hands. It was clear that not only everybody had a housekeeping or leadership role, but that everybody in the class wanted such roles in his or her turn. There was evidence of ability to think together, to make plans, to evaluate success or shortcomings, and to reach decisions that were acceptable to the group. Morale was high.

The preceding description is of an actual group of 25 five-year olds, engaged in an effective use of group planning. It could be multiplied many times, for good kindergarten teachers all over the country have found it possible for five-year olds to make plans, to carry them out, and to evaluate results at their level of communication. How many of these children are helped to retain and to strengthen these skills throughout their school career? The answer must be, all too few. Somewhere along the way, in most schools, children lose this precious ability to assume responsibility, to decide together what must be done, and to do it cooperatively. A core class in the secondary school must recapture some of the essential ingredients in this process in order to go into action as group problem solvers.

One of the essentials in the planning process is a feeling of security on the part of everyone in the class. A new class in a new school usually includes children from several elementary or junior high schools. They not only do not know each other well, but they do not know their new school either. An excellent beginning can be made by providing some orientation experiences which will help students get acquainted with each other, with their new school, with their teacher, and with the procedures they are to employ.

Dr. Rosalind Zapf, who has taught core classes for many years at Detroit's Denby High School, describes this orientation process as follows:

Launching the class. The first few weeks in a beginning core class are spent in a wide variety of activities, all having the purpose of helping the boys and girls become acquainted with one another, with the teacher, with the school, and with the many situations which they must meet daily and which are new to them on coming into a school with which they are not familiar. The teacher makes every effort to make her pupils feel at home. Opportunities are given for the boys and girls to learn each other's names, what they enjoy doing outside of school, and where they have lived and gone to school. Representatives of the different clubs are brought in to interest the newcomers in joining one or another. The school paper and yearbook are not only advertised; their preparation is explained and demonstrated. Several periods are spent in the school library where the librarian gives help in understanding how to use the facilities available. Invitations are also extended to the principal and assistant principal and a counsellor or two to visit the class and become acquainted with the boys and girls.

From the beginning the teacher makes every effort to find out all that she can about her boys and girls—their interests, their general reactions to situations, their home relationships, their existing friendships, their ability to make new frends, in fact, anything that might prove of value in understanding and helping them. She must in turn give much of this same type of information about herself in a friendly and easy way to her pupils so that they feel that they know her, not just as a teacher, but as a friend.

Just where the orientation period ends is hard to say. With some classes it is fairly accomplished in two weeks' time. With others it must be continued for a much longer time. Gathering information of the nature described above actually never ceases, although it is obtained as time goes on by less direct methods then during the initial orientation period. However, when a class seems to be on a reasonably friendly basis and good rapport has been established between pupils and teacher, the group is ready to go into action.[1]

Myrtle Toops, core teacher at the Burris Laboratory School at Ball State (Indiana) Teachers College, has also described the "getting acquainted" stage.

The first several days of school were spent in establishing friendy relationships and good rapport between students and teacher. A wide variety of activities with the sole purpose of helping the children get acquainted with each other, with the teachers, with the school, and with new situations which they would meet daily, were planned and carried out. Children were encouraged to tell of their hobbies, vacation trips, and interests. Organizations to which they belonged were reviewed. Often children organized in small groups for these discussions. Sometimes the entire group shared.

The arrangements of the furniture and the bulletin boards were cooperatively planned. The care of the room library and the care of the flowers and aquaria were planned. A survey of materials to be found in the room was made.[2]

A significant part of the process which these two experienced core teachers describe is that which involves getting acquainted with one's peers. This need to reduce social barriers is a vital part of any group process. Its real significance is not generally recognized. Each of us carries about him an invisible but very real barrier with which he protects himself from others. We develop this barrier to prevent others from finding out that we are not as good or as smart or as able as we would like them to think we are. Unfortunately, these barriers work both ways— they tend to prevent others from knowing us, but they also prevent us from communicating with others. The five-year olds described earlier in this chapter have not yet discovered this need to shield themselves from others. Consequently, they usually open themselves to new friends much more readily and skillfully than

---

[1] Dr. Zapf has served since 1942 as chairman of the core teaching staff at Denby High School. Her description of the core curriculum has also been presented in filmstrip form: *A Core Curriculum Class in Action*. Detroit: Wayne State University College of Education, 1948.

[2] Myrtle Dewey Toops, *Working in the Core Program in Burris Laboratory School*. Muncie, Indiana: Ball State Teachers College, 1955, p. 15.

older children or adults. Communication is a relatively easy matter in the kindergarten.

Adolescents have lost some of this skill in communication which they once possessed. They have had experiences, both in school and out, which have caused them to withdraw from others, to erect barriers between themselves and strangers. The barriers are not impenetrable in adolescence; they will not, however, melt away at once without some help. Situations are needed that help classmembers to get well acquainted with their peers. Resolving social barriers will help much to speed communication and thus to facilitate problem-solving and planning activities.

Some teachers ask the class to form small "get acquainted" groups of four. At the end of twenty minutes, each member introduces a new friend to the class, telling his name and hobbies or interests. He may add, "the most interesting thing I learned about —— in the past twenty minutes was ——."

In forming such small groups it may be well to structure them in such a way as to scatter those entering from any one previous school among several groups. This plan can also be useful in further, temporary grouping for such specific purposes as planning a get-acquainted party or in making proposals for improving the seating, room decoration, bulletin boards, and library. Other core classes use small groups for committee purposes, such as a temporary planning committee, a map committee to plot the locations of homes represented in the class, or committees for arranging visits to various parts of the school, inviting older students to speak to the class about school activities, making building drawings to help the class get acquainted with their new school, or taking care of special equipment in the room. Name tags may be useful at the early stages in getting the class launched. These may be lapel cards, or the easel cards which are placed on the desk in front of each student. Movable seats are a great help in speeding up the get-acquainted process. The class seating plan should be studied rather carefully for clues to helping students make new friends.

Many different get-acquainted games have been found useful

by core teachers. These include such a device as self-introductions, followed by a contest to see who can afterward introduce the largest number of students to the class. There are also a number of games such as cutting and matching puzzles, matching different colors of ribbons on name tags, and "who am I?" puzzles in which one student describes another and the class guesses his name.

The early remarks students make about their hobbies or special interests can become useful aids in remembering names and in forming new friendships based on common interests. The teacher should act like a member of the class at this point, and tell the students about some of his personal interests and hobbies, too. Core students often recall this early talk about hobbies as their first indication that "teachers are people."

An early party for the whole class can speed the process of getting well acquainted. This may take the form of a late afternoon or evening at the bowling alleys or skating rink, a movie party followed by snacks, a dance, or a series of social games followed by refreshments. The type of recreation must be selected with skill and sensitivity in terms of the maturity and interests of the students. It will be a better party if the students help plan it, for they can guess more intelligently than most adults what kind of a party their group will enjoy. A valuable chance to observe students engaged in group planning is presented by the class party. An estimate of their readiness to enter into further planning experiences can be formed from watching their behavior in planning the party. Such questions as the following might occur to the teacher throughout this early process of temporary grouping for social and orientation experiences:

Is My Group Ready for Planning?

1. Do they appear to be interested in the specific objectives they have set?
2. Are there evidences that they have had previous experiences in co-operative planning?
3. Are they succeeding in overcoming such initial barriers to group

unity as social cliques, religious or racial differences, and economic or nationality differences?

4. Are leaders beginning to emerge from the group?

5. Do they seem eager to assume some responsibility?

6. Do they see a need or reason for the small group or committee?

7. Do they feel comfortable about the process, and about the teacher's (new) role in it?

8. Do they exhibit some self-confidence?

9. Can they recognize and meet a problem without disintegrating? [3]

Orientation includes more than getting acquainted with the new school and with one's fellows. It includes also an understanding of what group planning entails, of what demands it makes on each member of a class, and of what role the teacher will play in any group planning process. If the students have been accustomed in their previous school years to a considerable amount of teacher-direction, they may not be "ready" in the sense implied by the foregoing questions. It may help to spend some time evaluating how well the planning went in the groups that were formed for socializing purposes.

Some teachers have gone on at this point to introduce the whole matter of "democracy" or cooperative planning, and to explore with students how it might work in their own class.

an introduction to "democracy"

Zapf describes an early unit on democracy, which serves in ninth grade core classes to prepare the way for group problem solving.

The first unit. The first actual unit of work is a unit on democracy. The purpose of this is two-fold: (1) to serve as an introduction to the ideas underlying a core class; and (2) to bridge the gap between strictly teacher-directed work to which pupils are largely accustomed, and work planned by the pupils and teachers together. A typical introduction to this unit follows:

TEACHER .

If someone were to ask you what kind of government we have in this country, what would you answer?

[3] Adapted from a report of a graduate class, Wayne State University, College of Education, 1954.

All hands up and a general laugh.

TEACHER

Well, Helen?

HELEN

It's a democracy, of course.

TEACHER

Is she right?

MANY VOICES

Sure.

HUGH

My brother says we aren't as democratic as we think we are.

BILL

My father says we call it that, but that it isn't really.

HELEN

I think it is, because we have a representative form of government, and so it's a democracy.

JACK

Sure. Everyone 21 or older can vote, can't they?

TEACHER

Let's hold it a minute and see if we are sure that we *agree* on what a democracy is. What would you say was a definition of a real democracy? If we agree on that we may have less trouble deciding whether or not we have a democracy in America.

JOY

That's easy—it's government of the people, by the people, and for the people.

TEACHER

How about it? Jane?

JANE

I agree with Joy.

BILL

Sure, we learned that long ago.

General murmur of assent.

TEACHER

Are we agreed on that then? All of us? Does anyone feel that this might not be all of the story?

MARGARET

Well, I don't know, Miss ————, but what about the people who can't get jobs? They're people, but it seems as though the government doesn't always care whether they have a place to live or not.

MARY

My mother doesn't vote.

STANLEY

And in some places a Negro can't vote.

DON

Oh, who cares anyway whether he can or not?

SUSAN

He's part of the people isn't he?

TEACHER

It sounds as though we aren't as ready to settle on the definition of democracy as we thought, doesn't it? Maybe we need more information to help us reach a decision. There are two movies in the building, one called, "Democracy," and the other called, "Despotism." [4] I wonder if you wouldn't like to see these before you come to a conclusion as to what democracy is.

The following class period is spent in the movie room, viewing the two films. From this develops a class discussion of democracy as we find it in our country and in our homes. Another aspect of this discussion is the degree of democracy found in the American schoolroom.

TEACHER

In the last few days we've been talking about democracy. Yesterday we spent quite a bit of time considering the question of whether we lived democratically in our homes and we came to some interesting conclusions. How about a quick review of these, Gail?

GAIL

Well, we found that in most of our homes there was a fair amount of shared respect, but not too much shared power or shared knowledge.

SHIRLEY

There were exceptions to those though; for example, when Bill said that his family all helped plan where they were to go on trips.

---

[4] Both films produced by Encyclopedia Brittanica Films, Inc., Willamette, Ill.

TEACHER

That's right, we did see a great many exceptions, and they are pretty important. Now, I'm wondering what you think about the degree of democracy we usually have in school classrooms.

General shout of derision.

DOUGLAS

That's one place you sure don't find it.

BILL

That's a laugh!

EDITH

How could you have a democracy in school? Somebody has to tell you what to do.

DON

They *make* you go to school, they *make* you learn stuff, they *make* you take exams, they *make* you keep quiet. Democracy—bunk!

TEACHER

I guess I'm beginning to see how you feel, but let's take a minute to look at each of the points we have begun to think are important. How about shared power? Have you had any experiences in which a teacher and you shared power?

ELSIE

I was chairman of a class for a week in Miss *A*'s class in grade school, so I guess that would be sharing power.

JUSTINE

But you could only do what she wanted you to do. That doesn't seem like sharing the power to me.

HUGH

Besides, it was only you two. The rest of the class still had to do what either you or Miss *A* said.

PHYLLIS

I think Edith was right. The *teacher* should tell us what to do.

JOY

In our school our class was allowed to plan a picnic without the teacher's help—just us.

TEACHER

Did it go off all right?

JOY

Sure. It was swell, but that was a once in a lifetime chance.

DON

But most of the time you have to do exactly as the teacher tells you or you get in trouble.

TEACHER

It sounds as though most of you feel that sharing power between pupils and a teacher is either impossible or is something that ought not to happen. Now think a minute. Could a class be set up so that the pupils would share running the class with the teacher? Could our class be set up that way? Would it be wise?

JACK

You mean we would help decide what we were going to do?

JANE

Do you mean that our ideas would count?

BILL

And what would happen at card-making time? Those who did what you liked would get good grades, and those who didn't wouldn't.

TEACHER

Do you really think I would mark you down when you didn't agree with me?

BILL

No-o-o, I guess not.

PHYLLIS

But how would we know what to do?

HELEN

I think we could talk things over and decide all together what to do.

DON

We would have to choose class officers to take care of the different things.

TEACHER

Do you mean, Don, that there would be responsibilites for a lot of people to carry?

DON

Sure—I guess we would all have some.

JANE

What if we decide to do something and it doesn't work?

JACK

We would know enough then not to try doing things that way again. We could chalk that up to experience.

ELSIE

What if the class decides to do something against school rules?

DOUGLAS

Maybe we would have to have a constitution and put down in black and white what the rules are for our class. That could include school rules.

TEACHER

You sound very much in favor of trying out a democratic procedure. But before we decide, let's look at the other two points—shared respect and shared knowledge. Let's think about these tonight and we'll talk about them tomorrow.

Several days are now spent in considering whether respect and knowledge are things that can be shared by the boys and girls and the teacher and if so, what kinds of behavior will best bring these about. Such methods as working in groups and having general class discussions in order to find out what other people are thinking about a problem are suggested. These are tried out in class and the successes as well as the problems that the pupils meet in using the techniques are discussed. The conclusion is reached that shared respect and knowledge are as possible as shared power in a classroom if a real effort is made to achieve them.

They decide further that even a small group has certain rights, and certain corresponding responsibilities, if they hope to form a democratic planning group. Following is a typical list of such "rights and responsibilities," drafted by a ninth-grade class:

Rights

1. To express our own opinions
2. To help make the rules
3. To help decide the goals of the group
4. To have a free vote
5. To question the opinions of others
6. To help decide what activities are to be carried on by us

Responsibilities

1. To abide by the rules made by the group
2. To accept responsibilities laid on us by the group
3. To take an active part in the work of the group

4. To work for the welfare of the group
5. To act in such a way as to be an asset to the group.[5]

Organizing for Problem-Attack

The next step is class organization in terms of election of class officers and writing a class constitution. It usually becomes clear early in the process of writing a constitution that it is necessary to establish the goals of the class. When this need is recognized, the class is divided into random groups, each group being responsible for preparing a list of goals. These items are then written on the board and a general discussion follows, in the course of which the class decides on those it feels should be retained on the final list. A sample ninth grade list follows:

Class Goals

1. Gain knowledge in topic selected
2. Do research well:
   a. Use all materials possible
   b. Take good notes
3. Be able to communicate through good writing
4. Be an active and worthwhile member of a working group:
   a. Participate in all discussions
   b. Present helpful ideas as often as possible
   c. Give full attention at all times
5. Get along well with classmates
6. Express thoughts freely and well
7. Improve ability to decide things for ourselves on basis of reliable information
8. Respect another's wishes and opinions
9. Develop self-reliance
10. Increase self-confidence
11. Listen to a discussion with an open mind
12. Develop self-control

Selecting the next unit. When the constitution is complete and the officers have been elected, a class is ready to approach the problem of selecting an area for study.

Establishment of Criteria

CHAIRMAN

Yesterday we decided that we were ready to pick out the topic we want to work on for the next few weeks. We agreed that we would each make a

---

[5] "Rights and Responsibilities" quoted by Zapf from her *A Core Curriculum Class in Action.*

list of the topics we were most interested in at home last night. What should we do now?

JANE

I think we should put them all on the board and then vote for the ones we want most.

DON

I think a committee should take everyone's list and put them all together first.

ELSIE

That would take too long. Why don't we divide into groups of seven or eight and each group can put the lists of its members together.

BILL

That will take too long, too.

TEACHER

Do you want to put every topic that is suggested on the list?

BILL

Sure, why not?

MARY

I think every one should be on.

CHAIRMAN

I showed my list to Doug and he thought a couple of mine shouldn't be on the list and I thought a couple of his shouldn't. I'll bet we'll have trouble that way.

DOUGLAS

I've been thinking. Is there any way we could decide ahead of time whether a topic should go on the list? Some of mine are sort of silly, I guess.

CHAIRMAN

Has anybody any suggestions?

Silence. No suggestions.

CHAIRMAN

Miss ———, what do you think?

TEACHER

Well, when people want to judge whether a thing is to be used or not, they decide on ways to measure its usefulness. We say that they decide on criteria for judging it. Maybe we could go at this by asking ourselves this question: "How can we tell whether or not a topic is a good topic to work on?" What would you say to this question?

JACK

I think a topic is good if knowing about it is going to tell me things that are useful to me. That's most important, I think.

CHAIRMAN

Helen, will you put these on the board? Then we can all see them.

JOY

I think it's just as important to learn about some things that are going to be useful to us later on in our lives too.

CHAIRMAN

Are there any others to be added? Margaret?

MARGARET

A topic should be interesting, too, if you are going to work on it for a long time.

STANLEY

I want to learn about things that are happening in the world today. Maybe that's what Jack meant when he said it should tell us things that are useful. But that might be something like learning how to make a soapbox racer if you wanted to enter the Derby. But I want to be able to understand a lot of other things that are happening too.

CHAIRMAN

Maybe we had better make Jack's point and yours separate even if they sound a lot alike. But I don't know how to say it.

JAY

Could Stanley's point be said this way: "Helps us to understand the world around us?"

STANLEY

That's it.

SUSAN

We had better be pretty sure we can find enough material on the topic we choose, too.

MARY

That's right. If we don't, we'll have trouble.

CHAIRMAN

Any others?

Silence.

TEACHER

How about choosing a topic that you haven't studied before? Would it be a good idea to add that?

HUGH

I think that should go on the list. If it doesn't, we might choose something like Transportation and we studied that for a long time last year.

SUSAN

I don't think it should go on the list because we might study a different problem about transportation and then we would be learning something new.

HUGH

That's different. If we haven't studied that problem and we want to, it's O. K. because then we aren't studying the same thing over at all.

CHAIRMAN

Any other points? If not, will you read the list of points for us, Helen?

HELEN

Criteria for Choosing a Topic
1. Knowledge of the topic should be useful to us now
2. Knowledge of the topic should be useful to us later in our lives
3. A topic should be interesting
4. Knowledge of the topic should help us to understand the world around us.
5. We should be able to find enough material on the topic
6. It should be a subject we haven't studied before

CHAIRMAN

Now that we have that done, we still have to decide how to select our topic to work on. But I guess that will have to wait till tomorrow.

As was indicated at the beginning of the group discussion just reported, the selection of an area of work is set in motion by having every pupil bring a list of possible topics to class. The next step is to have each pupil judge his suggestions on the basis of the criteria set up by the class. Following this, random groups are usually formed in order to assemble the various suggestions and to consider further the fitness of the items in terms of the established criteria. A final list is then put on the board and discussed.

These items are weighted by each pupil on a 3-2-1 basis, all items of greatest value in the eyes of the pupil being given a 3, those of least value, a 1. A composite of the weightings is then made and the four or five with the highest scores are set aside for further consideration.

Since the question of finding sufficient materials on any given subject is a real problem at times, this is investigated before the final decision is made. A day or two is spent in the library checking on possible resources for the four or five areas selected. Usually when reports are brought back to class, one or two topics are automatically eliminated due to the lack of resource material. The final selection of the area for study is made then by vote, or weighting of the remaining topics.

Preparation of the problem attack. When the topic has been selected, a day is spent in listing questions to which the class members feel they want to find answers. From an examination of these a general over-all problem is set up as well as sub-problems relating to it. These are usually stated in the form of questions. The class then divides into small groups on the basis of interest in the sub-problems. Let us assume that the selected area is *Juvenile Delinquency* and that the over-all problem is: *What is being done and what can further be done to solve the problem of juvenile delinquency?* The sub-problems chosen might be: (1) *What are the causes of juvenile delinquency?* (2) *What do juvenile delinquents do?* (3) *How may juvenile delinquency be prevented?* (4) *How is juvenile delinquency dealt with?*

Other kinds of approaches have been made to the selection of a problem for study. Some classes are limited to the general content of a textbook, or at least to one or more themes or areas of study for a given year. In such cases the limitations should be candidly acknowledged and choices for group planning should be made within the given framework. Even in the most rigidly limited class there are possibilities for group planning of such matters as:

Order of studying various units
Supplementary projects
Manner of reporting to class
Method of evaluation
Creative writing
Dramatic presentation
Films
Reading of related materials

Some teachers have found it possible to "cover" all the required content in a relatively short period of time, leaving a block of time for group projects that offer choices to students. Others have managed to set aside one or two days each week for group research on related problems that are chosen by the students. Still other teachers begin with the textbook and then graduate from it into more meaningful problems. Many textbooks offer such opportunities and suggestions for group research in connection with each unit. Such use of group problem solving is limited, and presents the hazard that students may not really accept the "problems" as their own. They may be reluctant to spend themselves on problems offered in the textbook. Yet if no other choice presents itself, this may be a way to begin a process which can encompass more territory as it succeeds and unfolds.

Other methods of arriving at problems for study have been tried successfully by core teachers who are not bound to a text or course of study. For example, the class may see a film, or take a trip which may start them discussing a social problem, and decide to study it more intensively. They themselves may have an experience, in or out of school, that will serve to launch a unit for study. One class heard an assembly talk on space travel, and that same day decided to work together for awhile on the possibilities and means of interplanetary exploration. Another heard, during the morning announcements, an appeal for clothing and food for Korean children, and undertook a study of Korea's geography and history. Still another class had made a practice of exchanging letters with children in other lands, and decided on a systematic study of all the countries where they had correspondents. A twelfth grade class discovered one day that they were all worried to some degree about the grammar they would be expected to know that fall as college freshmen—and entered eagerly on a study (and drill) on the forms and rules of English grammar.

Whatever the method of selecting a problem for study, it is likely that small groups of from four to eight students will either

(a) select a sub-problem related to the over-all problem, or (b) attack a special problem of interest to them, but not tied in directly with any larger problem. In either case, small groups will be formed for planning, carrying out, and appraising their problem or project. Rosalind Zapf continues with a description of such a small group "in action."

A Group in Action

EDITH

Is every one who is supposed to be in our group here now?

JACK

Tom was going to be on our group, but he decided he would rather work on the problem of how to prevent juvenile delinquency.

DON

Well, then I guess we're all here. How about having Bill act as chairman of the group?

STANLEY

I second that. How about the rest of you? In favor?

All heads nod except Bill's. He shakes his violently, but agrees to take the job. He appoints Shirley to act as secretary for the group.

BILL

Well, let's see. We chose the problem of finding out what the causes of juvenile delinquency are. How should we go about it?

MARGARET

Miss ———— said the other day that there are those steps to guide us in solving a problem and that we should try to follow them.

BILL

That's right, but I can't remember them. Anybody write them down?

EDITH

I did. Here they are. (1) What do we already know about the problem? (2) What do we think the answer is? (3) How can we get reliable data? (4) What facts have we found? (5) What conclusions can we draw from these facts?

DON

We can't do all that in one day, that's sure.

BILL

No, but we can get started at any rate. The first one is, *What do we already know about the problem?* I don't know very much except things I've heard. How about you, Jack?

JACK

My dad says it's because kids have too much money, but I heard a friend of his say it was because they didn't have enough.

DON

I read an article that said it was all the parents' fault.

SHIRLEY

My mother thinks it's because boys and girls don't go to Sunday school and church as much as they used to.

> *Margaret and Edith are talking together in an undertone and obviously not about the problem.*

BILL

Come on, Margaret. We'll never get this done if you don't pitch in and help. We've got to stick together. Stanley, you haven't said anything yet. What have you heard about this?

STANLEY

I heard a fellow on the radio blame it on poor homes. He said home environment. I think he meant homes where kids aren't happy and things go all wrong.

EDITH

That makes sense. I read some place that it was the school's fault when kids went wrong. But I think it's more likely to be the way Stanley said because you can take a lot outside if just your folks stick by you and things go all right there.

BILL

That sounds as if you were working on our second question, *What do you think is the answer to the problem?* Does anyone have any more on the first one before we go on to the second?

> *Several voices—Let's go on.*

BILL

O. K. Edith and Stanley think the cause of juvenile delinquency is unhappy homes. What about the rest of you?

MARGARET

I agree with that, but it isn't always true. Sometimes there is some other reason.

DON

I read that when kids didn't have enough chance at decent recreation they often got into trouble and I think that's true too.

JACK

I think those two are the main reasons—being unhappy at home and not having a chance for decent fun outside.

SHIRLEY

Should I write those two down as the things our group believe are the biggest causes of juvenile delinquency?

BILL

How about it? Should Shirley record those or are there others as big as those?

DON

I think that's good.

Others show agreement.

BILL

The third step then is to plan how to get information about this. It's the end of the period, though, so we'll have to get together first thing tomorrow and make our plans.

Another day or two is spent in planning ways of securing information and in making decisions as to the assignment of areas of work to different members of the group. Then the plans are put into operation and many periods are spent in the core room library and the school library, in interviews with people who may be able to give assistance, in trips to places where further information may be obtained and in writing letters asking for helpful materials. The members of the group come together frequently for a period of discussion and sharing of information. At the end of the fact-gathering period, the group formulates the conclusions to the original problem on the basis of the material collected. Comparisons are made with the original hypothesis which was based, as you recall, on the things the pupils had heard or read about the problem previous to a careful study.

Planning the presentation. It is necessary to make plans for presenting the material to the entire class since this is only a part of the solution to the original, over-all problem. The presentation is sometimes in the form of a panel discussion, sometimes a radio script, a play, a debate, or perhaps in the form of an oral report by each member of the group. When preparations have been made, a period of time is set aside for all group presentations. In the example used here, four group presentations would be made, each dealing with the special phase of juvenile delinquency which it had selected.

When all groups have presented their material, the attention is turned to the over-all problem established in the beginning and an answer to this is drawn up through general class discussion. Frequently this discussion brings new problems to light which are selected by an interested small group for further work, or even at times by the whole class. With a new problem before them, pupils again set the problem-solving process in motion.

Every teacher who has had some experience with the small group technique has become aware of some problems. One of these has to do with locating materials. The school library may not be adequate or specialized enough to have materials available for a whole class on a particular problem. The textbook, if any, may not deal adequately with a given problem. Encyclopedia material is often sterile and brief—and stereotyped.

All these resources, and many others, must be tapped for help. The teacher will want to assemble some material for a start, but students can benefit enormously from this search for resources, too. One thing which is a great help is a rich collection in the core classroom of books, magazines, clippings, posters, exhibits, pamphlets, and other expendable materials that are available on a free or inexpensive basis from many sources. A more adequate treatment of this problem of materials appears in Chapter 9.

The teacher will often need to give the class some help on recording notes. The use of 3 x 5 or 4 x 6 cards for collecting data involves some time-saving techniques which will help all students. The blackboard, and a bulletin board exhibit of well-written notecards may be helpful in explaining this process. It should be emphasized at this point with new or young students that the notes are not for the teacher, or even for the student himself—but for his group. Some students have been so conditioned by previous experience that they feel sharing materials is somehow dishonest.

Each small group will need to make a plan of work. This may include such items as the following:

Statement of problem of our group
Questions that need answers
Where can we find answers?
What do we already know?
Who will be responsible for each question?
What is our time schedule?

The group recorder should be responsible for keeping the plan of work available for the group to use in checking its own progress. The class planning committee, with a member representing each group, will propose deadlines or times for reporting the outcomes of group study to the class as a whole.

As the day arrives for groups to present their reports to the class, some other kinds of problems arise. The presenters may be more interested in their report than are the other members of the class. The students may not have learned as yet how monotonous a series of oral reports, all in the same format, can become. All groups may not terminate their work exactly at the same time. Some groups may be at work on projects that do not lend themselves at all well to class reporting. Some core classes have made such presentations a matter of group choice. If the grouping is on a basis of an over-all, class-selected problem, however, some kind of sharing seems indicated as in the case of any delegated committee plan. It behooves the teacher to help groups arrive at a lively, communicative kind of report that will be listened to, enjoyed, and really shared. Some excellent opportunities exist here for developing oral communication skills. There is a place, too, for the artistic and musical students, and for those gifted in constructing exhibits. The report can take the form of panels, debates, lectures, open-forum discussions, exhibits, tape recordings, glass slides, mimeographed reports, guided tours, pantomimes, dance, music, drama. Some groups have brought in resource persons for a planned interview as a part of their report to the class. There is a real challenge to creativity in the reporting process, which may contribute more value than the information conveyed in the report itself.

Evaluation. After groups have reported and the class has discussed the over-all problem—its significance in the light of new information now acquired, and possible cues for action of solving of the problem—it becomes appropriate to take a look at what has happened in this whole process.

Rosalind Zapf's account of her own ninth grade class deals with this evaluation process in the following manner:

TEACHER

At the beginning of the semester when we were writing our constitution, we listed twelve things that we felt we really wanted to achieve through our work in this class. Let's take a look at these today and see if we can judge how much we have grown in these through our work on the problem of juvenile delinquency. Perhaps we have failed rather badly. But whatever it is, let's be honest about it so that we can see where we need to put our effort in our next unit.

Class members take out copies of constitution and read through list of goals.

TEACHER

If you were to choose the one thing in which you think we did best in working on our problem on juvenile delinquency, which one would you select?

DON

I think we did best at doing research on our topic. Everybody had a lot of information and had read a lot of material.

BILL

I think so too, only there was something wrong in it. I read a lot of material, but I had an awful time when I wanted to use it.

TEACHER

Where do you think the trouble was?

BILL

I don't know, but I couldn't find the right facts when I wanted them.

SHIRLEY

I did the same thing. I think we need to learn how to take notes so they are of some use to us. Couldn't we spend a little time learning how to do that?

TEACHER

We certainly can if that is something that is bothering you. Let's keep that in mind for a later decision.

JACK

Well, I know one thing that I've learned to do a lot better, and I think we all have, and that is to talk to others more easily and to get along with the others better. We are all friends in here now and that helps you to talk and tell people what you think about a question.

MARGARET

Sometimes we're too friendly. We talk about things that haven't anything to do with our work.

JACK

I guess that's true because the group chairman had to call people back to work often some days.

EDITH

But even so, I think the boys and girls in our group learned a lot about working with others and the other groups must have too, because their presentations were very well planned.

TEACHER

Do you suppose that all of us have grown an equal amount in each of these items?

STANLEY

Of course not. You can tell that by watching the people in our class. Some still never take part in a discussion and some of us certainly haven't learned very much about self-reliance. I think each one is different.

TEACHER

Let's see how well each one of you can judge his own situation. Usually the teacher tells you how well or how poorly you have achieved the things you are supposed to in a class. This time, instead of that, you think very carefully about yourself as you have worked these last weeks, and you decide for yourself what points you are strong in and what points you are weak in. Write the word good, fair, or poor, after each of the twelve items in our list. Can you bring that to class tomorrow?

This is, of course, only a partial description of the evaluation process, consisting of a class discussion of the extent of individual

growth achieved during the unit. Often this process is followed
by each individual's rating of his own achievement in relation to
the goals he has helped to establish for the class. If these ratings
differ significantly from the teacher's own ratings of the student
on these criteria, a teacher-student conference is indicated. An
effort is made to review the basis each has used for the respective
ratings and to arrive at consensus on each criterion. A further
analysis of the techniques of individual appraisal appears in
Chapter 14.

Another kind of evaluation consists of a group's appraisal of
its own successes and failures. Such questions as the following
are often used by small groups in evaluating their work on a unit
or problem:

1. What have been the best features of our work together?
2. In what ways are we becoming more effective in our work as a
   group?
3. In what ways have we failed in our objectives?
4. How could we improve our ways of working together?
5. How can we make more effective use of each other, and of other
   resources?

Many variations of the above questions have been developed and
used by groups in core classes as they seek to evaluate their work.
This process of developing group evaluative judgments is not
an easy one. It cannot be avoided, however, because it is a basic
part of the group planning process. Even when it is poorly done,
much can be learned from these judgments. As an entire class
continues its work and matures in its critical judgment, the small
groups often become extremely skillful in the important business
of reaching a true consensus as to the strengths and weaknesses of
their work together. In view of the importance of critical judgment as an educational goal, the process of group evaluation can
scarcely be overstressed. It provides a means whereby the evaluative process can become educative in the sense that it helps to
change the learner's behavior.

Other kinds of questions may occur to the teacher—for his own
help in appraising the effectiveness of group planning in his class.

For example, the following questions have been helpful to some core teachers:

Will my group function adequately in my absence?
Does my group disintegrate in face of crisis?
Do all members share the group interest?
Are goals common to the group?
Is the motivation toward these goals realistic?
Is there mutual respect for all expressed points of view?
Is the group able to come to a friendly conclusion?
Is discipline self-imposed rather than imposed from without?
Does the situation permit the evolvement of real in-group leadership?
Is evaluation of group membership and group activities on an objective and continuous basis?
Is there self evaluation as well as group evaluation?
Is participation on a willing, interested basis?
Does the handling of the group tend to promote social and emotional maturity?
Good group handling tends to promote group continuity. Do your group members tend to remain with the group?
Is there carry-over into other activities of the group members?

An experienced core teacher will not expect to answer all these questions affirmatively. They represent goals which some classes take months or years to achieve. Yet the continuous, systematic appraisal of the progress achieved by a class at any given point will be helpful to the teacher as the students move on to another activity or unit.

Selecting a New Problem for Study

At the end of the evaluation process the core class is confronted with the question: What next? This may be answered in any of several ways.

1. The class may repeat the problem census procedures already described, selecting a new problem for study in terms of criteria which they have established.

2. They may return to a problem or unit which was second in priority in the earlier problem census.

3. They may evolve a new problem from the one just studied. For example, out of a unit on juvenile deliquency one may conceivably develop on "The role of religion in American life," or on "How does our local and state program of law enforcement work?"

4. The class may now decide to respond to some recent stimulus that suggests a new problem; e.g., a welfare drive on behalf of our Navajo Indians may interest them in a study of the history and modern problems of American Indians.

The selection of problems for study has been done in many different ways, even with a given class. It varies from class to class and from school to school in terms of the maturity level of the participants, the amount of freedom permitted the class and the teacher, the success or failure of previous planning efforts, the understanding and acceptance of the process by students and their parents, and many other factors. The attack on the problem, too, proceeds in different ways with each succeeding core class. In general, however, some such sequence as the following is used:

1. The problem is selected, as the culmination of:
   (a) An exploratory experience suggested by either the teacher or the pupils
   or (b) Another related or lead-up unit,
   and (c) A class problem census in which every effort is made to get all voices heard and to get at the real problems and interests of the group
   and (d) A careful checking of the problems against a list of class-developed "criteria for the selection of a problem for study."
2. The problem is clearly stated and defined.
3. Areas of study are decided upon in terms of:
   (a) Tentative solutions,
   (b) Natural research division,
   (c) Individual and group interests.
4. Needed information is listed.
5. Resources for getting information are listed.
6. Information is secured, selected, and organized.
7. Information is analyzed and interpreted.

8. Tentative conclusions are stated and tested.

9. A report to the total class is planned and presented.

10. The entire process is evaluated, including the validity of the conclusions.

11. New avenues of exploration toward further problem study are pursued.[6]

summary

In this chapter descriptions have been presented of core classes in action. We have noted the techniques for helping new students get acquainted with each other and with their new teacher, room, and school. Methods of orientation to the planning process itself have been presented. The problem selection and problem attack procedures have been described, followed by some suggestions for evaluation.

The following list of suggestions evolved by a group of core teachers at a state conference may serve to summarize the process of teacher-pupil planning:

1. Begin slowly, possibly with such a project as a party.

2. The teacher should study the group, especially its leaders.

3. Students should be helped to know each other better.

4. Students should be at first invited to plan specifics within the general framework.

5. An effort should be made to help students understand democracy and its purposes.

6. Pupils should help set goals and frequently assess their own progress.

7. A gradual transition should be provided from subject-matter teaching to pupil-teacher planning.

8. Students should be encouraged to look upon planning as a means of finding better ways to achieve their important goals.

9. Students should be helped to get a clear picture of themselves.

10. Flexibility and freedom are important.

11. Purposeful action should follow planning.

12. Students should be taught to appreciate individual differences.[7]

---

[6] Adapted from *Problem Solving*, Detroit Citizenship Education Study. Detroit, Michigan: Wayne State University Press, 1948.

[7] Michigan State Core Conference, April 1955; unpublished report of conference group.

It will be noted that this chapter has generally been confined to the *group operation* as distinguished from the *individual's* efforts in a core class. We have thus far been discussing the problem-solving method, and its application to real problems in our society, including the life of the school.

As important as this group attack on problems is, other rich experiences are offered in a good core class. In the next chapter we shall go on to the individual enrichment which contributes so much to the value and enjoyment of students in core classes.

SELECTED REFERENCES

Alberty, Harold, *Reorganizing the High School Curriculum,* Revised. New York: The Macmillan Company, 1953, Chapter XIII.

Alcorn, Marvin D., Richard A. Houseman, and Jim R. Schunert, *Better Teaching in Secondary Schools.* New York: Henry Holt and Company, 1954, Chapter 5, "Cooperative Planning."

A Primer For Common Learnings. Minneapolis: Minneapolis Public Schools, 1948.

Berger, Donald, "Planning in the Core Class," *Educational Leadership,* VIII (January 1951), pp. 208-214.

Educational Policies Commission, *Education for All American Youth: A Further Look.* Washington, D. C.: The National Education Association, 1952, pp. 237-251.

Giles, H. H., S. P. McCutcheon, and A. N. Zechiel, *Exploring the Curriculum.* New York: Harper and Brothers, 1942, Chapter IV.

Kelley, Earl C., *The Workshop Way of Learning.* New York: Harper and Brothers, 1951, Chapters III and VII.

MacConnell, Charles, Ernest O. Melby, C. O. Arndt, and Leslee Bishop, *New Schools for a New Culture,* Revised. New York: Harper and Brothers, 1953, Chapters II, III.

Miel, Alice, and associates, *Cooperative Procedures in Learning.* New York: Bureau of Publications, Teachers College, Columbia University, 1952, Chapters XIII and XIV.

Mudd, Dorothy, *A Core Program Grows.* Bel Air, Maryland: The Harford County Board of Education, 1949, Chapter IV.

Near Home—16 mm. sound film. New York: The British Information Service, 1946.

Noar, Gertrude, *Freedom to Live and Learn*. Philadelphia: The Franklin Publishing Company, 1948.

Practicing Democracy in the Classroom—16 mm. sound film. Wilmette, Illinois: Encyclopedia Brittanica Films, 1953.

Problem Solving, Detroit Citizenship Education Study. Detroit: The Wayne State University Press, 1948.

The Ohio State University High School Class of 1938, *Were We Guinea Pigs?* Chicago: Henry Holt and Company, 1938.

Toops, Myrtle, *Working in the Core Program in Burris Laboratory School*. Muncie, Indiana: Ball State Teachers College, 1955.

We Plan Together—16 mm. sound film. New York: Teachers College, Columbia University, 1949.

Wiles, Kimball, *Teaching for Better Schools*. Englewood Cliffs, N. J.: Prentice-Hall, Inc., 1952. Chapters 5, 6, 8.

Youth Learns to Assume Responsibility, Michigan Secondary Curriculum Study. Lansing, Michigan: The State Department of Public Instruction, 1944.

Zapf, Rosalind, *A Core Curriculum Class in Action*—Filmstrip. Detroit: Wayne State University College of Education, 1948.

Chapter 7

Enriching Individual Learning

introduction

In Chapter 5 some facts regarding individual differences were presented. It was pointed out that a startling range of differences exists for an entire class in terms of its command of the various academic skills and knowledges. Even more significant data were presented to illustrate the range of different skills and levels of knowledge within each individual in a class. Not only in academic skills but in emotional adjustment, maturity, personality, physical development, intelligence, interests, family background, and vocational aptitudes, *individuals differ*. A still more important fact is that most of the differences that exist within a given class will tend to increase, not diminish, as the individuals grow and develop.

This fact of individual difference has been recognized for many years. It appears, however, that the traditional secondary school has done very little about adapting instruction to this fact of difference. A step has been made in this direction with the elective program of the senior high school. This is helpful for those students who do not drop out of school before they can avail themselves of electives that are geared to their special interests and abilities. The guidance movement has helped to alert teachers to the need to study their students as individuals, but this is generally impossible to accomplish for 150 to 200 students, or the number confronting teachers daily in a departmentalized school.

The core curriculum offers some help on this problem of studying individual differences and then adapting instruction to these differences. Not only is the core teacher responsible for a smaller number of different individuals, but he also has a longer block of time daily, and usually more continuous semesters of association with his groups than does the teacher of five separate subject classes.

In the preceding chapter attention was given to the techniques of group planning in a core class. The small group technique can be helpful in locating individual interests and abilities, and in finding channels for their effective growth through use. The boy or girl who is a "natural" leader quickly comes to the fore in the small group; the student who should develop leadership traits gets a chance too, in the day-by-day operation of a group in which he feels secure to try out his wings. The element of interests—in various topics or subjects—is provided for by the choice of a group and by the subsequent planning within the small group. The variety of roles that are natural and needed in a group's operation tends to create a constructive place for every member. Not only is there an opportunity for the "talker," but also for the "maker" and "doer." Not only the student who writes well, but also the student who can interpret dramatic roles or build models or take care of the room has a job to perform on behalf of his group.

A cooperative group enterprise encourages and accepts individual differences, for it is built upon them. The success of a group depends on the unique backgrounds and abilities which are contributed to the group enterprise by each member. Without these differences, the group could not succeed. Indeed, if it were possible to have a group entirely composed of identical individuals, such a group would be stymied from the start. The very essence of group-planning is individual difference, which permits of different contributions to the progress toward solution of the group's problem. Kelley and Rasey point this out in their book *Education and the Nature of Man:*

> The opportunity to specialize, to perform separate functions better than any one cell could do them all and to perform these functions for others while others were doing different tasks for them, is the basis for all living tissue or organism above the level of the single cell. And so it is when people do things together. Their uniqueness is what gives individuals value in social organization. If people were all alike, had the same abilities, there would be little value in association. None could learn from others; none could perform tasks which others could not do for themselves.[1]

Thus the successful operation of problem-groups in a core class provides many opportunities to take account of individual differences.

There are other kinds of experiences possible in a core class, besides group problem solving. The additional time span enjoyed by most core classes makes possible a wide variety of activities, often unrelated to group activity. The longer period of time seems to encourage a more creative approach to instruction. There is time both for small group activities and for individual and total-class experiences which may relate only incidentally, if at all, to a problem or topic selected for class study.

speech activities

Evaluations which have been made of core curriculums usually reveal a significant command of oral discussion skills in the students. This ability to communicate orally is emphasized by the small group technique, and in other ways in core classes. There are many opportunities to speak to the entire class, in the process of making reports of group progress, as a member of the

---

[1] Earl C. Kelley and Marie I. Rasey, *Education and the Nature of Man.* New York: Harper and Brothers, 1952, pp. 90-91.

rotating class planning committee, as class chairman, as representative to the school student council, or as member of any of the numerous special committees which have specific assignments for the class.

Many core classes have periodic programs, "just for fun" or in celebration of special days. These programs, sometimes a regular weekly feature of the core class, place a premium on speech talent and its development. Students volunteer or are asked to read stories, plays, or poems to the class. A group of students presents a one-act play for the occasion. The role of introducer or master of ceremonies is passed around to give many students experience. Mock debates or panel discussions provide merriment for the class, but also give students some chances to develop oral skill. In one core class an hour just before noon each Friday was set aside for such a program, at which time the group ceased thinking of itself as a "class" and became a "club." During a school year, every one of the forty students appeared in some role on the program, and many appeared several times. The program was kept a secret from all but the program committee and the participants selected for that day. Songs, plays, skits, pantomimes, burlesque debates, and readings of poems or stories was the usual kind of thing included in these programs. There was usually at least one game, too, which was selected with a view of its possible contribution to both fun and speech training.

Other kinds of speech opportunities develop in a core class. Many class discussions, planning, evaluation, analyses of a film or TV show, or commenting on current events, go on every day. Many core classes have a regular radio or television newscast scheduled as a daily, fifteen-minute feature of the class. Following this newscast, students take turns in leading a class discussion of the new developments in the news.

Many core classes invite their parents in for an occasional program. This helps interpret the work of the class to parents, and at the same time offers valuable experiences in speaking to adults. Other core classes have formed a kind of speaker's bureau, selecting student panels to appear before teachers or parents to evaluate the methods of learning which they are currently experiencing.

The alert core teacher is constantly creating opportunities for members of the class to communicate orally, and helping them to develop into better speakers. In one core program in the New School at Evanston Township High School a thirty-page pamphlet was developed by Dr. Karl Robinson, designed to help students master necessary speech techniques in core classes.[2]

For many boys and girls, the development of effective oral communication is dependent directly upon their own acceptance by their peers. One high school core teacher has contributed the following description of a boy who was helped by his classmates to learn how to share his special area of competence with them:

Richard was a small boy with a thatch of black hair thrust angrily awry. Behind a cloak of dark, impassive eyes lay the mystery of a mind which persevered against the odds. Most boys of Richard's limitations would have left long before. He could not read. He could scarcely write his name. He spoke in faltering phrases difficult to understand. All our clever instruments indicated that he had measurable intelligence quotient somewhat below sixty-five. Still he stayed.

Beyond the elementary school there was no special opportunity program in our school system for boys and girls of Richard's rank. But we did not deny to anyone the opportunity to enter high school. We welcomed them all, trying sometimes futilely to find a challenge for each one.

Richard entered my core class along with twenty-five other boys and girls who had the usual range of possibilities to be found in a high school class— the brilliant, the average, and the slow. But Richard was behind them all. I tried to find small jobs for him to do about the classroom, yet there must have been many dark hours while he sat with his massive, Sphinx-like patience, a spectator to most of the verbal activities of the class.

The other boys and girls were not hostile toward him. Quick to sense his limitations, they considered him somewhat of a strange duckling. Their conversations with him were always pseudo-serious, like those most adults

---

[2] Karl F. Robinson, *Speech Techniques for the Core Curriculum: The Oral Report* Evanston, Illinois: Northwestern University Press, undated.

have with small children. Often they came to me to ask, "Why is Richard so 'funny'?"

Richard, however, was not discouraged. He came with cheerful consistency, always with a broad smile and labored greeting. When he came early, we talked of baseball. He was a great baseball fan. Somehow within his fragile web of perceptions, those strands having to do with baseball held fast. He knew the game. He knew the players. He knew their batting averages. He knew who had won the world series for several years back. He seemed to know more about baseball than any other boy in the room.

Gradually the other boys and girls came to realize Richard's one talent. By World Series time they had involved him in several spirited discussions on the relative merits of the Yankees and Dodgers. And Richard was holding his own in the give-and-take. I was surprised to note that the tone of condescension was absent in the other boys' remarks to him. They were talking with him on equal terms, no longer with tongue-in-cheek. His predictions met the same democratic derision as those of the other boys.

I cannot recall all the subtle shifts that came afterwards, but there were small tokens of acceptance which came with no prompting from me. On one occasion the class was working in small groups, rehearsing plays they had written on historical periods. I knew that Richard had been stage manager for his group. But one day when I returned to the room after half an hour's unexpected absence, I found that Richard's group had written him into the script. They had given him one line, printed in letters an inch high, and one of the girls had taken him aside to teach him his part. Some time later we made a tape recording of a choral reading piece. Richard was assigned a part, and the fact that he came in on cue with a small voice valiantly trying to be strong and clear gave us all a feeling of warm satisfaction. On another occasion when short talks were to be presented before the group, Richard's talk became a concern of the whole class. Unknown to me, special preparation was made in study hall. "It seemed as though the whole school was working to make sure Richard was ready to give his talk," the study hall teacher told me later.

When Richard stood before the class to give his talk, he was poised and confident. As he demonstrated with labored explanations how to hit a baseball, his peers, who had secretly tutored him, sat in breathless expectation. By standards applicable to the other students, he gave an excellent talk. Richard had now won the right which other children assume—the right to be taken seriously.

I could detect in Richard's classmates no touch of glory in what they had done. In this and other ways too tenuous to observe they had been able to relate themselves to this seemingly strange yet wonderfully purposive boy. I would like to believe that they saw in this least of God's children a part of the grand design, and that as a consequence of living in an environment that valued highly the human personality, they had found some capacity for tolerance and charity for their fellow man.[3]

experiences in reading

Much reading is done by each member of a group, seeking data or evidence that will help the group with its problem. This research activity leads group members to use encyclopedias, almanacs, atlases, history and geography texts, biographies and autobiographies, current analyses of the American and world scene, state and local histories and volumes on government, pamphlets published by industry, labor, and government, and magazines and newspapers. All these, and other kinds of reading matter become source material for members of a group at work on a problem.

Other kinds of reading occur in a core class. Many core classrooms have a library of several hundred books of literature, social science, and science. Free reading periods and attractive book displays encourage students to read poetry, plays, novels, short stories, biographies, and other kinds of books for sheer enjoyment. In the New School program referred to earlier,[4] four kinds of reading programs were emphasized: *Interest Reading* of sports, hobby, and leisure time interest materials, *Core Reading* supplementary to the topics being studied, *Challenge Reading* of the classics, and *Current Reading* of newspapers and periodicals.

The core teacher recognizes that his class represents many levels of reading ability, and he accepts the task of helping all individuals to progress in reading skill. This means that the room must contain some reading material of simple word power but of

---

[3] Harvey Overton, "We Opened the Door, Richard," *Teaching Core,* Wayne State University, Detroit, 3:3, January 1955.

[4] Described in Charles M. MacConnell and others, *New Schools for a New Culture,* Revised. New York: Harper and Brothers, 1953, pp. 36-38.

adolescent interest, for the use of retarded readers. Such "slow" readers may have to have some individual help in oral reading. If clinical help is available, the core teacher refers the most difficult cases to the clinic, but in most situations the responsibility falls on the core teacher to start where each student is, and help him progress through encouragement and success to the goal of becoming a better reader.

Other students need to have material that is advanced in vocabulary and concepts, well beyond their present grade level. They need to be challenged to go beyond the class in their individual reading. These students do not present as serious a problem procedurally; they can often go ahead on their own if they are helped to get material that is of interest. The core teacher makes suggestions and follows up with counseling and opportunities for sharing new knowledge and understanding with the class, as well as with the teacher.

At all levels of reading comprehension and speed, there are needs which students have in common. The core teacher makes it his business to improve reading skills of the entire class in such ways as the following:

1. He helps provide in the core class experiences in living that arouse curiosity and challenge interest.

2. He makes available a wide variety of materials. He seeks continuously for new materials that will interest someone in the class.

3. He studies reading scores and listens to oral reading to find out what deficiencies need correction.

4. He provides time in class for students to look at books and magazines and get started in reading them.

5. He encourages students to use the room library at noon or after school.

6. He uses pressure-free techniques that encourage sharing with others the enjoyment of the books students read.

7. He emphasizes and constantly seeks success and satisfaction, not failure.

8. He helps students learn to scan material in a book to discover whether it is of interest.

9. He helps students form standards of taste, to separate wheat from chaff.

10. He helps students learn to recognize propaganda and to distinguish opinion from fact.

11. He seeks the help of parents and of the students' other teachers in encouraging more and better reading.

12. He uses films, live plays, radio, and television to stimulate a taste for a particular story or book.

13. He gives daily evidence to the class that he himself enjoys reading and he gives out a contagious enthusiasm.

It should probably be noted that even the most effective core teacher will not work miracles of sudden conversion of every student into a competent reader. This area of reading skills is perhaps the most difficult, complex task that slow learners face. The core class is no panacea. The chief advantages of the core teacher may be his freedom to *accept* all levels of skill, to lend *reality* to learning, to insure feelings of *satisfaction* and *confidence,* and to provide a *flexible program* which permits all to progress at their individual rates.

experiences in writing

Both in reading and in writing, the learner's most important initial handicap is his own fear that he cannot achieve.

"So long as he sees himself as one who cannot, he is lamed and blind to his own enhancement. He cannot try. This we believe is the right word." [5] Thus the core teacher's major task is to build self-confidence by encouragement and a "succession of successes." This will mean, among other things, that he will avoid the common practice of red-penciling a student's written efforts in such a way as to confirm his conviction of his own ineptitude. It means that the teacher will find something good to say about whatever a student writes, before he begins to help him correct his weaknesses. It means, most of all, that the teacher *accepts* all the students at whatever stage they have arrived, and

[5] Marie I. Rasey and J. Wilmer Menge, *What We Learn from Children.* New York: Harper and Brothers, 1956, pp. 36-37.

then builds their interest and self-confidence in the art of written communication.

Many opportunities exist in a core class for various kinds of writing experiences. There is the writing of research notes for sharing with the small group. There are creative challenges in writing scripts for oral presentations to the class. There are letters to be written to sources of material or other help. There are autobiographies, individual logs for periodic self-appraisal, invitations to one's parents to come to class for a program, reports to parents about developments in the core class and about the student's own growth over the past marking period or semester. There are group projects to which each individual contributes his ideas and language.

Many core classes put together at regular intervals a class newspaper or magazine, which provides an outlet and a stimulus for the creation of poems, stories, and essays. Such a project offers a number of other related responsibilities which students with gifts other than writing may assume. School assembly programs and other public presentations may offer special challenges to the interested, gifted young writers. The Junior and Senior Scholastic magazines regularly publish the efforts of young writers, and have also put them together in an anthology entitled *Saplings*.[6]

art and music

The lengthened period and freedom of the core class makes possible such activities as crayon work and painting, costume-design, model-building, scrap books, posters, bulletin board arrangement, and other kinds of art activities. These may grow out of the creative efforts of a problem-group which is preparing its report. They may relate instead to other special projects of the class, such as the newspaper or the preparation of a corridor exhibit. In many cases they are simply done during periods set aside for individual activities in the room.

Music has an important place in the core class. Some classes do a great deal of group singing, usually in connection with a regular

---

[6] Pittsburg, Pennsylvania: The Scholastic Publishing Company.

program or a special day observance. One class made a systematic study of folk music, soliciting the aid of the music teacher in learning to sing the songs and in understanding their origin and significance. Listening to records was an important part of this learning experience. Other core classes have set aside a regular weekly period for listening to great music, and for discussion of its meaning.

hobbies and collections

The preceding chapter referred to the discussions of individual hobbies through which students in a core class first get acquainted. In many classes these individual hobbies become a continuous and regular part of the class program. Hobby shows or formal exhibits may occasionally be planned. Additions to an individual collection may be presented and enthusiastically discussed. Interested students may pursue independent research on their own hobbies as a means of increasing their own enjoyment, for example, of a stamp or coin collection.

science experiences

The world of science offers many fascinating leads for individual study and for class sharing periods. Some schools have arranged the science classes in such a way that the science teacher is available as a consultant during the core classes. One entire class became involved in a discussion about finger-nail soil used in criminal investigation. They adjourned to the science room and spent thirty minutes making smears and studying them with microscopes.

Another class obtained the assistance of the science teacher in building an aquarium for their core classroom. Individuals in core classes have secured similar help in identifying rocks, plants, birds, or leaves or in securing materials about the fascinating world of physical and natural science.

One core class developed its problem-solving approach from science. The class was at first relatively structured for three periods daily, the last of which was devoted to science. The boys and girls became so interested in their individual and small group research about turtles and other creatures that the "science" period gradually extended. As their projects and learning became more enriched, the students developed their own books on their subjects, illustrating them in artistic fashion and writing scholarly papers to go with the drawings. They gave talks about their subjects to the class, and later to at least a dozen adult groups in the community and on a near-by university campus. The project finally provided significant growth in science knowledge and understanding, in care of live specimens, in language skills, in illustrating by drawings, in constructing exhibits, and in planning and working together.

A core class is quite likely to have at least one or two boys in it whose major interest is in science. Sometimes there are several individuals with such an interest and aptitude. The core teacher who is alert will use this special bent as a means of maintaining and enriching the student's skills in reading, speaking, writing, and in other ways of sharing his enthusiasm with his classmates.

other individual experiences

Many other activities are developed by ingenious core teachers. When the class goes out on a field trip there are various responsibilities which individuals can assume—making the arrangements for the bus, getting clearance from the office, "casing" the trip in advance to note the desired route, or developing safety rules. The classroom itself is a constant challenge in terms of housekeeping and improvement. There are draperies needed on the windows, and the class decides to earn some money and make the draperies itself. There is a bulletin board that calls for a new exhibit, there are the chairs to restore to their original order, there is the library to check on, there is the core newspaper file to keep straight.

The class plans a program for the parents next Friday. The cookies must be baked and the boys of one group surprise everyone by turning out an excellent batch of oatmeal cookies. Host and hostess roles must be assigned, the room arranged, the invitations prepared, the telephone follow-up planned and executed, the program developed and (sometimes) rehearsed. The tea must be made in the home-making laboratory and cups, plates, and napkins secured. Extra chairs will have to be brought from the band room.

The kids have been cutting across Mrs. Donaldson's lawn opposite the school and some of the flowers have been trampled. The core class discusses this for a while and decides to ask Mrs. Donaldson if she would let them repair the damage. New plants are obtained and set out, the worn places are seeded and a little white fence is built to remind people to take a few additional steps and save the flowers.

Bud came into the ninth grade core class from a rural one-room school. It soon became evident that Bud had few of the conventionally expected skills. He spelled and wrote very badly. His reading score on the Iowa test was fourth grade level. He spoke shyly and was handicapped by a slight stutter. His physical coordination was poor, probably due to his recent rate of growth.

In social relationships Bud did not exactly shine. He made friends with great difficulty. He was not only shy, but seemed suspicious of the advances made by the other students. The core teacher and the planning committee talked about Bud one day.

"What can we find that Bud can succeed in?" asked one student who had been a member of his group for a week. "When we play the word game he falls out first every time and just sits there and watches."

"Do you think that bothers him at all?" another asked. "He seems to enjoy it."

"Well, I don't think anyone could like always being the first one to fall out."

"I think Bud is a good guy," a boy put in quickly. "He never crabs and it isn't his fault if he can't do things."

The teacher pondered this conversation all of that day for she had been wondering how to help Bud find a real place in the class.

A hike was planned that week Friday. The trail led up the creek to a sand dune about a mile from the school. Second growth timber covered most of the trail and the group expected to see some small game and perhaps pick some late flowers. A surprise was in store for everybody. Hardly had the students entered the wood when Bud pointed out a wood-chuck's hole. From that point on, he became hike leader. He helped the students identify birds and small animals, shrubs and flowers and trees. He showed them the effect on bark and tree growth of prevailing wind and rain direction. He taught us many bird calls. He caught a garter snake and told us how valuable it was to farmers. Bud knew more wood lore than anyone in the class.

From that day on, Bud's status in the class was assured. He seemed to be reconciled to his failures in some activitives, for he had established himself as a leader in an important field. He made friends and his whole attitude toward the class changed. He even started to keep a spelling notebook and build his vocabulary. Even his marks in his other classes improved.[7]

In summary of this chapter, it might be stated that any educative and enjoyable activity which helps individuals to grow and learn is possible in a good core class. Perhaps the basic problem in all educational method is that of identifying and providing for individual differences. Wiles has titled one chapter in his book, *Teaching for Better Schools,* as follows: "Teaching Is Skill in Individualizing Instruction." He sums up that chapter with the following specific suggestions:

1. Study the cumulative record of each child.
2. Compare achievement score with ability indices.
3. Examine a pupil's creative production for words and symbols and topics that are used frequently.
4. Listen to pupils talk about themselves.
5. Provide opportunity for a choice of activities.
6. Visit each pupil's home, if possible.
7. Help each pupil learn as much as possible about his values, attitudes, purposes, skills, interests, and abilities.
8. Be willing for pupils to say what they think.
9. Reflect for students their beliefs and values.
10. Analyze with pupils their interpretations of their in-class and out-of-class experiences.
11. Organize class activities around individual or group study of problems important to the individuals involved.

---

[7] Unpublished report, Michigan Secondary Curriculum Study. Lansing, Michigan: State Department of Education, 1942.

12. Help each pupil to state his purposes, immediate and long-term. Share with pupils the information available about his present status.
13. Clarify with pupils the limitations (in time, materials, and resources) of the situation.
14. Ask each pupil to formulate a plan of work.
15. Encourage each pupil to collect and share materials.
16. Make possible the collection of information in out-of-class situations.
17. Use record-keeping as a way of helping the individual student to organize his learning.[8]

It may occur to the reader that such provision for individual differences is a condition of good teaching in any class or situation, and is not particularly unique to a core class. It is true that good teachers at every level and in all subjects have sought for many years to identify and provide for the differences in abilities and interests of individual learners. To the extent that they have sometimes failed to achieve this goal in conventional programs of instruction, the cause may be due to one or more of the following factors:

1. With five or six single-period classes each day, a teacher may not have time to get well enough acquainted with each pupil to discover his "differences."

2. Adherence to a single basic textbook or expectations regarding materials that must be "covered" by all students may seriously limit the teacher who attempts to adapt instruction to differing ability-levels and differing interests.

3. Policies regarding marking and promotion may create artificial standards which substitute for and inhibit the development of more realistic individual standards for each learner.

4. The single daily period allowed for conventional classes in secondary schools provides little time for cultivation and pursuit of individual interests, or indeed for development of individual skills.

The core class has more time and flexibility, and the core teacher has fewer students. Operating in a climate of experi-

---

[8] Wiles, Kimball, *Teaching For Better Schools*. Englewood Cliffs, N. J.: Prentice-Hall, Inc., 1952, p. 286.

mentalism, with some freedom to study each learner and to adapt instruction to his unique purposes and needs, the core teacher is in a position to try out some of the techniques of individualized instruction. There is now time, not only for the group planning activities described in Chapter 6, but also for a wide variety of individual projects, research, construction, and reporting. It is possible for a core teacher to discover and make maximum use of the unique contributions of each boy and girl. It is feasible for the core teacher also to help each individual to grow in his command of basic skills, by beginning where he presently is and challenging him with next steps.

How can such a wide variety of activities be included in the daily plan of a core class? Perhaps an actual example will help. The following schedule of one week's activities was adopted by a tenth grade core class during its business session of the preceding Friday:

Monday   8:30   Radio news report. Discussion led by Janet.

8:55   Business meeting (President Tom). Report of committee on Friday's club program, Mary B. Report of Committee on magazines, Jane. Report on this week's high school assembly, Jack. Distribution of evaluation forms for week, Mary D., secretary of planning committee.

9:30   Committee work on problem now under study by our class: "What is America Like?" (Committees: Peoples of America, Land and Conservation, Literature, Stage, and Radio, Business and Industry, Sports.)

11:00   Free reading and activity period. Newspaper work, crafts, etc.

11:30   Dismissed for lunch.

Tuesday   8:30   Radio news report. Discussion led by Pete.

8:45   Business Meeting. Announcements by Mr. Johnson.

8:50   Committee work by our five problem committees.

11:00   Free reading and activity period. Newspaper, crafts, etc.

11:30   Dismissed.

Wednesday   8:30   Radio news report. Discussion led by Laura.

                 8:45   Business meeting. Announcements by Mr. Johnson. Report of Sadah, our Student Council representative. Discussion of report. Recommendation of two matters for Sadah to present and urge action on at next week's Council.

                 9:45   Progress report, Committee on Land and Conservation. The committee also gave us a brief "listener's test" to check on how much we learned from the report. This was followed by an oral evaluation of the report, led by President Tom.

                11:00   Free reading and activity period. Planning Committee met.

                11:30   Dismissed.

Thursday   8:30   Radio news report. Discussion led by Wallace.

                 8:55   Problem Committee Work.

                10:00   Progress report by committee on "Peoples of America." The committee is going to make its final report in the form of a play about prejudice. Criticisms and suggestions by class.

                11:30   Dismissed.

Friday   8:30   Radio news report and discussion, led by Phyllis.

                 8:55   Business meeting. Announcements: Tom. Collection of evaluations of week's work: individual and group. Report of Planning Committee on next week's plan. Discussion and adoption of tentative plan for next week. Collection of Student Activity Ticket payments. Banking in Thrift Bank.

                10:00   Club Program. Chairman, Mary B. Refreshments: cookies and milk. Songs of many lands. Records, followed by group singing. Harmonica duet, Barbara and Bob. Original story, read by Wilson K. Original play: "Manners Make the Man" Author—Roger. Cast —Tom, Mary D., Phyllis, Elaine, Bill, Jack, and Mr. Johnson. Distribution of the "Blah-Blah," our weekly core newspaper.[9]

---

[9] Unpublished report, Michigan Secondary Curriculum Study. Lansing, Michigan, 1943.

Certain continuing threads appear in this schedule. The class began each day's work with a radio newscast and a discussion of it. This was followed, every day except Thursday, by a brief business meeting. Group work on the current problem of the class was next in the order of the day except on Friday, when time was set aside for a weekly club program. Other items fitted into the week's schedule were free activity periods Monday, Tuesday, and Wednesday and problem committee reports on Wednesday and Thursday.

Such a schedule would be likely to differ from week to week, as projects develop and needs vary. In one core class, for example, an entire week was used in conducting house-to-house surveys of opinions on the topic "What Our Community Needs Most." The sample schedule given will serve, however, to indicate the variety and flexibility that characterize a good core class.

summary

In summary of this analysis of the core class in action, the characteristics of the day-by-day program may be listed as follows:

1. The program is flexible, and can be changed with the group's changing purposes.
2. It is democratically planned. Every member's voice is heard in the process of making the plan and judging its success.
3. It provides for a maximum amount of student leadership in various roles.
4. The teacher is freed from the chairmanship and directing role and becomes participant, advisor, technician, and individual counselor.
5. A wide variety of creative educative activities are provided for all.
6. There is a direct tie with the total school activities, with the community, and with world events.
7. Materials for study are readily available in the room.
8. The students are able to leave the room or even the building in search of further materials.
9. The problems under study are real to the students. Their interests and purposes have been the chief criteria in selecting the problems.

10. The skills of democratic citizenship and the guidance of youth in wholesome living are the real goals of the program.

It is possible for a teacher to expect too much from new core students. Many of them have been subjected to years of classroom experience in which they were in a passive, nonparticipating role. They cannot be expected suddenly to develop the skills of cooperative planning and to assume complete responsibility for their own acts. Many core teachers try to bridge this gap by beginning with a large measure of teacher-direction and then increasing student participation in planning as rapidly as possible. Teachers often make the opposite error and underestimate the ability of boys and girls to assume responsibility and plan effective learning experiences for themselves. Continuous evaluation by the group should make it possible to avoid either of these mistakes.

In the next chapter an analysis will be made of the core teacher's role as a guidance counselor.

SELECTED REFERENCES

Alcorn, Marvin D., Richard Houseman, and Jim R. Schunert, *Better Teaching in Secondary Schools*. New York: Henry Holt and Company, 1954, Chapter 14.

Association for Supervision and Curriculum Development, *Fostering Mental Health in Our Schools*. Washington, D. C.: The National Education Association, 1950, Chapter V.

———, *Toward Better Teaching*. Washington, D. C.: The National Education Association, 1949, Chapter V.

———, *Creating a Good Environment for Learning,* Washington, D. C.: The National Education Association, 1954, Chapters 4, 5.

Havighurst, Robert J., *Human Development and Education*. New York: Longmans, Green, and Company, 1953, Chapters 13, 14, and 15.

Kelley, Earl C., *Education for What Is Real*. New York: Harper and Brothers, 1947, Chapter V.

———, and Marie I. Rasey, *Education and the Nature of Man*. New York: Harper and Brothers, 1952, Chapters 9, 10, and 11.

Lane, Howard and Mary Beauchamp, *Human Relations in Teaching.* Englewood Cliffs, N. J.: Prentice-Hall, Inc., 1955, Chapters 9 and 10.

MacConnell, Charles, Ernest O. Melby, C. O. Arndt, and Leslee Bishop, *New Schools for a New Culture,* Revised. New York: Harper and Brothers, 1953, Chapters III and IV.

Miel, Alice and associates, *Cooperative Procedures in Learning.* New York: Bureau of Publications, Teachers College, Columbia University, 1952, Chapter XV.

Rasey, Marie I., and J. W. Menge, *What We Learn from Children.* New York: Harper and Brothers, 1956, Chapter II.

Redl, Fritz, and William W. Wattenberg, *Mental Hygiene in Teaching.* New York: Harcourt, Brace, and Company, 1951, Chapter VIII.

Robinson, Karl F., *Speech Techniques for the Core Curriculum: The Oral Report.* Evanston, Illinois: Northwestern University.

Sands, Lester B., *An Introduction to Teaching in Secondary Schools.* New York: Harper and Brothers, 1949, Chapter XIV.

Stratemeyer, Florence, and others, *Developing a Curriculum for Modern Living,* Revised. New York: Bureau of Publications, Teachers College, Columbia University, 1957, Part IV.

Wiles, Kimball, *Teaching for Better Schools.* Englewood Cliffs, N. J.: Prentice-Hall, Inc., 1952, Chapters 11 and 12.

Chapter 8

Guidance in the
Core Curriculum

WHY GUIDANCE?

Before it is possible to understand guidance in the core curriculum it will be necessary to see guidance in its relation to education itself. The roots of the guidance movement as well as those of the core curriculum are deeply imbedded in the developmental phases of our educational ideas and practices.

why has guidance developed?

Guidance has been a recent development in American education; its historical beginnings lie well within our twentieth century. Prior to the turn of the century practically all youth attending the secondary school expected to go to college; therefore, the work of the secondary school was considered to be essentially college preparatory, and the curriculum was predominantly academic in nature. Since colleges thought of their task as mainly that of the preparation of youth for professional leadership in civil government and the few time-honored professions, their curriculums were restricted and tended to be quite similar. This in turn led to somewhat uniform college entrance requirements. The high schools, thus discouraged by the limiting uniformity of college entrance specifications, tended to restrict their curriculums to those general subjects thought to prepare their students best to meet prevailing college entrance requirements.

About 1900 there began a popular movement toward greater educational opportunity for all, which profoundly affected the secondary school. Enrollments in the secondary school increased rapidly, approximately doubling each ten years from 1900 to 1940. There was a notable change as well in the character of those who now entered high school. Many had no ambition to go to college, and therefore had no interest in meeting the highly academic requirements of college admission standards; they were interested in more practical learning that would fit them for immediate vocational activities.

Along with this shift in the character of the interests and abilities of those attending the secondary schools came two major changes in the schools themselves. During the second and third decades of this century a popular movement got underway to expand the secondary school curriculum to meet the varied needs of pupils with a wide range of vocational abilities and interests. It was not uncommon to find the larger high schools offering as many as one hundred to two hundred separate subjects; sometimes even more. It became possible for the pupil at the beginning of his high school career in such school situations to choose from a wide range of curriculum offerings a pattern of subjects that would lead to one of many skilled or semi-skilled vocations. The second change in the schools was the natural shift in urban centers from small to large schools often with several thousand students.

Under these conditions it was but natural for confusion and maladjustments to develop. Pupils were selecting the wrong subjects—i.e., that did not lead to the vocational goals desired.

Others found themselves enrolled in courses far beyond their abilities or interests. In these schools, where the teaching staff was made up of specialists in narrow subject areas, the pupil was much on his own with little help in selecting the best school program to meet his needs, abilities, and interests. The rapid increase in subject failures, pupil frustrations, and school dropouts forced the public and the schools to give attention to these problems.

how did guidance begin?

Practically all authorities on the movement agree that it began toward the end of the first decade of this century, and that the first approach to this problem was made outside of the schools. Frank Parsons is credited with the initiation of vocational guidance in 1908 in Boston. He began by giving out-of-school youth some vocational placement counseling. At first his main emphasis was upon giving youth help in finding jobs for which they were fitted in terms of their abilities, interests, and technical skills. He urged upon the schools the need to develop such services as a regular part of the school's educational program. In 1914 Jesse Davis, a teacher in the Grand Rapids, Michigan, schools, sought to teach educational and vocational guidance through English composition courses, in which he had pupils explore their own interests and abilities, the nature of certain vocations, and the degree of knowledge and skill competencies required in them, the opportunities for advancement, and other desirable or undesirable aspects of particular vocations that should be of concern to the prospective employee. His plan was publicized in a small book printed in 1914, *Vocational and Moral Guidance*. The shift to an emphasis upon educational guidance as well as upon vocational guidance received its first major impetus with the appearance in 1918 of Brewer's *Vocational and Educational Guidance*. Prior to 1920, and even much later, the principal concern of guidance was vocational in nature. Educational guidance was largely concerned with vocational fitness and training. It was but natural that the early attention to guidance should be with these more obvious, immediate, and pressing needs of youth.

WHAT IS THE MODERN CONCEPTION OF GUIDANCE?

why has the guidance concept changed?

In the early beginnings of the guidance movement, the nature of occupations was little understood except in the cruder, more superficial aspects of the particular vocation. Again, only the more obvious educational needs to qualify an employee for a given job were recognized. Consequently, guidance at first was concerned principally with the wise selection of a vocation and the selection of the courses thought necessary to a proper training for the vocation in question.

During the second decade of the century the results of numerous studies on the larger problem of individual differences began to be published, such as Thorndike's historic volume on *Mental Work and Fatigue and Individual Differences and Their Causes,* which appeared in 1914. Since that time numerous studies and a wealth of information have been accumulated on this complex subject. The results of these studies have added measurably to the effectiveness of vocational guidance: they have also led to the realization that man is such a complex being and is different in so many ways that guidance must find vocational choice and preparation but a small part of the total task imposed upon it.

The radical changes in the conception of the nature and function of education that have taken place within this generation forces upon us a new look at guidance. Among the first pronouncements of major educational significance in this connection was the report of the Commission on the Reorganization of Secondary Education entitled *Cardinal Principles of Secondary Education* made in 1918. The purposes of education as visualized in this report made preparation for college a secondary, almost incidental function of the secondary school, and emphasized the civic-social-ethical factors of living as the primary responsibility of secondary education. The change in educational thinking and direction so sharply pointed up in this most famous report has been emphasized repeatedly in subsequent pronouncements of responsible educational groups. Possibly the most complete, if not indeed the most advanced, of such statements is to be found in the several publications of the Educational Policies Commission of the National Education Association, and particularly as elaborated in *Education for All American Youth,* released in 1944, and revised in 1952.[1]

Henceforth, it was not enough that the individual be guided into the right vocation or advised properly as to which courses to elect out of the profusion of offerings available so that his education would provide the correct vocational training needed. Now everything that made for competent social behavior as an effective citizen became a part of guidance and the larger responsibility of education.

what are the dangers inherent in the
older guidance concept?

It is clear from the forgoing discussion that the newer conceptions of education understood man to be a far more complex being than previously had been assumed true. Education, therefore, became concerned with this total person who differed so much within himself and with others.

Still, the guidance movement continued to stress the vocational needs of youth, often giving scant attention to the social and inner personal needs of boys and girls, and in some situations virtually ignoring a wholeness in its approach to individuals. Even worse, in many instances the functions of the guidance specialist were regarded as separate and distinct from that of the teacher. This danger of failing to see the "wholeness" of the educative process is clearly pointed out by Lloyd-Jones:

Take, for instance, the important points proclaimed vigorously in every book on student personnel work: that personnel work is interested in the

---

[1] For a more extended discussion of the development of the guidance movement see Glenn E. Smith, *Principles and Practices of the Guidance Program.* New York: The Macmillan Company, 1951, Chapter 2.

whole person, not only his mind or his economic productivity, and that personnel work contributes to the personalization of education. The very specialization, however, to which personnel work itself has fallen victim, as described above, has threatened to nullify these basic claims of personnel work. On the other hand, we talk piously of the whole student, and on the other we proceed, because of the way our professional expertness has developed, because of the size of the units within which we work, and because of the organizational forms personnel work has taken, to divide the student up amongst the experts, thus contributing directly to the depersonalization of personnel work and education.[2]

how is modern guidance defined?

At least in basic theory, if not always in organization and practice, modern guidance does take into account the wholeness of the individual in the educative process. Arthur J. Jones, long recognized as a leader in the guidance movement says:

Viewing the life of the individual as a whole, guidance may be said to have as its purpose helping the individual to discover his needs, to assess his potentialities, gradually to develop life goals that are individually satisfying and socially desirable, to formulate plans of action in the service of these goals, and to proceed to their realization.

This practically identifies the purpose of guidance with that of education. It places major emphasis upon the development of the whole individual who is now functioning and will in the future function in a social environment. It is a useful concept because it stresses the unity of one's life and reveals the impossibility of separating one aspect of life from another.[3]

The modern all-inclusive conception of the nature of guidance is expressed by another guidance specialist in these words:

The keystone of the school program is guidance—personal assistance to individual boys and girls in making their plans and decisions about careers,

---

[2] Esther Lloyd-Jones and Margaret R. Smith, Editors, *Student Personnel Work as Deeper Teaching.* New York: Harper and Brothers, 1954, p. 6.

[3] Arthur J. Jones, *Principles of Guidance,* 4th Edition. New York: The McGraw-Hill Book Company, 1951, pp. 77-78. This writer devotes an entire chapter to a discussion of the meaning of guidance which all interested in this problem should read. For further discussion of this issue see: Lefever, Turrell, and Weitzel, *Principles and Techniques of Guidance,* Revised. New York: The Ronald Press Company, 1950, Chapter 24; Smith, *Principles and Practices of the Guidance Program,* Chapters 1-2.

education, employment and all sorts of personal problems. . . . Guidance is . . . the high art of helping boys and girls to plan their own actions wisely in the full light of all the facts they can muster about themselves and about the world in which they will work and live.[4]

Another writer emphasizes the broad aspects of guidance thus:

In guiding our youngsters we must enable them to learn how to live with themselves as well as how to live with others. There is a narrow line that somehow or other must be found. Otherwise, schools are preparing them not for democratic living but for a totalitarian existence. Throughout this book we are going to be concerned with the uniqueness of the individual. It is a guidance responsibility to enable the child to understand and accept himself and to understand and accept his needs for belonging and for group participation so that he can make wise decisions about how he will maintain his individuality and at the same time enhance the society in which he lives.[5]

This same writer has spelled out his definition of guidance in a five-point statement:

1. Guidance is the organization of information by the school about the child and his community for the purpose of helping the child learn to make wise decisions concerning his own future.
2. Guidance is the organization of life experiences within the school situation so that the child is provided with situations in which he feels completely accepted, in which he is enabled to "take stock" of his potentialities, accept his limitations without threat, and develop a realistic picture of himself and the world around him.
3. Guidance is the provision for satisfactory group experiences in which successful leadership and membership roles are learned and in which the group is able to set goals and solve problems dealing with interpersonal relations.
4. Guidance is the provision of opportunities for the child to understand and value his uniqueness and his relatedness to others.

---

[4] Franklin R. Zeran, "The Pupil-Personnel Program," in Paul B. Jacobson, Editor, *The American Secondary School.* Englewood Cliffs, N. J.: Prentice-Hall, Inc., 1952, pp. 284-285.

[5] Ira J. Gordon, *The Teacher as a Guidance Worker,* New York: Harper and Brothers, 1956, p. 5.

5. Guidance is the provision of the above experiences and opportunities for all children.[6]

Still another quotation may help to clinch the contemporary "wholeness" concept of guidance.

The knowledge that each child presents a unique pattern of characteristics and requires unique treatment lies at the heart of our guidance philosophy. With individual differences as our starting point, we view guidance as relating to all those things which adults do *consciously* to assist an individual child to live as fully and as effectively as he is able. . . . Guidance involves both helping the child adjust to a required pattern and adjusting the pattern better to fit the child.[7]

The reading of these statements of very broad ideas about guidance must make clear the all embracing nature of the modern meaning of guidance.

how are the concepts of education
and guidance related?

It would be difficult indeed to find any definition of education presented by a responsible educator today which did not in essence embrace all that is implied in the foregoing definitions of guidance. More than two decades ago one of the authors of this book defined *education to be the adjustment of man to his environment, which contemplates man's adaptation to and the reconstruction of his environment to the end that the most enduring satisfactions may accrue to the individual and to society.*[8] In this definition education is conceived as pointing both a process and a goal as is true of the function of guidance presented in the several statements on the preceding pages.

---

[6] Gordon, *The Teacher as a Guidance Worker*, pp. 3-5. See also a list of 46 such guidance activities in Clarence C. Dunsmoor and Leonard M. Miller, *Principles and Methods of Guidance for Teachers*. Scranton, Pennsylvania: International Textbook Company, 1949, pp. 36-41.

[7] Association for Supervision and Curriculum Development, *Guidance in the Curriculum*, 1955 Yearbook. Washington, D. C.: The National Education Association, 1955, p. 13.

[8] Nelson L. Bossing, *Progressive Methods of Teaching in Secondary Schools*. Boston: Houghton Mifflin Company, 1935, p. 12; see Revised Edition, 1952, p. 10.

Guidance, like education, has undergone change in meaning and function. When education was thought of as largely a mastery of quantities of subject matter, and the curriculum as a confusing array of discrete subjects, guidance came into being as a means of helping youth select the right subjects to qualify for specific vocations.

Now education is conceived to be the guidance of the pupil in his learning activities so that he may have those types of learning experiences which will provide him with the personal and social skills necessary for happy and effective living in a democratic society. Education thus becomes all pervasive in its impact upon the learner. Since no two pupils are now regarded as alike in abilities, interests, or maturity, and by these same tokens the personal and social needs of individual pupils must vary within a large orbit of common needs, education becomes highly personalized as it tries to meet both the individual and group needs of each pupil. As the guidance movement has tried to adjust its thinking and program to meet the obvious needs of the "whole" but highly complex person to be educated, the guidance function, as defined by guidance authorities, for all practical purposes becomes identical with the total educative program of the school. There appears, then, to be a direct overlap, if not a major duplication of function, within the educative agencies that have grown up in the school.

What Is the Place of the Teacher in Guidance?

This apparent overlapping or duplication of functions points sharply the respective places of the teacher and the so-called guidance specialist within what appears to be a commonly accepted educative task.

It must be crystal clear to the reader of this book that the educational point of view stressed throughout its pages makes the task of the classroom teacher envelop the activities now considered by guidance specialists to be the special concerns of guidance. It cannot be too often or too emphatically repeated that the teacher in modern education is concerned not with teaching subjects *per se,* but with the guidance of youth in those behavioral adjustments which will enable him to live successfully and happily in his present environment, and develop competencies for future living. This is the essential task of the teacher. The teacher has no other real justification as a member of the school staff.

1. The centrality of the teacher in the guidance function now seems generally accepted alike by leaders in education and special proponents of guidance. There is scarcely a contemporary book coming from the press on methods of teaching, or bearing directly upon the place of the teacher in modern education, that does not have a chapter devoted to the guidance responsibilities of the teacher, or at least a discussion of the teacher's responsibility for guidance. A recent book on *Guidance in the Curriculum,* written by a group of educators and including but one professional guidance counselor, expresses the point of view quite forcefully in these words:

> Classroom teaching is regarded as inseparable from guidance; the teacher guides as well as teaches. . . . The authors take the position that classroom teaching should not be separated from guidance; that, instead, guidance should be regarded as an essential aspect of the work of every classroom teacher. The teacher . . . stands second only to the parents in the weight of his responsibility for guiding the development of the pupil.[9]

A professional guidance leader agrees with this point of view in these words:

> It becomes increasingly necessary for guidance to become a preventive program, to become a program which is concerned at the teacher level with all the children in the school. . . . the great responsibility for carrying on effective guidance will rest in the classroom where it belongs.[10]

Of similar import are the words of Strang, long an exponent of guidance:

---

[9] Association for Supervision and Curriculum Development, *Guidance in the Curriculum,* 1955 Yearbook. Washington, D. C.: National Education Association, 1955, pp. 5, 12, and 13.

[10] Gordon, *The Teacher as a Guidance Worker,* p. 6.

Obviously personnel work is not an "extra," a fad, or a frill; it is an essential part of good education. It has always been so. Wherever and whenever teachers have been concerned with helping each individual to realize his potentialities, they have exemplified the personnel point of view and have rendered guidance services.[11]

In a recent summary of educational writing on the subject of guidance, Arbuckle makes these trenchant observations:

> One of the major findings of the past few years is evidence to indicate that the teacher *can* function as a guidance worker, *is* in many schools functioning as guidance worker, and to be completely effective, *must* function as a guidance worker.
>
> In the vast majority of the articles that have been written on the problem of guidance in schools, however, the major question is no longer, "Is the teacher a guidance worker?" but rather, "How can the teacher function most effectively as a guidance worker?"
>
> The characteristics of the good teacher and the good counselor are, according to many articles, almost exactly the same. Many writers have pointed out the changing role of the teacher, who is no longer considered as a mere imparter of information, and they discuss the newer point of view and its implications. Mental hygienists writing on self-understanding for teachers point out the impossibility of the good teacher not being a guidance worker, and some have pointed out that the teacher is a mental hygienist or guidance worker whether he thinks he is or not.[12]

2. There is a practical aspect of the guidance problem which, under the circumstances, makes a discussion of the relation of the teacher to guidance irrelevant in the light of modern educational thinking. Hamrin has clearly demonstrated that unless the teacher functions in the guidance role most schools will have no guidance services.[13] This is one of the anomalous situations

---

[11] Ruth Strang, *The Role of the Teacher in Personnel Work,* Fourth Edition. New York: Bureau of Publications, Teachers College, Columbia University, 1953, p. 33.

[12] Dugald S. Arbuckle, "The Classroom Teacher's Role in Guidance," *Guidance, Counseling and Pupil Personnel,* Review of Educational Research, April 1954, 24:181, 182. See also discussion in Janet A. Kelley, *Guidance and Curriculum,* Englewood Cliffs, N. J.: Prentice-Hall, Inc., 1955, p. 420 ff.

[13] Shirley A. Hamrin, *Chats with Teachers About Counseling.* Bloomington, Illinois: McKnight and McKnight Company, 1950. See also discussion in *Guidance, Counseling, and Pupil Personnel,* Review of Educational Research, April 1954, 24:183-184.

that emerges from the newer conception of guidance as an integral part of the basic educational process, and the older assumption that only the specialist could do guidance work. The recommended standards of the National Guidance Association that there should be one guidance specialist for every 350-400 students would leave most schools without a guidance worker, particularly in the secondary schools where a majority of the schools enroll less than 200 students.

3. There does remain a very practical problem of how the teacher can relate his guidance functions with those of a guidance specialist where such specialists are employed. In the complex nature of the educational task as now understood, the teacher who would be fully competent to discharge his responsibilities in maximal degree would have to possess the qualities of a superman. The educational task of the teacher, as now conceived, is one of the most complex and exacting responsibilities assigned to any professional group.

No one can hope to be an expert in every phase of education. It is this fact that has led to the development of specialized functions in the school, aided and abetted initially by our tendency to think of education more or less as a collection of separate parts, and our failure to see the interrelated wholeness of the total educational process. There is a place for the specialist or specialists in this total educational process. The specialist must see his particular responsibility as dovetailing into that of the other members of the educational staff. And they in turn must look upon him as a complementary facet of their area of special responsibility.

One educational administrator and writer, accepting the modern theory that education and guidance are essentially synonomous functions, has taken the position that basic face-to-face guidance must remain the responsibility of the teacher. He has utilized his guidance specialists as service arms of the teacher. It is they who can advise with the teacher as to the proper use and diagnosis of test materials, and can counsel with the teacher on health, home, or other living conditions that affect the behavior of particular pupils. For the teacher these specialists become a welcome supplement to his own less specialized competencies.[14] With much this same point of view as to the function of the guidance specialist, another writer has listed seven ways in which such specialists can serve the teacher as a valuable resource person:

1) To help plan and supervise the gathering of such facts as are essential to the understanding and guidance of each individual pupil in the school system.

2) To help teachers interpret and use these facts (assembled in individual cumulative records) in solving their problems in the guidance of children.

3) To assume direct responsibility in the guidance of a child only when principals and teachers are unable to solve the child's problems.

4) To coordinate and integrate the work of the teacher and the various specialists who deal with the child—that is, the guidance consultant should be the liaison worker who unifies all the efforts which school personnel put forth for the child's welfare.

5) To help teachers and parents plan and carry on a continuous program of education to increase their knowledge and understanding of children.

6) To help parents and teachers discover the implications and applications of such knowledge for ways of dealing with children in homes and schools.

7) To help teachers and parents understand the dynamic interrelationships between guidance and instruction, to the end that mutual adjustment of school to pupil and pupil to school may be a continuously evolving process.[15]

4. It is one thing to see how the guidance specialist may be of assistance to the teacher, and quite another to spell out the particular guidance functions which the good teacher will accept as a part of his responsibilities. Two recent writers have tried to indicate what activities the teacher might look upon not only as

---

[14] Paul R. Pierce, *Developing a High School Curriculum.* New York: American Book Company, 1942, pp. 217-218.

[15] Association for Supervision and Curriculum Development, *Guidance in the Curriculum,* 1955 Yearbook. Washington, D. C.: National Education Association, 1955, p. 104. See following pages for extended discussion of these points.

good teaching activities but also as typical activities accepted in the teacher's guidance role. Strang has listed seven of these areas of teacher guidance activities:

1. Using Personal Relationships
2. Building Self-Esteem and Competence
3. Individualizing Instruction
4. Guiding Daily Learning
5. Sharing Educational Goals with Students
6. Discussing Common Problems
7. Following Through on Student Needs[16]

Every teacher who accepts the modern educational point of view would recognize these seven kinds of guidance activities as the responsibility of every good teacher, as a part of his educational task. There is nothing unique about them that would set them apart from the normal instructional routines of the good teacher. Good teachers could not ignore them.

A similar list of good guidance-teaching activities has been suggested by Faunce:

1. Studying the needs, interests, abilities, and problems of each individual in a class
2. Analyzing the relationships that exist between individuals and subgroups in a class
3. Helping groups of students to discuss, analyze, and define problems of current interest that they need to solve for themselves
4. Guiding students in working on the solution of real-life problems in the classroom
5. Deepening their insights and enriching their interest in the world about them
6. Helping students to evaluate their own growth
7. Guiding students in the techniques of group self-control
8. Giving students insights into their own behavior
9. Helping them to make increasingly wise choices among alternatives
10. Helping them to learn from their own mistakes

---

[16] Ruth Strang, *The Role of the Teacher in Personnel Work*, Fourth Edition, pp. 115-124. The entire section should be read as each of the seven points listed above is discussed in detail.

11. Helping them to respect themselves and others
12. Helping them to get along well with others.[17]

This list of good guidance-teaching activities simply refines the shorter list given above by Strang. However, the refining of these items tends to sharpen for the teacher what is both good teaching and good guidance. It should be clear that guidance is a natural function of good teaching; and that the good teacher can go about the task of helping boys and girls develop skills in meeting and solving their personal and social problems, secure in the realization that in so doing he is meeting his teaching-guidance responsibilities.

WHAT IS THE UNIQUE PLACE OF GUIDANCE IN CORE?

The unique place of guidance in core grows out of the educational concepts upon which both core and modern guidance are based. The fact that core is based upon the principle that learning takes place through experience and manifests itself in the change in the behavior of the learner needs no elaboration to the reader of this book. The fact of the further shift in concept from an emphasis upon the subject-matter curriculum, with its major concern for encyclopaedic knowledge, to the experience curriculum with its natural emphasis upon the personal and social problems of the learner as the center of education and its core, needs only to be recalled here to clarify the issues involved. The newer ideas of guidance are based largely upon these central learning and educational concepts.

The unique place of guidance in core thus flows from the implications of the concept of learning and the curriculum implicit in the core idea. Learning is thought of as a matter of adjustments—and involves the pupil's satisfactory adjustments within his personal and social relationships. This is the major emphasis of guidance. Further, the philosophy of the core stresses the importance of the personalized aspects of the teacher-pupil relation-

---

[17] Roland C. Faunce, *Secondary School Administration*. New York: Harper and Brothers, 1955, pp. 135-136.

ship in the adjustment process, which, again, is at the heart of the guidance theory. It is these aspects of the educational bases of core that give guidance an important place in the core curriculum concept.

How Does Core Facilitate the Activities of Guidance?

There are at least four ways in which core facilitates guidance activities.

1. The organization of classes into large block-time units, sometimes technically called the multiple-period organization of classes, has been a major contribution to guidance. It has been a characteristic of core types of administrative organization to group pupils into classes extending over two to three of the usual class periods of 45-50 minutes. These larger time units for classes make many guidance activities possible which require more than the brief period of traditional school practice. The longer class period also provides a more leisurely atmosphere conducive to the personalization of the learning activities and individual counseling.

2. The popular form of longer block-time class organization makes it possible for the teacher to know the pupils better. Where the class hour is 45-50 minutes in length, the teacher would probably have at least five, and most likely six or seven class periods per day, with 30-35 pupils per class. This would provide the teacher with a probable minimum of 150 pupils, and more likely upwards of 200 pupils per day passing through his classes. Such daily pupil teaching loads are justified only on a production-line notion of education. Such situations make guidance activities almost impossible and defeat any conception of personalized guidance.

Where the large block-time class period is used, the core teacher may have but two classes with a total of not more than 60-70 pupils daily. This makes possible easy acquaintance with each pupil and some awareness of the personal needs, interests, and abilities of each member of the class. Such a class situation enables the teacher to personalize the educational process, discover personal problems or anticipate them, and thus through proper planning or counseling provide help when needed. This provides a most favorable guidance-learning environment. Teacher-pupil planning is thus made possible and encouraged.

Strang has recognized the special opportunity for guidance activities in the core type large-block-time organization:

> The core-curriculum provides for an ideal fusion of guidance and instruction. Under the core-curriculum form of organization, one of the core teachers has major responsibility for knowing each student in the class and helping each to get the experiences he needs. The person in charge of a core group of thirty or forty pupils is appropriately called "teacher-counselor." He might well be called "teacher-counselor-curriculum reviser" because he is constantly getting suggestions for changes in the curriculum as he gains understanding of individual pupils.[18]

3. A third feature of the core curriculum organization that contributes to the guidance activity is the growing tendency to extend the vertical length of the teacher-pupil relationship. Whereas the traditional school practice is to limit the teacher's contact with the pupil in terms of the length of time required to complete a subject, often a one-semester contact, the tendency in the core organization is to keep the teacher and the core class together one or more years. In this way the core teacher has a longer time in which to study each pupil and to gain some understanding as well of his home and community background. This makes possible a better basis of sequential guidance of the learning experiences of the pupil as well as a more intelligent sequence of counseling activities.

4. An important contribution of the block-time and extended period of teacher-pupil contact features of the core curriculum is the opportunity it provides for the use of classroom methods better calculated to help pupils develop skills with which to solve

---

[18] Ruth Strang, *The Role of the Teacher in Personnel Work*, Fourth Edition, pp. 44-45.

their personal and social problems. The use of problem-solving methods, teacher-pupil planning, and individual and group approaches to problem situations provides excellent opportunities for the teacher to guide the learning experiences of boys and girls, and in the highest degree contribute to their guidance needs. It is a way by which the teacher may apply certain methods or classroom techniques that will strengthen or build up desirable behavior characteristics. Indirect as well as direct personalized guidance may thus be used by the skilled teacher.

5. The nature of the core curriculum itself contributes directly to the guidance function. The organization of the core curriculum around the personal and social problems of the pupils provides a direct means of helping pupils understand themselves and their problems, and provides the basis for teacher guidance of the pupil in the discovery of effective ways of solving these problems.

What Resource Tools Are Available to the Core-Guidance Teacher?

All teachers, of course, should be concerned with the resources available for instruction and guidance. The core teacher, in the very nature of the concepts of education accepted, becomes vitally interested in every device or agency that will contribute to his effectiveness in the instructional and guidance activities which he recognizes as his responsibility as a good teacher.

1. School records are important aids to the core-guidance teacher. In almost every school it is now possible to find records of the intelligence levels of pupils, achievement profiles, and at least minimum health data about each pupil. These become indispensable to the teacher as a basis for guidance.

In our better schools, and particularly in the schools organized on the core basis, there has been a definite trend toward the development of the "Cumulative Folder" or "Cumulative Record" for the maintenance of pertinent data about a pupil. The kinds of data that should be included in such a folder or record and recommended by guidance authorities may be listed as follows:

1. Family background
2. Physical health and disability
3. Mental-emotional health
4. Social adjustment
5. Achievement profiles and other academic records
6. Intelligence test scores
7. Aptitude test scores
8. Personality test records
9. General and special interests
10. Social and so-called extracurricular school activities
11. Community social activities
12. Employment record
13. Samples of classroom work such as specimen writing, outlines, and so on.
14. Anecdotal records
15. Pupil and parental conference data

These records should be kept up-to-date so that they become a vivid growth-picture of the pupil. Samples of the pupil's work should be carefully filed at intervals to show clearly the developmental progress made. All responsible for the development of this file, and particularly the core teacher, should add to the data with a view to its utility by future teachers and guidance specialists who may at some time take over responsibility for the continued guidance of the pupil.

Such data as these records contain can be of inestimable value to the alert core teacher, and should be readily available to the teacher at all times. While some argue that these data should be kept in a central office and in the counselor's files when such a guidance specialist is employed, all agree that the sole purpose of such records is utilization. In the core organization it would seem that maximum use can be made of such data only when they are immediately available in the core teacher's files. Since the major guidance responsibility for a particular group of pupils in the core curriculum rests with a designated core teacher, it would seem to facilitate the guidance activities of the teacher to have the records immediately available when needed.

One objection to making such records so readily available to the teacher is the fear that teachers will not always respect the highly confidential nature of these files and fail to keep them from prying eyes. It may be assumed, however, that teachers, especially core teachers, competent to use such files have had sufficient training in the use of such confidential records that they recognize the nature of their responsibility in both handling them and safeguarding them from unprofessional use. Such records, of course, the professionally minded teacher will keep under lock and key.[19]

2. The administrative leaders of the school, the superintendent and principal in the small school, and the principal and supervisors in the larger schools, are able to provide much help to the teacher. Their knowledge of the pupil in his all-school relationships and frequently in his community environment can help the teacher by giving valuable supplemental data not found in the cumulative folder. And where such folders are not available their knowledge of the over-all school relations of the pupil makes the administrative staff a valuable resource aid in carrying on effective instructional and guidance activities.

In the twofold aspect of successful adjustment of the pupil it is necessary for the teacher to remember that at times the school must make some adjustments to the pupil. Where the special needs of a pupil require that the school waive a regulation or give some other special consideration to extraordinary needs, the teacher must have recourse to the administrative leadership for guidance assistance. Guidance is not a one-way activity—the school must give as well as demand. In such situations there must be cooperation between the administration and the teacher if the pupil is to receive effective educational guidance.

---

[19] For helpful suggestions to teachers in the use of cumulative records see Ruth Strang, *The Role of the Teacher in Personnel Work*, Fourth Edition, Chapter 12; also Association for Supervision and Curriculum Development, *Guidance in the Curriculum*, Chapter 8.

3. The teaching staff is another valuable resource aid to the guidance activities of the core teacher. At this point the core teacher is uniquely at advantage over the traditional teacher. As was made clear earlier in this book, the educational concept that lies back of the core curriculum is that all teachers are engaged in a cooperative educational task. They are generalists, not narrow specialists, as is true in the traditional, subject-matter curriculum. Consequently, each teacher is concerned with the total education of every child in the school, and considers himself obligated to contribute in every way possible to the education of every pupil. Every teacher, therefore, welcomes the opportunity to help other teachers with information or suggestions that will enable them to give better guidance to their pupils.

Often previous teachers of the pupil in question can throw light on the pupil's earlier problems, behavior, and experiences that may make more intelligence guidance possible. Too, other teachers in the school may be able to add their observations of the pupil which can be a valuable aid to the teacher in counseling or guiding the learning activities of the pupil more advantageously. In the contacts of other teachers with his pupils, the core teacher has possible rich sources of guidance assistance.

4. The parents provide another rich source of guidance help to core teachers. With more time scheduled in the core for the teacher's contact with parents, it is possible to utilize parental assistance in guidance not so readily available to the teacher in the traditional school organization.

There are many ways in which such contact can be of help in teacher guidance; three of the major ways are touched upon here briefly. (1) Many teachers have learned much about their pupils by an hour or two in conference with these pupils' parents, at the school conference, in the parents' homes, or both. Often many of the social and educational attitudes found in the children are reflected in the parents. English usage, care for appearance, and cultural background are more vividly portrayed in such visitations than are recorded in the cumulative record or reported by fellow teachers and administrators. Such conferences may provide a basis for understanding a pupil's attitudes and behavior and thus give clues as to the best means of approaching the pupil's difficulties. (2) Cooperating parents can answer many puzzling questions the teacher has not been able to answer within the immediate school environment. The teacher, for example, can learn the extent to which there is a definite carry-over into the home situation of attitudes and behavior patterns the teacher has been trying to develop in a pupil. (3) These teacher-parent, face-to-face conferences make possible the enlistment of the parents in the efforts of the teacher to carry on preventive or corrective guidance procedures. Many instructional-guidance goals can be reached successfully with particular pupils only when the full and enthusiastic cooperation of the parents has been secured. Possibly no source of help in the teacher's guidance activities can be more valuable than that of the assistance and cooperation of parents.

5. Many agencies in the community can render yeoman service, assisting the core teacher in his guidance activities. These have been discussed in considerable detail in other sections of this book; all that is necessary here is but a reminder of this important source of assistance.[20]

6. Last but not least, where the school is fortunate to have the benefit of a guidance specialist the core teacher will find him an invaluable resource person. Trained in certain areas of guidance techniques further than the average core teacher, the specialist can counsel the teacher in troublesome situations, interpret data significant to the case, and in some situations gather as part of his responsibility as a guidance specialist source data helpful to the core teacher. In extremely difficult cases he may cooperatively assist the teacher in direct counseling with the pupil, his parents, and others important to the case.

Beyond these immediate services to the core teacher in his

---

[20] For detailed discussion of this problem in other sources see Association for Supervision and Curriculum Development, *Guidance in Curriculum*, Chapter 10; Gordon, *The Teacher as a Guidance Worker*, Chapter 4; and Strang, *The Role of the Teacher in Personnel Work*, Chapter 3.

guidance problems, the specialist should be establishing community contacts, gathering data concerning the pupils of the school which may be later useful to the teacher in his guidance activities. Also he should be rendering a type of in-service training to help teachers develop more competence in the skills and techniques of specialized areas of guidance and counseling.

How Shall the Core Teacher Be Trained for the Guidance Function?

The core teacher may well ask what would be the ideal preparation for teaching-guidance responsibilities. Ira J. Gordon, a guidance specialist, believes the guidance teacher should possess at least four general competencies: a genetic understanding of (1) the growing maturing child, (2) the forces in the community and the family that help mold the pupil's personality, and (3) the influence of the peer group in shaping his attitudes and behavior as well as the part the learner plays in the interaction of himself in the matrix of his social environment; also (4) personal skill in observation and analysis of pupil behavior in the milieu of these complex factors that enter into his growth and development as a person; and ability to (5) participate effectively in group processes, counseling pupil and parent, and (6) define and solve school problems, which are regarded as basically a form of action research.[21]

The core teacher may well react to the above suggestions that the competencies visualized by core curriculum leaders for the well-prepared core teacher include all these and more. The function of the core teacher in a modern school includes all that is narrowly defined by some as guidance plus all that enters into the guidance of the learner toward becoming a well-adjusted individual, capable and functioning at all points as an efficient, socially minded member of the democratic community.

---

[21] Adapted from Gordon, *The Teacher as a Guidance Worker*, pp. 10-12. In this connection the reader should read pp. 6-12 for a complete picture of a fully qualified teacher guidance worker.

To state it in another way, the basic educational preparation now required of the good core teacher would involve:

1. A broad acquaintance with and understanding of the culture of which he is a part; its antecedents as well as some clues to its future direction in the context of a total world outlook.

2. A thorough understanding of what is now known about the nature of the learner, the nature of the learning process, and the psychological forces that operate in group relationships.

3. A full awareness and understanding of the social forces within and without the community environment that influence the developing behavior reactions of the growing boy and girl.

4. An understanding of and skill in the use of the most approved methods of effectively guiding the behavioral development of pupils both in and out of the classroom.

5. An understanding of and skill in the use of those devices and techniques commonly employed by the guidance specialist.

6. Finally, a deep respect for, an abiding faith in, and a warm personal outgoing concern for, people as persons; this quality may or may not in full be the product of the conscious, direct training of any institutional agency.

All these educational qualities and skills the core teacher must have to fulfill his responsibilities as a core teacher; with them, he automatically qualifies to serve as well in the guidance-teacher role. In the chapter which follows, an analysis will be made of other roles played by the core teacher as he learns to work more effectively with his students.

SELECTED REFERENCES

Arbuckle, Dugald S., *Teacher Counseling*. Cambridge, Mass.: Addison-Wesley Press, Inc., 1950.

Association for Supervision and Curriculum Development, *Guidance in the Curriculum*, 1955 Yearbook. Washington, D. C.: National Education Association, 1955.

Bernard, Harold W., *Mental Hygiene for Classroom Teachers*. New York: McGraw-Hill Book Company, 1952.

Blum, M., and B. Balinsky, *Counseling and Psychology: Vocational Psychology and Its Relation to Educational and Personal Counseling.* Englewood Cliffs, N. J.: Prentice-Hall, Inc., 1951.

Buhler, C., F. Smitter, and S. Richardson, *Childhood Problems and the Teacher.* New York: Henry Holt & Company, 1952.

Carleton, R. E., "Teaching and Guidance Can Be Mixed: Oil, Water, and Baloney," *Clearing House,* 25:408-409, March 1951.

Chase, Elizabeth, "Oil and Water: Teaching and Guidance Can't Be Mixed," *Clearing House,* 25:210-211, December 1950.

Corey, Stephen M., *Action Research to Improve School Practices.* New York: Bureau of Publications, Teachers College, Columbia University, 1953.

Department of Elementary School Principals, *Guidance for Today's Children,* Thirty-third Yearbook. Washington, D. C.: National Education Association, 1954.

Detjen, E. W. and M. F., *Elementary School Guidance.* New York: McGraw-Hill Book Company, 1952.

Dunsmoor, C. C., and L. M. Miller, *Principles and Methods of Guidance for Teachers,* Revised. Scranton, Pennsylvania: International Textbook Company, 1949.

Foshay, Arthur W., and others, *Children's Social Values.* New York: Bureau of Publications, Teachers College, Columbia University, 1954.

Gordon, Ira J., "The Class as a Group: The Teacher as Leader," *Educational Administration and Supervision,* 37:108-118, 1951.

————, *The Teacher as a Guidance Worker.* New York: Harper and Brothers, 1956.

'Guidance and Counseling," *Review of Educational Research,* 27:192-202, April 1957.

"Guidance, Counseling, and Pupil Personnel," *Review of Educational Research,* 24:181-189, April 1954.

Hamrin, Shirley A., *Chats with Teachers About Counseling.* Bloomington, Illinois: McKnight and McKnight Company, 1950.

Jones, Arthur J., *Principles of Guidance,* Fourth Edition. New York: McGraw-Hill Book Company, 1951.

Kelley, Janet A., *Guidance and Curriculum*. Englewood Cliffs, N. J.: Prentice-Hall, Inc., 1955.

Lane, H., and M. Beauchamp, *Human Relations in Education*. Englewood Cliffs, N. J.: Prentice-Hall, Inc., 1955.

Langdon, G., and I. Stout, *Teacher-Parent Interviews*. Englewood Cliffs, N. J.: Prentice-Hall, Inc., 1954.

Little, Wilson, and A. L. Chapman, *Developmental Guidance in Secondary Schools*. New York: McGraw-Hill Book Company, 1953.

Lloyd-Jones, Esther, and Margaret R. Smith, *Student Personnel Work as Deeper Teaching*. New York: Harper and Brothers, 1954.

Miel, Alice, and others, *Cooperative Procedures in Learning*. New York: Bureau of Publications, Teachers College, Columbia University, 1952.

Morris, Glyn A., *Practical Guidance Methods for Principals and Teachers*. New York: Harper and Brothers, 1952.

Pepinsky, H. and P., *Counseling: Theory and Practice*. New York: The Ronald Press Company, 1954.

Traxler, Arthur E., *Techniques of Guidance,* Revised. New York: Harper and Brothers, 1957.

Strang, Ruth, *The Role of the Teacher in Personnel Work,* Fourth Edition. New York: Bureau of Publications, Teachers College, Columbia University, 1953.

Wall, B. D., "The Progressive Teacher and Guidance," *Progressive Education,* 29:197-199, April 1952.

Williamson, James E., "Teaching and Guidance Can Be Mixed: Teaching and Guidance—No Boundaries." *Clearing House,* 25:414-415, March 1951.

Chapter 9

The Role of the Teacher

What about the "Traditional" Teacher?

Much has been said and written about "traditional" teachers. Sometimes they are referred to as "old-fashioned," or "authoritarian," or "subject-matter minded." Criticism usually gives rise to defense, and something resembling a debate is launched. If the traditional teacher resents being called old-fashioned, he may retort that the modern teacher has gone overboard for untested, new-fangled ideas. If the self-confessed traditional teacher is accused of being authoritarian, the counter-accusation is heard that the "modern" teacher has turned his job over to the kids and is not assuming any role as a professionally trained leader. If the traditional teacher is said to rule over students with an iron hand, and obtain control by obedience to the teacher, the reply may be that the modern teacher is encouraging bedlam and does not have any kind of control at all in the classroom. Thus the debate may wax warmer, and more heat than light is often generated.

It was pointed out in an earlier chapter of this volume[1] that teachers cannot usually be categorized as (consistently) authoritarian or democratic in their methods. Every teacher has on occasion employed an authoritarian role. He may do so intentionally, when he observes that the students are not yet ready to supply their own controls or to make their own plans. He may also discover some day that he has unintentionally regressed into an authoritarian role because habit is powerful and new roles are hard to learn.

It appears that classroom democracy is a hard-won goal, and that most teachers are moving along a continuum toward their own conception of good teaching and learning. Any given teacher is not, always and forever, fixed at a given point on this continuum. It is a mistake to categorize people as though they always behaved the same way. It is a mistake, for that matter, to attempt to improve education by name-calling—as we throw such terms as "traditional" at people.

On the other hand, there *are* differences between teacher-actions which fall at opposite ends of the "democracy-authoritarianism" continuum. It may be helpful to core teachers to examine some of these differences. As we do so, it should be noted that we are discussing actions and roles that are sometimes played by all teachers, but not necessarily always adhered to by any particular teacher. We are examining the extreme on the role-continuum. In the interests of clarity we must fall back on the perhaps hypothetical phrase "traditional teacher," who is imagined for our purpose to have adopted all the roles at the extreme end of the scale.

the chairman

Consider the conventional relationship of a teacher to his group. He usually assumes the chairman's role. As chairman, he announces the nature of the lesson to be studied, assigns the tasks, determines the resources, and delimits the goal in terms of daily class periods. As chairman, he "hears the lesson," that is, he asks

---
[1] See the early section of Chapter 6.

the questions and expects to hear correct replies. Communication is between each student and the chairman, rarely among students as a group. Again, as chairman, the teacher supplies any introductory remarks he deems necessary, and then inserts transitions between various parts of the lessons; at the appropriate point he also personally supplies the summary or conclusion. On occasion, he may even repeat his own version of the answer after the student has given his version, if such substitution will pave the way more neatly for the (teacher's) transitional statement that follows. Since the teacher serves as chairman, he must stand at the front of the room, where he can see every student. Since communication is between the teacher and the class, there is no need for students to see the other students' faces.

the chief source of information

The teacher is often regarded as a sort of live textbook. He is expected to be able to answer any and all questions about the lesson, on the spot. It is obvious that this responsibility compels him to keep the lesson within the scope of his own information. He may, if he encourages questions, find himself the target of a curious game engaged in by the more verbal students—consisting of catching the teacher in a mistake. The whole point of this game is the assumed infallibility of the teacher in "his" subject. Some teachers have learned to ignore or evade questions from certain members of the class. Some have sorrowfully abandoned the whole business of "letting" students ask questions. Some teachers, on the other hand, have become so successful at the game that they subtly encourage it. In the light of the enormous increase in human knowledge in all fields, it would be both reasonable and honest for us all to say to our students, on occasion, "I don't know; let's find out." These six little words are hard ones to utter when we have once cast ourselves in the role of one who knows.

evaluation

The traditional teacher is the only evaluator in the class. He tends to assume sole responsibility for estimating the degree of individual growth students have achieved. As chairman, he has set the goals for the class. As a specialist in a subject, he has usually limited these goals to mastery, or at least effort toward mastery, of materials or skills within that subject. Since the students neither established the goals nor defined the subject area within which they would work, it is usually assumed that they could not set up any criteria for evaluating their growth. They are likely to depend on the teacher for the whole process of evaluation. Their chief clue about their own progress consists of their marks, which they come to anticipate with eagerness and/or dread. There are some other clues in the teacher's attitude toward them —remarks or facial expressions or choice of who is to recite. All these evaluative clues derive from the teacher. In general, no one helps the students themselves systematically to form reasonable appraisals of their own progress.

group controller

Finally, the traditional teacher is completely responsible for the discipline, or control of the class. If he is a skillful and interesting leader, this responsibility may not appear onerous; yet the significant fact is that the teacher alone is having the experience of group control. No one else in the class has the opportunity to learn it by actual experience. In fact, the tradition usually develops that discipline is the teacher's business. Students do not consider it the proper thing for them to concern themselves about their own behavior, or that of others. In some traditional classes that are poorly taught, the control of the group gradually assumes greater proportions until it is the teacher's chief daily concern and there is time for little else to go on.

It should be made clear that the teacher whom we have been describing is usually neither malevolent nor autocratic by nature. He does not operate in this way through considered choice. In fact, he is likely to be filled with good will toward children and may be actuated by an earnest desire to give his best to his teaching. If he dominates the classroom, it is because he is the logical product of a series of experiences that have served to make him an autocrat. The philosophy of learning to which he has been exposed has so conditioned him that the autocratic role appears to be his only road to security in teaching. He has not yet had any experiences that would give him a comfortable feeling in a situation where children are helping to plan. He may even lack the insights that would make teacher-pupil planning possible. In short, he is a victim of the tradition that the teacher's task is to control and direct his pupils.

The teacher of a core class has usually grown up in this same tradition. His whole pattern of training and experience probably tends to make him the chairman and chief resource person of the class. The students, too, have been conditioned by many years of school experience to expect the teacher to plan their activities and to answer their questions. If he yields to these influences and remains the answerer of their questions, chairman and arbiter of all their class sessions, and chief maker of decisions for the group, he will achieve little success in helping students to grow through the experience of cooperative attack on a group problem.[2]

If, on the other hand, the teacher remains in the background and merely observes what goes on, he may not contribute much to the group's achievement and the problem-attack may even degenerate into a state of anarchy.

What Is the Role of the Core Teacher?

Let us first examine the role finally achieved by many experienced and skillful core teachers, since their status in their classes may suggest the direction in which many other teachers are moving. We can then examine the stages by which teachers have progressed toward the goal.

1. the teacher as participant

In the first place, the teacher is the oldest and presumably the most mature member of the group. The counsel of the ex-

---

[2] As we have pointed out in Chapter 5, no learning that is worthy of the name can proceed unless there is a genuine drive to learn. The teacher is therefore confronted with the task of discovering and developing these drives, which lie at the base of all group activity.

perienced core teacher is listened to with attention and real respect, not because he has insisted upon such listening but because the group has learned that he usually has some worthwhile ideas that will help them. Yet they know that they can ignore his counsel if they decide to do so, for that, too, is a part of their respect for him. He operates as a member of the group and makes suggestions on the same plane as other members. He earns respect and attention by the merit of his contributions. When a course of action is decided upon, he accepts responsibility like other members of the group. He no longer assigns tasks for students to perform. He helps them to develop their own assignments in contributing to the attack on a real problem. He even assumes some assignments himself.

The entire Unified Studies Class was gathered around a table near the windows, where their teacher was earnestly painting a small model airplane.

"I don't see how you ever got it together," sighed one of the girls.

Miss Morrison smiled, perhaps a little grimly, and looked at Henry, who was a member of the Model Plane Committee.

"It isn't really a very good plane," she said, "but I'm glad I made the effort."

"It's O.K., Miss Morrison," said Henry quickly. "After all, you gotta learn stuff like this by just doing it."

Sometimes the skillful core teacher deliberately withholds his own suggestions at certain stages in the planning process. He usually does this when it becomes evident to him that the old pattern of group dependence upon the teacher is again manifesting itself. He wants the group to have the experience of puzzling over a solution, and of learning through this experience how to solve the problem on its own. As the group grows in ability and confidence under skillful leadership, such tactics are less often necessary. The students will eventually reach the stage where they can even reject the teacher's suggestions and still respect him as a member of the group. Thus, the first role of the good core teacher is that of participation, not as dictator or observer, in the planning, executing, and evaluating of group projects.

The eleventh grade core class had finished its problem census, and was in almost complete agreement about the selection of the next unit—Imports and Exports of Latin America. The one dissenter was Miss Thomas, the teacher.

The chairman looked at her in a perplexed way.

"What do we do now?" she inquired helplessly.

"Well," said Miss Thomas, "what would you do if Sue or Jack were the one person who objected?"

"We'd try to talk them into it," replied the chairman.

"Or you could ask me to say once more why I object to this unit," Sue put in quickly.

"Maybe we could get a compromise worked out that way," a voice suggested.

Miss Thomas smiled.

"Well, I told you yesterday that this unit seems pretty big to me—and since none of us knows much about it, maybe we should explore it a bit first and then try to decide again whether it meets our seven criteria for selecting problems for study. I guess I'll have to admit that I wish I myself knew more about it, so I could tell just what we're getting into."

"That exploring idea sounds O.K. to me," said Jack thoughtfully. "Then we'll all know more about it, and that means Miss Thomas will, too."

The chairman went to the blackboard. "What suggestions have you for exploring this topic?" she asked the class.

2. the teacher as friend and counselor

The second role of the core teacher is that of friend and personal counselor to every student in the class. As a result of the characteristically longer period of class time and the reduced number of different students in a core teacher's daily load, he has time to study each individual. Instead of being responsible for five classes and perhaps a home-room group in addition, the core teacher may have one or two sections totalling sixty students at most. He can get rather well acquainted with each individual in such an assignment, particularly if he stays with the same students for more than one year. He is likely to have much useful information about each student in his own file, and he can make constant use of this information. He will visit most of his students' homes, and will meet their parents also on various occasions, for example through the room parents' club for each core section. He will have seen his students react to all kinds of social situations as a result of his participation with them in picnics, games, theater and bowling parties, and in other kinds of social affairs.

The core teacher's relationship to the class becomes increasingly guidance-oriented as he moves away from the traditional roles mentioned earlier in this chapter. He will not think of himself basically as one who imparts information, but as one who helps the learners to acquire their own information as a means of fulfilling their own purposes. He will stop making assignments and checking the mastery of subject matter and will start helping boys and girls to develop their own assignments and to evaluate their own progress. Thus, as has been indicated in the preceding chapter, the very essence of teaching in a core class involves the release of a teacher into the guidance role.

The core teacher is likely to have shed another traditional role —that of sole disciplinarian, which has stood in the way of effective classroom-centered guidance. The control of discipline and the drive for achievement have passed to the group, and thus released the teacher-pupil relationship from much unfortunate pressure. It is now possible to do friendly, nondirective counseling because the core teacher has achieved a nonpunitive relationship with the group.

The effective core teacher really likes to be with boys and girls and is welcomed by them as a sincere friend and counselor, to whom they readily bring personal problems and whose help they seek first, among all the adults they know.

Nine boys and girls from three different schools were discussing the advantages of the longer period used for their core classes.

Sally had just entered our school by transfer this year.

"I came from a big school, where I didn't know anyone," she explained. "I feel as though I had really gotten acquainted with Miss S———."

"She's a good Joe," chimed in her classmate, Herbert. "She acts like one of the gang. You'll catch yourself telling her stuff you'd never dream of telling to a *teacher*."

The core teacher would thus perform the basic guidance function in the secondary school, through his individual counseling contacts with his core students, through his study of group relationships in the core class, and through the kinds of problems that the core class undertakes to study. Units like Boy and Girl Relationships, You and Your New School, Propaganda and Public Opinion, Preparing for a Home and Family, Choosing a Vocation, and Building a Philosophy of Life are frequently pursued by core classes in senior high schools. It is difficult to imagine a more promising milieu for the provision of sound guidance than a core class engaged in study of such real problems as these.

3. *expediter*

The master teacher in a core class is more than a group member and counselor. He is also an expediter of the group plans and projects. He knows what resources are available, and where they may be found. He can help students to use the library, the periodical index, the city directory. He is acquainted with the numerous sources of free material on various topics, and has accumulated much of it over the years. He can help them make necessary contacts with resource persons in the community and state. He provides liaison with the school administration and can smooth the way for the class to achieve its purposes by interpreting the program to other teachers and to the principal.

A group of teachers in the cafeteria became involved in a favorite topic.

"I'll be up late tonight correcting themes," said the English teacher. "I'm glad I don't assign them every day."

"My term papers in history have got to be returned tomorrow," chimed in another.

"You two should complain," said a mathematics teacher. "I have five sets of math papers to correct every night." He continued with a wink. "Now if we were only core teachers like Clara Johnson. I understand they don't assign anything and don't have any homework to do."

Miss Johnson chuckled without resentment, but also without much mirth. "You should just follow me around for one week," she said. "Monday night my core kids and I went bowling, and all but four of them were there. Tuesday after school I had three parent conferences, and I spent that evening telephoning the planning committee members to change the place of our weekly luncheon to the Kewpie Hamburger because they're washing walls at my house. Wednesday night I had a talk with the principal about a trip we're taking to the Art Institute, and Thursday evening I was where you were—at P. T. A. As for papers, I spent the week-end curled up with group reports. Anyone want to swap classes with me?"

It should be noted at this point that helping a class to locate resources is vastly different from supplying ready answers oneself, or from pointing out answers in a textbook. The core teacher does not pretend to know all about the various fields his class may choose to explore. To do so would be humanly impossible. The teacher learns early in the process to say "I don't know—let's find out." There is no loss of prestige involved in such a statement, when the enterprise is a cooperative one and the teacher is not posing as an expert in a subject field. Instead of being a subject matter expert, the good core teacher is an expert in adolescent development, in guidance, and in group problem-solving. He may not know all the answers, but he knows how to help students find answers. Of course, if he *can* supply a simple answer to an occasional question, he does so. To evade a sincere question from a friendly group of which one is a member would be hypocritical and destructive of good human relations.

4. technician

The teacher serves another important function. He is a technician in the group process that the class is struggling to master. He understands the principles of group planning and group activity. He has had the experience of failure and success himself as member of adult groups. He is interested in this vital business of learning to plan and work together, and he has learned many of the necessary techniques by reading and by experience. Group and individual evaluation, too, is a field of which he has achieved reasonable command.

The planning committee for Core 2 was gathered around Mr. R————'s desk, discussing plans for the next week. Betty was insisting that not enough students had taken part in the discussion of group reports which had occurred the preceding period.

"Why don't they say something?" she exclaimed. "Why can't we get any discussion out of them after a perfectly good bunch of reports?"

"Well," said Elise, "I don't want to insult anybody in the other four groups, but I'll admit that I wasn't much interested in any of them except our own."

Tom broke in: "Do you suppose we're pulling farther apart all the time? At the start when we set up those topics they sounded interesting enough."

"What we need," said John thoughtfully, "is somebody to keep us on the track. Why don't you outline all of the topics for the groups, Mr. R———?"

"Oh no!" Betty interrupted, "excuse me, Mr. R———, but it seems to me we ought by now to be able to make our own outline and stick to it. What do you think?"

Mr. R——— spoke slowly. "I feel sure you are right about that, Betty. Yet we were one group in our major goals at the beginning, as Tom said. How would it be to throw this question to the whole class for discussion on Monday morning?"

"That's O.K.," said Bill, "but I think you should help our groups, to see how their separate problems fit into the class plan that we started with. Could you join us on Monday?"

The skillful core teacher is a student of adolescent psychology. He understands what makes boys and girls behave as they do. He has learned much about child growth and development through reading, observation, and experience. *He understands because he cares.* He knows that Tom is worried about his small stature and that he wonders whether he will ever grow up tall. He understands Sarah's shyness because he has met her domineering mother and heard her speak (in Sarah's presence) about her two older children, who "were not shy like Sarah." He knows why the boys in the class are louder and more given to exhibitionism when certain girls are present. He is aware of the cliques that form and reform in the class, the leaders who are sought after by all, the pairs who cover up their loneliness by preferring each other's sole company, the isolates who are rejected by all. He knows much about the boys and girls in his class: much that stands revealed in their natural, unrestrained conversation and behavior in an informal learning situation; much that comes out through their choices of companions, of activities, and of reading. He has been with them at parties outside school, and at the movies. He knows boys and girls, and he is a skillful technician in helping them develop group unity and aid each other's development through their work and play together.

We have undoubtedly been idealizing the core teacher's role as a means of discovering the goal toward which we are working. The skillful teacher of a core class, we have said, is (1) a participating member of the class group, (2) a friendly counselor, (3) an expediter of the group's plans, and (4) a technician in the group process.

5. *disciplinarian*

The teacher has at least one more role, which is seldom understood and often abused. Idealistic observers sometimes tend to assume that all control of behavior, all decisions regarding the individual's role in the group, can be assumed by the students. Indeed, that is the happy situation we seek to achieve. In the process of its achievement, however, situations will arise that will thrust the teacher back into the role of enforcer of group decisions, or even of decider of issues in a few cases. For example, there is the fairly familiar case of the rebellious individualist who rejects the group's plans and insists on working alone. Such a student may feel insecure in a cooperative classroom climate because of a long personal history of conflicts. The skillful teacher will seek, in his role of counselor and friend, to help the student to overcome his insecurity and to achieve the plane of acceptance in the group. In his other role of expediter of the group's plans, he may have to make and enforce some decisions for the individual. There are some persons who are too disturbed and too maladjusted to be helped immediately by their peers.

Such cases will be relatively rare as teachers and students gain increased skill in cooperative planning. When difficulties do develop, the good teacher deals patiently and understandingly with the individual. His ultimate goal is always the development of courage and responsibility in the student; self-control will follow. The teacher knows how easy it is for a person to surrender to others all responsibility for his own behavior. He therefore seeks constantly to develop that sense of responsibility in the student, even though he may be compelled to start by making some decisions for him. Even as he begins in such a fashion, however, he keeps constantly before him the twin goals of self-control and group responsibility. There is no other sound purpose that can lead a group in the direction of successful discipline. There is no discipline that has any validity in a democratic culture except self- and group-discipline.

How can a group develop this responsibility for self- and group-control? Through no other means than through satisfying experiences, gradually extended and intensified as the group matures. Authoritarian control does not provide these experiences; instead it progressively encourages the group to surrender to the teacher the sole responsibility for controlling their behavior. When the external controls are removed, aggressive behavior is quite likely to boil up and it becomes painfully evident that the group has learned nothing about control. Laissez faire situations are equally unsatisfactory, since they provide no experiences in control at all.

On the other hand, the democratic approach to discipline implies a steady, if gradual progress toward group control through definite structuring in that direction by the core teacher. Since he knows that group discipline can be learned through satisfying experiences, he undertakes to provide situations in which such satisfactions can be had. Since he knows, further, that analysis of these successes will help set the stage for their repetition and extension, he encourages continual evaluation of the group's successes and failures at self-control. There will be such failures, in every class. Some individuals will find it hard to adjust to a cooperative enterprise. Occasionally, hostility patterns will be temporarily carried into the classroom from outside. Small groups will sometimes exhibit a puzzling antagonism toward some individual, or toward other groups. In the junior high school years, sex antagonisms will often be openly expressed. Even a good core class will, on a particular day, seem to disintegrate for no apparent reason. Successful core teachers are aware of such problems and are ready to cope with them in such a way as to build morale, not destroy it still further. If they decide that they must "take over" the class for a while, they do so with the resolution to re-establish group self-control as early as possible. Sometimes a bit of humor will help. At other times a change in class routines may be indicated. There are situations where seats and group membership must be altered. There may even come a day when one or more youngsters must be removed from the class for a while, just to make it possible for the class to pull itself together. Throughout such efforts to restore order and morale, the good core teacher never loses his faith in youth's basic goodness, or in the process of growth toward group self-control. Whatever he may have to do temporarily as a "classroom manager," he never loses sight of his main goal of helping boys and girls to work together on their common goals.

The specter of anarchy frightens the inexperienced teacher. He visualizes a situation where the class is out of control, and he may exert more authoritarian pressure than he would if he felt secure and confident of the group's capacity and goodwill.

Neither students nor teachers want anarchy or disorder in a class. Boys and girls are as eager as adults for the security that results from order and accomplishment. When a condition of real anarchy develops, it is usually the result of a misunderstanding by the teacher of his role in the group. He may have resolved to cease being an autocrat and failed to visualize any alternative role except that of spectator. As one crisis succeeds another without any serious attempt at a solution by the group, the morale of the class will steadily degenerate because of the abdication of the teacher.

It is often asserted that such conditions result from a teacher's trying to move too rapidly. It is more often the case that he has moved in the wrong direction, for anarchy is as much the antithe sis of democracy as is autocracy. The three involve separate and distinct techniques. The teacher, we repeat, need not become a mere observer when he ceases to be a dictator. He should become an active and respected participant in group planning, a friendly counselor, a marshaller of resources, and a technician in the group process. Such a teacher need not fear that a condition of anarchy will develop for any length of time. If such a condition appears, it immediately becomes the chief challenge to the group process, the mistake through which the class can learn. As such, even disorder may serve a valuable function.

The experienced core teacher can bring about an astonishing change in group discipline in a relatively short time. Indeed, the widespread use of student leadership throughout a school has often been known to raise school morale and improve general discipline outside the classrooms. The goal of group and self-control is not, therefore, a remote ideal to be constantly sought but rarely attained. On the contrary, such classroom discipline is quite common in schools where intelligent efforts are made to attain it. The constant goal of the core teacher is to help students to become increasingly responsible for their own learning—and for their own control, which will naturally be more easily achieved when the learner's own purposes are being engaged. The students must really "buy" the classroom activity and feel that it is theirs before they will organize for self-control.

The professor who was visiting the core class was engaged in conversation with the core teacher in the open doorway of the classroom. The bell rang, but the interested conversers continued.

Presently the visitor felt a light touch on his arm. It was the core class chairman, one hand on the open door.

"You'll excuse me," the boy said, politely but firmly, "but I'd better close this door so we can get on with our work."

stages of progress

Other kinds of transitional stages appear in a core teacher's progress toward the ideal. The class may be quite inexperienced in group planning and execution. While they are acquiring those important skills, the teacher may have to assume the central leadership role. It is obviously impossible to move faster than the group can move. Yet it is hazardous to begin by setting authoritarian patterns, for such patterns have a tendency to persist. More mistakes are probably made through lack of faith, through assuming that boys and girls cannot plan and work together, than through beginning on the assumption that ability and goodwill are potential in every group. Even at the start, a good core teacher invites the class to assume at least some responsibilities in planning. If they cannot decide the problems that they will study together, they can at least help to decide how they will organize for such study, where they will obtain needed help, and how they will report their findings. Classes that cannot be trusted to make such rudimentary decisions as these are rare. Through the opportunity of group planning, with the chance to learn alike from their mistakes and their successes, groups will develop more rapidly than is commonly assumed.

Much has been said in the past about the teacher's role in motivating instruction. It is usually assumed that certain subject matter must be set out to be mastered, and that the skillful teacher will arouse the student's interest in the subject matter to such a point that he will attack and perhaps master it. If such salesmanship fails, we fall back on the familiar pattern of extrinsic rewards and punishment, of which marks and failure are the common symbols.

It should be noted that this task of motivating students, as conventionally understood, has no significance for the successful core teacher.[3] There are no sacred or indispensable items to be inserted into the course of study for a core class. By definition, the core class is a class wherein a cooperative attack is made upon real problems, arrived at by teacher-pupil planning. Motivation for this attack resides in the nature and significance of the problems undertaken and in the process itself. If a problem or area for study has to be sold to students, it cannot have been a

---

[3] The reader may wish at this point to review the section on motivation in Chapter 5, pp. 119-125.

real problem in the first place. Thus the core teacher becomes a partner with her students in a creative enterprise.

The following analysis by Gertrude Noar emphasizes the challenging and difficult role that the core teacher assumes during the problem-selection phase of group work.[4]

There is a definite part to be played by the teacher during these discussions. It is true that she must refrain from directing the choice, and certainly from imposing her will upon the children. If she does so, the children become cynical as the result of frustration. As their doubt of the teacher's sincerity increases, they are apt to become aggressive and hostile. Their active interest and participation in discussion will sink to a low level.

On the other hand, it is equally true that the teacher must never lose sight of her responsibility for postponing choice until all the facts are before the class. She also has the right to lead and to guide thought and discussion. To her falls the task of leading the class to see the triviality of one problem as contrasted with the serious nature of another. She must be sure that the fact that the class has already had some experience in one suggested area, but that the other offers virgin soil, is not overlooked.

At times pupils may ask the teacher directly for her opinion or even for her preference. A direct answer from her may be possible if her rapport with the group is almost perfect, but it exposes her to the necessity of accepting a decision contrary to her stated choice, if strong pupil leaders are not entirely on her side. Should such a situation arise, the teacher's stature with her group will increase if she can accept defeat without rancor or resentment.

It often happens that after a center of interest has been selected and the unit of work has been planned, a small group of children intensely interested in an alternative problem remains dissatisfied and rebellious. Under such circumstances the class can discuss the problem, and with guidance, will usually plan to have these children go ahead with their topic provided they keep the class informed, join with the class in such activities as trips, and listen creatively to all committee reports. At other times the antagonism will disappear if the teacher makes a special effort to give the dissenters interesting things to do which will gain prestige for them.

Occasionally it is advisable to give the entire class the opportunity to

---

[4] Gertrude Noar, *Freedom To Live and Learn.* Philadelphia: Franklin Publishing Company, 1948, pp. 32-33.

explore briefly this special interest. This will suffice in cases where the problem is beyond the ability of the group or where usable materials are not available and the teacher must become the source of information.

The development of a single question of enough significance and of sufficiently general concern, upon which a whole group is eager to work, is a difficult but exciting experience.

conclusion

In this chapter we have examined the several roles of a teacher in a core class. We have emphasized the fact that a teacher need not, in rejecting authoritarian roles, move in the direction of becoming a passive observer while the class lapses into anarchy. He may choose instead the difficult but exciting roles of *participant, friend* and *counselor, expediter* of plans, and *technician* in the process of democratic planning, execution, evaluation, and group control. He can and should become a skillful group leader who helps young people by insuring "that group experience meets the needs of the individual members and at the same time keeps the whole group moving toward its goal." [5]

In short, the core teacher is dedicated to the role of sound leadership in the most indispensable processes of democracy. To the degree that he performs that role with insight, patience, and skill, his students will become progressively more competent and courageous in meeting and solving the problems of life.

As the teacher participates in group planning with his students, and helps to expedite their plans, the need for materials and resources for such planning becomes evident. The chapter which follows will include discussion of such resources for classroom learning, and of the core teacher's role in planning for their use.

SELECTED REFERENCES

Alberty, Harold, *Reorganizing the High School Curriculum,* Revised. New York: The Macmillan Co., 1953, Chapter X.

Association for Supervision and Curriculum Development, *Creating a*

[5] Rudolph M. Wittenberg, *So You Want To Help People*. New York: Association Press, 1947, p. xiii.

Good Environment for Learning, 1954 Yearbook. Washington, D. C.: The National Education Association, 1954, Chapter VII.

————, *Group Planning in Education,* 1945 Yearbook. Washington, D. C.: The National Education Association, 1945.

Cantor, Nathaniel, *Dynamics of Learning.* Buffalo, New York: Foster and Stewart Company, 1946, Chapters V and XI.

Giles, H. H., S. P. McCutchen, and A. H. Zechiel, *Exploring the Curriculum.* New York: Harper and Brothers, 1942, Chapter IV.

Kelley, Earl C., *Education for What Is Real.* New York: Harper and Brothers, 1947, Chapter VII.

————, and Marie I. Rasey, *Education and the Nature of Man.* New York: Harper and Brothers, 1952, Chapter 13.

Lane, Howard, and Mary Beauchamp, *Human Relations in Teaching.* Englewood Cliffs, N. J.: Prentice-Hall, Inc., 1955, Chapter 15.

MacConnell, Charles M., Ernest O. Melb, C. O. Arndt, and Leslee Bishop, *New Schools for a New Culture,* Revised. New York: Harper and Brothers, 1953, Chapter VI.

Noar, Gertrude, *Freedom To Live and Learn.* Philadelphia: Franklin Publishing Co., 1948, Chapter VI.

Miel, Alice, and associates, *Cooperative Procedures in Learning.* New York: Bureau of Publications, Teachers College, Columbia University, 1952, Chapter XVIII.

Rasey, Marie I., and J. W. Menge, *What We Learn from Children.* New York: Harper and Brothers, 1956, Chapter VI.

Sheviakov, George, and Fritz Redl, *Discipline for Today's Children and Youth.* Washington, D. C.: The National Education Association, 1944.

Wiles, Kimball, *Teaching for Better Schools.* Englewood Cliffs, N. J.: Prentice-Hall, Inc., 1952, Chapter II.

Wittenberg, Rudolph M., *So You Want To Help People.* New York: Association Press, 1947, Chapters I, II, and III.

Chapter 10

Using Resources in Core Classes

The core curriculum makes it possible, indeed necessary, for the teacher to disregard restrictions of prescribed subject matter. It provides freedom and time for a group of students and a teacher to plan the work of the class together. This work usually consists of an attack upon real social, civic, and economic problems that the group recognizes as important. The attack upon these problems presupposes an acceptance of the problems by the students and the teacher.

WHY PREPLANNING?

This kind of group problem attack constitutes a real learning situation. Actually, as we have pointed out in Chapter 5, no true learning can go on until the learner has perceived a purpose for it.[1] To the extent that the core curriculum makes it possible for

---

[1] This point of view, generally accepted in educational psychology, is well set forth in Earl C. Kelley, *Education for What Is Real*. New York: Harper and Brothers, 1947, p. 68.

teachers to discover the true purposes of the students, and to build a learning situation geared to those purposes, it is on a sound psychological basis. It seems clear that students must help to plan the curriculum of the core if it is to take account of their purposes. Suggestions for this kind of teaching have been set forth in Chapters 6 and 7.[2]

Many teachers have accepted the concept of teacher-pupil planning as an ideal. Even experienced teachers, however, raise certain questions about the application of the concept. They inquire how they can make sure that boys and girls will develop a real purpose for all the areas of desirable knowledge or skill, and how they can be sure that important parts of a good curriculum will not be omitted. How can the teacher be sure that the students' interests will develop at the proper time to build a logical sequence of problems for study?

Questions such as these must be considered by schools launching a core curriculum. Core teachers must at least have faith that the answers to such questions can be developed by experience with a group of boys and girls.

is it a real learning sequence?

The logical sequence of learning experiences for which some people yearn is often an artificial one. If the pattern of learning makes sense only in terms of topics and subject areas neatly complementing preceding topics on paper, there is no certainty that any learning will take place. If learning fails to occur, the "scope and sequence" argument loses its weight. There is no point to an elaborate plan for learning experiences that do not produce learning. It is quite possible for teachers to project plans so detailed in their logical pattern as to ignore or circumvent the learner's purposes, upon which true learning must be built.

In the last analysis, the curriculum of general education must have for its source the learner himself—his interests, his drives, and his purposes. These purposes include those of the culture

---

[2] See also H. H. Giles, *Teacher-Pupil Planning*. New York: Harper and Brothers, 1941.

in which we live, for no individual, adult or youth, lives in a vacuum. It is therefore reasonable and possible for us to extract all of the necessary elements of the core curriculum from an average class group of young people.

preplanning has its place

The above principle is a sound one. It is supported by the known laws of learning and by the succesful experience of hundreds of core teachers. It does not follow, however, that there is no place for preplanning by teachers in the core curriculum. In fact, core teachers often do more planning than do subject-matter teachers, but of a different kind. They seek, through their own planning, to become more effective participators in group planning, better friends and counselors, more efficient expediters of group plans, and more skillful technicians in group process.

How Can One Preplan?

studying the community

The good core teacher has done a considerable amount of planning before he first meets his class, in terms of the community setting in which the children live. He knows that problems for study will emerge from that setting, and that he must understand it. He has explored the history of the community and its region. He knows its chief agricultural and industrial products, its land forms and land uses, the businesses that it supports, and its cultural resources. He knows something about the people of the community—their ethnic backgrounds, their level of education, the kinds of homes they live in, and the churches and lodges they attend. He has developed understanding of the potential growth and probable future trends of the community as a clue to the problems that will accompany such development. Finally, he has acquired some insights into the economic and social problems that confront the community today and with which young citizens should be concerned.

One entire high school faculty spent four days in a preschool conference exploring the nature of the community, its trends, its resources, and its needs. The first session began with a presentation by a local citizen of the history of the town and of the county. He had made a lifetime hobby of local history and presented many interesting facts about the community's background. During the discussion that followed his address, many ideas were presented as to how data like these could be used in various classes.

A committee of teachers then reported upon a study, made during the previous semester, of community resources that could be used in high school classes. Over one hundred places and persons were included in this annotated list. It was agreed that the report should be embodied in a mimeographed manual titled *Community Resources for Instruction.* The manual was later distributed to all teachers. The committee decided to continue its work during the present school year, in consequence of various new challenges that emerged from the discussion.

The core teachers held two meetings during the preschool conference to launch a unit on community resources. They felt sure that unit materials on this topic would be useful in core classes because of the perennial concern of core students with community problems.

As a result of the core teachers' work on the resource unit, a special reserve shelf of community materials was set up in the high school library. Many new titles suggested during the conference were ordered for this collection. Also added were two scrapbooks made by student committees in core classes the previous year. One was called *The People of Our Town.* The other was on the subject of vocational opportunities in the local community.

The new core teacher who is fortunate enough to attend such a preschool conference can begin his year with a considerable degree of orientation to his new school community. He will confront his new core class with considerable knowledge of community backgrounds.

studying the children

The new core teacher will know not only the community, but also this new group of youngsters with whom he will live for a year or more. Files from the previous year will be handed on to him, often with interpretation from the previous teacher. He will know which pupils are exceptional readers who will require constant challenge, and which are so retarded that they will need special help in the selection of suitable reading materials. He will have read anecdotal information revealing their interests, their ambitions, and often their fears. He will have analyzed data on their health, their home background, and their relationships with their classmates and adults. He will have looked over samples of their individual work and reports of their group work of the past year.

The core teacher who takes his guidance function seriously will seek information about other important aspects of the child's development. The answers to such questions as the following make a significant contribution to the preplanning phase of instruction.

Has he had a chance to learn what the school takes for granted—especially language, manners, ways of playing with others, obeying rules, concepts like "cooperation"? If not, what has he learned in these and related areas?

What particular expectations and pressures has he had to meet thus far, particularly in his family and play group? To what special pressures has membership in a minority group subjected him?

What values has he taken on? What does he consider "success"?

What kind of a self does he value? What does he expect of others?

What concepts has he acquired about everyday realities—what a family is, or what a community is?

What ways of expressing feelings has he developed? How does he feel about the things which happen to him?

How has he learned to relate himself to others? What does he expect in his relations with others? [3]

---

[3] Elizabeth Hall Brady, "Children Bring Their Families to School," *Fostering Mental Health In Our Schools,* 1950 Yearbook, Association for Supervision and Curriculum Development. Washington, D. C.: The National Education Association, 1950, pp. 27-28.

Data on these questions and others like them can be available to the new teacher in the form of anecdotal observation records, autobiographies, results of written work cast in the various versions of "wishing-well" questions,[4] sociograms showing group leadership,[5] acceptance and rejection patterns, reports by teachers of home visits, and many other kinds of written information. Amplification and interpretation of data like these should be achieved through case conferences with the teachers who had the youngsters the preceding year.

To provide time and opportunity for this pre-planning based on the children's stage of development, many schools have arranged pre-opening conferences in which clinical sessions are conducted between present and past core teachers. In some schools the teachers exchange assignments for one or more days during the preceding semester in order to give both children and teachers the chance to get acquainted before school opens. Pupils are also sometimes brought into the next grade and sectioned with their new core teacher for a day of orientation during the previous semester.

WHAT RESOURCES EXIST IN THE SCHOOL?

the room library

Experienced core teachers tend to develop classroom libraries. Such room libraries become increasingly adequate as a result of efforts made over a period of years. They include some materials that remain permanently in the classroom, as well as other materials borrowed from various sources for periods of one day to one semester.

The room library might include one or two daily newspapers, current periodicals, a pamphlet file on personal, social, economic, and political problems, and a collection of books selected for

---

[4] See, for example, *The Wishing Well*, Bureau of Educational Research, Ohio State University. Columbus: Ohio State University Press, 1945.

[5] An excellent brief treatment of the sociometric test and the sociogram is included in A.S.C.D., *Fostering Mental Health In Our Schools*, pp. 203-225.

their relevance to the typical problems that students face and recognize. Additional books and bulletins can, of course, be secured as the specific problems emerge. The responsibility for securing such supplementary materials is an important one for students to assume.

The classroom library is often built up by a rental fee that students pay in lieu of textbook costs. Some core classrooms have several hundred books, collected over the years in this manner.

The books in core rooms are likely to be of three general types: (1) general reference or textbook collections, retained in the room because of their constant use for study of recurrent problems or skills; (2) special reference books on a particular problem, borrowed for the period of study of that problem area; and (3) fiction and nonfiction books, chosen from a variety of interest fields and written for various levels of reading skill—this last collection is used by core students during free-reading periods.

Posters, pictures, models, films, records, transcriptions, and other visual and auditory learning aids are used intensively in a core class. These materials, too, are usually obtained by students in the process of seeking information or preparing to report to the class on a specific problem.

the school library

Most school librarians are eager to make materials available to the core teacher, and to acquire the new books and periodicals that will be most useful in the classroom. The good core teacher is well acquainted with the resources that are available in the school library, and submits regular requests for classroom loans and for new purchases. For facilitating such requests, some schools use a small card on which the core teacher can record her requests, in order to give the school librarian advance notice. The card contains space for the following data: (1) date, (2) name of core teacher, (3) titles requested for loan, or (4) titles requested for purchase, and (5) nature of unit or activity for which materials are desired. The purpose of the last item is to enable the school librarian to suggest other appropriate items that may be of assistance.

Core students will keep the school librarian busy in their continuous search for materials. The librarians in many schools report that the students from core classes are among their most persistent and most regular clients.

text materials

The textbook is rarely used as an instructional guide by the experienced core teacher. Many teachers retain it as a temporary or transitional measure, but even this limited kind of use raises many problems. If students buy the textbook, it is inevitable for them to wonder why it is not used more often. If it is used often, it tends to establish a theme or framework for the course, thus placing limits on the process of teacher-pupil planning.

One compromise measure has been used by some core teachers. Instead of a single basic text, a dozen copies of each of several texts or anthologies are purchased by a classroom-materials fee. This fee is often arrived at by computing the net annual cost of using all of the textbooks usually purchased for the classes replaced by the core course. This net annual cost figure is the difference between the new purchase price and the average resale price after one year's use. The class materials fee is the total of the net annual cost figures for all texts used. With this fee it becomes possible to buy many different books, as well as subscriptions to a newspaper, to magazines, and to various loan-services for instructional materials.

How Can Pupils Discover Resources?

The following partial account of a unit taught recently in a junior high school core class illustrates the pupils' resourcefulness in searching for materials.

The children decided that the problem of where to get the information had to be explored before anything else was done. They mentioned first the necessity for reading—books, newspapers, magazines, and pamphlets. These were to be consulted in the classroom, school library, public library, at home, and in the Sunday schools. The following conversation occurred: Teacher—"Does everyone have to learn all these things?" John—"That would take a very long time." Mary—"If each one decides what topic he likes best we would be formed into committees." Bill—"Then each committee could tell the rest of the class what they found out."

The teacher had brought into the class as much material as she could gather on the various phases of the subject. She indicated to the children what there was and permitted them to spend the remainder of the period browsing. She advised that each child write down the names of publications which seemed especially devoted to the phase of the topic to be explored by the committee of which he was a part. They were soon busily at work and many times one child would say to another: "This won't help me, but it is good for the part you have to look up."

The teacher opened the planning with the question: "Are printed materials the only things from which you can learn and is reading all you want to do?" Animated discussion of how we learn and where, followed. This was finally summarized by listing the activities to be planned.

1. Pay visit to places such as churches of at least three kinds—Catholic, Protestant, Jewish.
2. Ask parents to come to class to talk about such topics as, "My Life in Italy and the United States."
3. Hear a radio program or playback record.
4. See a movie either in school or outside.
5. Bring to school family treasures brought from "the old country."
6. Get a "big" speaker to tell us how things are related to democracy.
7. Bring pictures for bulletin boards.[6]

A ninth grade core class recently reported, in the language of a student recorder, the methods and materials used in their topic study:

Before the members of our class selected the topics a list of suggestions was put on the board to help us. This list was made up of suggestions made by the boys and girls and teachers. From this list the area of work was selected which was of most interest. The members of the class then divided into groups, with each group selecting a thing on which they were most anxious to work collecting their material.

---

[6] Gertrude Noar, *Freedom To Live and Learn*. Philadelphia: Franklin Publishing Company, 1949, pp. 117-118.

At last we were on our own and we had to struggle for ourselves. Material must be collected from every possible source by ourselves. No one was there to place the material in our hands. We had no textbook. It was our responsibility.

We now have learned extremely well how to get material from the school library and the public libraries. Some of the students went down to the main public library to search even deeper into the mystery of our topics.

A lot of the pupils sent away for information on their topics. The teacher often brings in any books, material, or clippings she happens to find that will help us.

Our topics, we discovered, were both interesting and educational with fascinating titles such as "Youth Movements," "Nazism," "Democracy," "The Orient," and many more.

Core has taught us to work and think for ourselves successfully. It has enabled us to work in a truly democratic way. With the help of our teacher and our fellow students, we succeeded in gathering satisfactory information about our problem.[7]

It is the responsibility of schools to provide adequate instructional materials. Even in those schools where students contribute a materials fee, an annual budget for supplementary materials will pay rich dividends. In addition to the pupils' contribution and that of the school, the alert core teacher will enrich the classroom resources by writing for free materials to the many private and public agencies that publish them.

What Are Some Out-of-School Resources?

Resources exist, however, that go far beyond the printed word or the visual aid. When a group of students plan, with their core teacher, an attack upon real personal or community problems, the classroom walls melt away and the whole community becomes their laboratory.

Every town has many citizens who can aid the students in

---

[7] *This Way To Democracy*, unpublished manuscript, report of a year's work in a core class. Edwin Denby High School, Detroit, 1943.

their study of problems: the banker, who comes into a core class to explain the procedures used in mortgaging a home, and follows it by inviting the class to visit the bank and study its operations first hand; the newspaper publisher, who makes an annual hunting trip to the Hudson Bay area and has some beautiful color films that students want to see as they study the natural resources of North America; the city manager, who willingly accepts an invitation to come and discuss with the class their plans for improved housing and traffic control in the community; the state conservation officer, who explains the problem resulting from the lowering water table; the rabbi, who discusses with the class the conventions and ritual of the Jewish faith.

All of these are actual examples of ways in which core classes have used citizens of their community in helping them attack a problem. Many other similar examples could be quoted. Such citizens are usually glad to be of help to a class and will respond willingly to such a request. They are especially glad to work with a group of students who have already studied the questions. A careful plan for the use of such human resources should be developed in advance by the group. Such a plan might include the method of presentation, the questions to be presented, and a plan for evaluating the effectiveness of the program.

When several sections of core classes in one school are employing community resource persons in this manner, it is wise to develop a coordinated plan. In some schools a handbook of community resource persons has been developed by the core teachers and brought up to date from year to year. In one school this handbook was a loose-leaf notebook containing over one hundred typed pages, listing such persons and places in the community and including a paragraph describing their possible contributions to the instructional program.

When one or more core classes decide to use such a person from outside the school, some teacher or administrator is asked to record the request, the date, and the purpose. It is then announced in the faculty bulletin in order to permit maximum use of the visitor. The students, however, are encouraged to make the contact themselves as an educative experience.

In making visits to places in the community, some additional planning and coordination may be needed by an administrator or teacher designated for this purpose. This is especially true if bus transportation is required, or when a given place is visited frequently.

Core classes are able to go directly to some community resources because of their longer block of available time. One group of core students, for example, became interested in surveying their community in connection with their study of housing. They spent nearly a month conducting the housing survey and building a large scale model which was used in reporting their findings.[8] Another core class landscaped and developed a creek channel near the school in order to have available a permanent instructional resource. Students in still other core classes have visited court-houses, slum sections, museums, art galleries, radio stations, erosion gulleys, farms, factories, and a host of other places in search of information. The groups have usually developed a plan for such visits, including the types of information sought as well as the details of organization for the trip itself.

In some cases core classes have saved the necessary funds for much longer trips in order to study economic or social conditions that are not available near home.[9] Such excursions are the more valuable because they have developed as a phase of the students' search for real knowledge about a real problem. It is probably unnecessary to add that the group must plan longer excursions of this kind with great care.[10]

---

[8] For many additional illustrations of community service activities performed by students, see Paul Hanna, *Youth Serves The Community*. New York: Appleton-Century-Crofts, Inc., 1936. A bibliography on youth services may be found in M. R. Mitchell, "Youth Has A Part To Play," *Progressive Education,* 19:87-109, February 1942.

[9] See, for example, Charles M. MacConnell, Ernest O. Melby, and C. O. Arndt, *New Schools For A New Culture.* New York: Harper and Brothers, 1943, p. 43.

[10] Excellent suggestions on the development of school excursion programs are contained in the Ninth Yearbook of the National Council for the Social Studies, *Utilization of Community Resources In the Social Studies.* Washington, D. C.: The National Council For The Social Studies, 1938, pp. 73-83.

What Are the Class Resources?

We have been discussing such instructional resources as books, films, and persons and places in the community, but perhaps the most valuable resources in the kind of learning that goes on in a core class are the persons in the class—both students and teacher. In no other kind of learning is the focus so directly upon people and their contributions. In conventionally taught classes there is little opportunity for children to learn from each other. In fact, a handicap is often placed upon such learning, in the form of penalties for cooperation. Students who help each other are considered to be hindering, not aiding, the morale of the group. Communication is carried on from each student to the teacher, not to his fellows in the group.

In the core class, however, there is maximum emphasis upon the development of the individual through his contribution to the group's progress in attacking a problem. When this process uncovers a unique ability, skill, interest, or command of information in some area, these contributions are swiftly geared to the group's purposes. The assumption inherent in the core curriculum is that each individual has a unique and valuable contribution to make to the group. It is the task of skillful teaching to discover and facilitate these contributions. The most valuable single resource of the group is truly the persons in it.

How Can the Resource Unit Be Used?

It has been noted that the role of the core teacher in pre-planning is to discover resources and techniques to help pupils learn through a group attack upon real problems. In the effort to achieve this end, core teachers are turning to the development of resource units.

The resource unit is a device that can give teachers the security they seek without prescribing subject matter and thus depriving the learning process of its real essence—the purpose of the learner.

The resource unit has been defined by Professor Harold Alberty as "a systematic and comprehensive survey, analysis, and organization of the possible resources (e.g., problems, issues, activities, bibliographies, etc.) which a teacher might utilize in planning, developing, and evaluating a learning unit."[11] Biddick suggests a somewhat different interpretation in defining a resource unit as "a record of exploration made by a teacher or a group of teachers of the needs of pupils within some broad area of living, of ways in which it is believed these needs might be appropriately met, and of ways for determining whether or not they have been met." [12]

The resource unit may be employed to provide a unified approach to some particular problem, such as atomic energy.[13] A school faculty may further extend its development of resource units until they constitute an over-all curriculum plan for general education.

It is at once clear from the definitions given that the resource unit is much more comprehensive than a teaching, or learning, unit.

A teaching unit is developed by one teacher and one section of students around a specific subtopic selected for study. A resource unit is developed by a group of teachers, preferably representing several subject areas, around a broad problem area. For example, a resource unit might be developed in the problem area, *Understanding and Respecting Others*. Included in such a resource unit would be materials for a series of teaching units in human relations. One such teaching unit might be *The Negro in Modern American Life*. Another might be *The Nature and Cause of Prejudice*. Still another might be *The Spanish-Speaking Americans*. Many other teaching units might be drawn from this

---

[11] For this definition, and for many of the suggestions used subsequently regarding the resource unit, the authors are indebted to Dr. Harold Alberty, of Ohio State University. See his *Reorganizing the High School Curriculum*. New York: The Macmillan Company, 1947, Chapter IX.

[12] Mildred Biddick, *The Preparation and Use of Source Units*. New York: The Progressive Education Association, 1939, p. 3.

[13] See for example Harold Hand, *Living In The Atomic Age*. Urbana: University of Illinois Press, 1946.

one resource unit. The resource unit is intended to help a group of teachers to plan the ways in which they and their pupils may enrich their study of a given problem area.[14] It leaves to the teacher and the pupils much of the responsibility for specific planning of a given core class.[15]

Let us suppose that the students in a core class have proposed as a problem for study the role of the Negro in modern American life. If earlier classes have studied the same problem, it may be that a resource unit on interracial relations has already been developed by the core teachers, and can be used as a basis for further planning of a teaching unit. If not, a beginning might be made at once by several teachers of a given grade level in which the problem has been raised. Special teachers of the same grade level should help. The art teacher, the music teacher, the mathematics and science teachers, and other subject specialists can be helpful to the core teachers as they work out the resource unit.

The teachers would usually develop a brief statement of the problem and its significance to the students. They would pool the questions that students were asking about the problem and about related problems into a list that would remain open for revision and addition.

The teachers would then work out a list of goals or objectives to which such a study of human relations might contribute. This list of goals should be based upon the students' own purposes and should, like the questions they have raised, be open to constant revision.

Next, the group of teachers might develop a list of learning experiences that would contribute to the solution of the problem in ways that would achieve the students' and teachers' purposes. These experiences would include reading, writing, speaking,

---

[14] A somewhat different approach to the resource unit is represented by the series, *Problems in American Life.* This series of resource units has been developed by the National Association of Secondary School Principals and the National Council for the Social Studies, 1201 16th Street, Washington 6, D. C.

[15] The resource unit technique has also been used in Denver, Santa Barbara, Minneapolis, and other city school systems as a guide for helping to orient teachers to unit instruction. See, for example, the *Santa Barbara County Curriculum Guide for Teachers in Secondary Schools,* Vol. IV. Santa Barbara, Cal.: Schauer Printing Studio, 1941.

listening, and observing; they might also include computing, acting, singing, playing, surveying, manipulating, creating, discussing, summarizing, and evaluating. They would be a reservoir upon which not only the core teacher, but also the teachers in art, music, health, science, and mathematics might draw for teaching units on intercultural relations.

The learning experiences might be divided into such categories as *initiatory, developmental, and culminating* activities. Or they might be classified as *preparatory, investigational, and evaluative* activities. Whatever the division, there would be a list of possible learning experiences centering around the definition and development of the problem, investigation of the problem presentation or summary of findings, and evaluation of results.

It seems clear that this part of the resource unit, like the three already mentioned, must be left open to subsequent revision by groups of students. In practice, this experience section will usually emerge originally from activities actually planned and carried out by students and teachers as the resource unit is being developed. Subsequent use of the list should result in constant enrichment and revision by other groups of students.

Finally, the teachers would develop a list of usable and obtainable materials bearing on the problem of intercultural relations; this list would also be subject to constant revision through the typical initiative of students who are eagerly attacking a real problem.

Thus, the resource unit might consist of five parts:

1. A statement of the problem and its significance to students
2. A list of questions raised by students about the problem
3. A statement of the purposes of students and teachers alike in attacking the problem
4. A list of learning experiences, including evaluation activities, that have proved helpful to students and teachers in attacking the problem
5. A list of materials which have proved useful in attacking the problem

Meanwhile, the core class or classes from which the original impetus for the resource unit was derived will have proceeded with their study of the Negro in modern America through the use of a teaching, or learning unit, developed from day to day through teacher-student planning. The goal-statements, the pupil activities, and the materials developed in this teaching unit on one specific problem in the field of interracial relations will contribute constantly to the work of the group of teachers who are constructing the resource unit. At the same time, other classes in the school may be working on units that relate to the general problem of this resource unit. Thus the classroom ideas, activities, and discoveries produced by various specific learning units flow continuously into the resource unit and enrich it considerably. It is thus possible for teacher-pupil planning to enter indirectly into the development of a resource unit as well as into the teaching units which are drawn from it. For the purpose of insuring this enrichment, resource units should be kept flexible by loose-leaf construction or by the flow-sheet device.

The following are suggested criteria for constructing and evaluating a resource unit:

1. The resource unit should recognize students' needs and interests
2. It should include specific ways in which students can participate in planning, developing, and evaluating the work
3. It should provide suitable socializing activities
4. It should explore community resources that will be useful in developing the learning unit
5. It should be based upon sound principles of learning
6. It should be practicable under prevailing school conditions
7. It should stimulate professional growth in democratic ways of working with students
8. It should provide the students with experiences that call for reflective thinking
9. It should be organized for easy use by the teachers
10. It should be based upon a definite philosophy of education

11. It should be developed by several teachers representing as many subject fields as possible
12. It should contain many more suggestions than any class is likely to use
13. It should be suited to the students' maturity[16]

students help plan

Through all these criteria runs the important thread of teacher-pupil planning. The resource unit, we repeat, is not a substitute for teacher-pupil planning. It is rather a vehicle for facilitating such planning. If it is used as a dynamic, flexible device that grows and changes as each successive class group draws upon the suggestions it contains, it can become a stimulus to group planning by students as well as teachers. If it is permitted to become prescriptive or rigid, it will constitute almost as real a barrier to teacher-pupil planning as a textbook or course of study.

some sample problems

What kinds of problems do pupils and teachers study in core classes? The following list of problems was proposed as a basis for resource units by a group of ninth and tenth grade teachers:

1. Entering a new school
2. Understanding and respecting other members of our democratic society
3. Conserving natural resources
4. Food and health
5. Choosing an occupation
6. Getting along better with people[17]

The Minneapolis Common Learnings program has resulted in the development of a number of resource guides. The following list of titles suggests the scope of problems most persistently raised in these classes:

---

[16] Adapted from Alberty, *Reorganizing the High School Curriculum*, pp. 272-276.

[17] This list of problems formed the basis for the brief sample source units developed by 58 Michigan teachers in 1945. Published in *Planning and Working Together*. Lansing, Michigan: State Department of Public Instruction, 1945, pp. 62-111.

Conflicts Between Ideals and Practices
Driver Education and Training
Home and Family Living
Minneapolis City Government
Natural Resources for Minnesota
Orientation Unit for Seventh Grade
World in Which We Work[18]

Areas appropriate for the development of resource units will arise naturally out of students' concerns and questions, if they have an opportunity to raise questions. Such resource units, over a period of years, can provide a more functional basis for the scope and sequence of learning experiences than can any course of study. For example, core students have expressed concern and raised problems in such varied areas as the following:

1. Understanding myself and others
2. Getting along with people
3. Building better home and family life
4. Adjusting successfully to school
5. Getting and earning a living
6. Conserving natural resources
7. Building world peace
8. Understanding nuclear fission
9. Maintaining health
10. Analyzing propaganda
11. Learning to play
12. Taking my part in democratic government
13. Communicating with others
14. What can you believe?
15. Shall I go to college?
16. Knowing our community
17. Overcoming our prejudices
18. Knowing our Latin-American neighbors
19. Understanding Russia

---

[18] Minneapolis Public Schools, *A Printer For Common Learnings*. Division of Secondary Education, Minneapolis Public Schools, 1948, pp. 23-25.

20. Learning about the Far East
21. Buying insurance
22. Planning a home
23. Raising children
24. Understanding the American heritage
25. Understanding democracy and communism

This list could be considerably extended. When boys and girls realize at length that their interests and concerns are important in the core class, they usually propose for study the same problems that are confronted by the total culture. A curriculum based upon such problems is on the high road toward successful learning. A group of teachers who have planned resource units based on the more persistent of these problems have laid a good foundation.

WHAT ARE SOME ADDITIONAL PLANNING AIDS?

grade-level planning

The kind of planning that we have been describing cannot be accomplished by one teacher working alone. It is doubtful that it can be achieved by reliance on meetings of teachers after school hours. High school core programs are increasingly turning to the device of group planning of resource materials by all of the teachers of a given grade level, and are providing time for such planning.

A common practice is to schedule all teachers of a given grade level to be free of classes for a certain period during the day. This is accomplished in a variety of ways—through large group activities such as physical education, music, or study halls, through split sessions, or through the provision of substitute teachers for some of the classes involved. Time is also frequently obtained through preschool and postschool conferences, through credit and noncredit workshops, or through released time for in-service education purposes.

Whatever the device, it appears promising to develop resource materials through the cooperative efforts of a team of teachers working at a given grade level. Such a team would certainly include the core teacher. It should also include the science, health, and mathematics teachers, and teachers of art, music, and other exploratory fields.

the resource file

The work of such a team of grade-level planners would be the development of resource materials. These might take the form of resource units like the ones already described, or they might consist of less formally organized materials that have proved useful in past units and will probably be found useful again. Such resource files would contain much fugitive material of the consumable type—pamphlets, periodicals and reprints, pictures, posters, charts, maps, graphs, letters, radio scripts, and newspaper articles.[19] The files would also contain past teaching units and outstanding samples of classwork done in connection with various units. Among these materials might be summary reports, scripts, and other end-products of past group work on a problem that may prove useful to future class groups.

Such resource files can readily be assembled by any interested group of teachers and pupils who are willing to pool their materials for the general welfare. The materials should be classified for ready use, centrally filed for easy access, and kept up to date by continuous additions and periodic pruning. Those materials that were originally published for propaganda purposes should be clearly identified to avoid misinterpretation. Even they are useful, however, when they are used intelligently.

The cooperative development of such resource files by a grade-level group of teachers will insure a much richer set of instructional materials than could be developed by any one core teacher. It will have the further advantage of promoting their use by all teachers of a given grade level. This may make a

---

[19] Lists of free or inexpensive learning materials are available from the Educator's Progress Service, Randolph, Wis., as well as from many business and industrial corporations, the book columns of national educational journals, and so on.

significant contribution to the goal of the core program—the integration of the total learning experience of the child's day with the real problems of living here and now.

conclusion

The core teacher has a positive challenge in preplanning, a challenge met by his study of the community, the children themselves, and the learning resources that are available to help them in their study. He need not work alone at this task, but may be a member of a team of teachers, all concerned with the same goal: assisting the children in their study of problems without selecting the problems themselves or solving them in advance for the pupils. With such an approach to planning, the core teacher has laid the foundation of a rich and real learning experience.

SELECTED REFERENCES

Alberty, Harold, *Reorganizing the High School Curriculum,* Revised. New York: The Macmillan Company, 1953, Chapters XIV and XV.

Association for Supervision and Curriculum Development, *Fostering Mental Health In Our Schools.* Washington, D. C.: The National Education Association, 1950, Chapter 16.

———, *Toward A New Curriculum.* Washington, D. C.: The National Education Association, 1944, Chapter V.

———, *Toward Better Teaching.* Washington, D. C.: The National Education Association, 1949, Chapter III.

A Primer for the Common Learnings. Minneapolis, Minnesota: Minneapolis Public Schools, 1948.

Hanna, Paul, *Youth Serves The Community.* New York: Appleton-Century-Crofts, 1936.

Illinois Secondary Curriculum Program, *Guides to Curriculum Planning.* Springfield, Illinois: The Department of Public Instruction, 1950.

Krug, Edward A., *Curriculum Planning,* Revised. New York: Harper and Brothers, 1957, Chapters VII and VIII.

Leonard, J. Paul, *Developing The Secondary School Curriculum.* New York: Rinehart and Company, 1953, Chapters 15 and 16.

Miel, Alice, and associates, *Cooperative Procedures in Learning.* New York: Bureau of Publications, Teachers College, Columbia University, 1952, Chapter V.

Mudd, Dorothy, *A Core Program Grows.* Bel Air, Maryland: The Harford County Board of Education, 1949, Chapter IV.

Noar, Gertrude, *Freedom To Live and Learn.* Philadelphia: The Franklin Publishing Co., 1949, Chapters 12, 13, and 14.

Olsen, Edward G., *School and Community Programs.* Englewood Cliffs, N. J.: Prentice-Hall, Inc., 1949, Chapters 2-7.

Planning and Working Together, Bulletin 337. Lansing, Michigan: State Department of Public Instruction, 1945, Chapters VII-VIII.

Quillen, James, *Using A Resource Unit.* Washington, D. C.: National Association of Secondary-School Principals, 1942.

Romine, Stephen A., *Building The High School Curriculum.* New York: The Ronald Press Company, 1954, Chapter 9.

Santa Barbara County Curriculum Guide for Teachers in Secondary Schools, Vol. IV. Santa Barbara, California: Scharrer Printing Studio, 1941.

Utilization of Community Resources in the Social Studies, 9th Yearbook. Washington, D. C.: The National Council for the Social Studies, 1938, pp. 73-83.

Chapter 11

Learning How To Teach Core Classes

Administrators who are developing a core curriculum sometimes feel that teacher education institutions are not organized to turn out good core teachers. Colleges and universities do need to give serious consideration to the kinds of experiences that will enable young people to become more effective core teachers. Traditional programs of teacher education take little account of this new need for core teachers; often they even seem to be going in the opposite direction. Instead of receiving an integrated program of general education, the future core teacher is usually exposed to a series of unrelated disciplines, even more disparate and departmentalized than the program of the traditional secondary school. Instead of offering the student experiences in the skills of teacher-pupil planning, the traditional program usually subjects him to four years of professorial domination, lectures and listening, assigned readings and reports, cramming for terminal examinations based on subject-matter mastery. Instead of presenting the methods of group process and techniques of guidance, we require a series of separate, subject methods courses. Finally, we often place the future core teacher in separate subjects even for the practice teaching contact.

How Can Colleges Prepare Core Teachers?

An increasing number of colleges and universities have recently, however, launched programs of preparation for core teaching. These programs, developed in response to the rapidly swelling need for core teachers, have generally represented efforts to break away from the methods and curriculum described above, in order to meet certain special needs of core teachers. A recent monograph of the A.S.C.D. has set forth the following competencies of an effective core teacher:

—Understanding the adolescent and helping to meet his needs
—Using major fields of knowledge as resources for studying and solving common problems
—Providing leadership in the use of democratic group processes
—Counseling and guidance
—Organizing and utilizing learning materials[1]

This report then goes on to present some understandings and abilities, grouped under each of these five categories, which a core teacher should seek to develop:

Understanding the Adolescent

—Ability to provide activities and learning opportunities in which pupils are encouraged to affiliate with each other, both for solving mutual problems and for having fun together
—Ability to make some measure of approval and success possible for every learner
—Ability to provide the pupils with constructive means of releasing aggressions
—Ability to sense developmental levels of adolescents and to gear experiences to these levels

---

[1] Association for Supervision and Curriculum Development, *Preparation of Core Teachers*. Washington, D. C.: The National Education Association, 1955, p. 21.

—Ability to begin with the immediate and concrete in the learner's present world and to help him develop from them patterns of generalization

—Ability to help adolescents identify their problems and to gear learning to real (individual) purposes

Using Major Fields of Knowledge as Resources

—General knowledge of such fields as history, literature, natural science, economics, sociology, government

—Ability to identify major current social, economic, and political problems or issues

—Ability to draw upon and use major fields of knowledge in solution of current problems

—Ability to relate various fields of knowledge to a problem area

—Ability to locate materials, persons, places, and other resources useful in helping solve current problems

—Ability to organize resources in effective form for later use

Leadership In Group Processes

—He must be able to help the class achieve the level of rapport and mutual respect needed for effective group planning

—He must be able to give the class some orientation to the planning process, and a reasonable degree of security in using it

—He must be able to help the class to formulate and adopt clearly stated goals for its work, for any given unit and for longer range objectives

—He must be able to help the class conduct a problem census, explore the possible problem areas, and achieve consensus in the selection of areas for study

—He must be able to help groups organize for effective work, to choose leaders, develop a plan of work, define a problem, set up hypotheses to be tested, secure resources, keep records, formulate conclusions, evaluate results

—He must be able to help the class to evaluate its growth in relation to the various skills, concepts, understanding, and knowledge which may be established as its goals

—He must be able to help the class to learn and use techniques of self- and group control

Counseling and Guidance

—Ability to listen, to "draw out" the pupil, to help him formulate his own conclusions and make his own decisions

—Ability to make suggestions without either dominating the interview or putting words in the pupils mouth

—Ability to wait patiently for results

—Ability to accept all youth warmly, without condoning their every act

—Ability to structure opportunities in a classroom in such ways as to build up and strengthen personality

—Ability to interpret data from tests and other sources that help in understanding students

—Ability to identify and help re-structure group relationships

—Ability to help members of a group assume responsibility for their own (disciplinary) control

Organizing and Utilizing Learning Materials

—Broad knowledge of several subject fields that have a bearing on contemporary problems

—Knowledge of the community and its personal—and place—resources

—Knowledge of sources of free and inexpensive materials

—Ability to select and organize materials around broad problems of current concern

—Ability to identify, without salesmanship or compulsion, the actual problems or concerns of adolescents

—Ability to gauge student interest, reading power, and developmental levels in selection of materials

—Ability to devise varied possible opportunities for experiences that will enable students to utilize resources

—Ability to work cooperatively with administrators, librarians, fellow teachers, and local citizens in developing resource materials[2]

In the effort to prepare core teachers who have such understandings and abilities as these, a number of colleges and universities have recently launched programs specifically aimed at helping to meet the demand for competent core teachers. The total number of such programs has increased significantly from the three or four which could be found across the country in 1950. The A.S.C.D. bulletin already quoted presents the curriculum requirements of eight such programs. Many others have been developed, both during the preparation of the bulletin and

---

[2] A.S.C.D., *Preparation of Core Teachers*, pp. 22-32.

subsequent to its publication. Certain common trends appear in these college programs:

1. They generally emphasize the objective of broad preparation in a number of subject fields, as opposed to intensive specialization in one field.

2. They tend to emphasize skills in guidance and in group problem solving.

3. They seek to reveal to the prospective core teacher the relationship of the various subject fields as they are used in solution of current problems.

4. They usually provide early and systematic practice teaching experiences in core classes in secondary schools.

Many of these programs are of graduate level and are thus aimed at the in-service teacher. There is increasing basis for hope that the needs listed earlier in this chapter will be presently met in the pre-service curricula from which new core teachers will graduate.

Meanwhile, it is evident that the basic need is one of in-service education. New core curriculums cannot usually be staffed with new teachers, even if that were desirable. The core classes have been, and will continue to be largely staffed with teachers now in service, especially in such widely required fields as English, social studies, and science. The problem, therefore, is how to help experienced teachers adapt their methods and change their points of view in order to become good teachers of core classes. Teachers who are experienced in core work usually assert that they learned by starting to teach core classes.

The role of in-service education therefore assumes considerable significance in schools that are attempting any departure from conventional types of instruction. If most high schools are to launch a core curriculum, using for the most part the teachers they now have, and helping them to become more effective through the process of experimental growth and evaluation, the experiences that those teachers have while teaching core classes are very important. It might almost be stated that the success of a core curriculum hinges upon the extent to which a vital program of in-service education is planned and developed throughout the period of the experiment.

Accordingly, it is a common practice for an effective core curriculum to be accompanied by, and perhaps built up through, a systematic program of in-service education. Such programs can be found in city and county school systems in states across the country. The A.S.C.D. monograph presents descriptions of such practices in Garrett, Harford, Baltimore, and Prince George's counties, Maryland; in Dade county, Florida; in Minneapolis, Minnesota; in eight Michigan schools; in forty-four Wisconsin schools; in New York City; Elizabeth, N. J.; Evanston, Illinois; Portland, Oregon; Battle Creek, Michigan; Sunburst, Montana; Springfield and Kansas City, Missouri; Philadelphia, Pennsylvania; and in the Ohio State Laboratory School in Columbus, Ohio. Certain generalizations are presented, based on analysis of these and other in-service programs for core teachers. These "principles" are:

1. An in-service education program for core teachers should at some time involve all teachers in the school—not just core teachers.

2. An in-service education program for core teachers should be directed toward further development of the competencies needed at the pre-service level.

3. An in-service education program for core teachers should provide for a schedule permitting meetings on school time—e.g., for grade level and department meetings, conferences, institutes, and workshops.

4. An in-service education program for core teachers should provide for the participation of lay people.

5. An in-service program for the education of core teachers should be centered upon problems identified by the group concerned.

6. An in-service program for core teachers should be focussed upon the common needs, problems, and interests of adolescents in this society.

7. An in-service education program for core teachers should give consideration to the contribution of special services in an adequate core program.[3]

---

[3] A.S.C.D., *Preparation of Core Teachers,* pp. 91-95.

time for planning

Certain of these principles appear to have high priority in any program of in-service preparation for core teaching. The third principle, which mentions "time for planning," is an important one. Provisions should be made for such planning to take place during the "regular" school day. Morning and afternoon meetings can be arranged, at least partly on school time, by the location of the core teachers' "free" period. Teachers can be released for committee or grade-level meetings by use of substitutes or cadet teachers. Early dismissal once a week is used in many school systems. The summer months, too, may be used for curriculum development when teachers are placed on twelve-month contracts.

It has been the general experience of schools introducing the core curriculum that additional vacation time was necessary to prepare a teaching staff properly to introduce and carry on the reorganization program. A workshop of from three to six weeks in the local school system, with several expert consultants from outside the system, has been used in large cities; or where a teacher training institution was located in the community, a cooperative arrangement has been effected whereby a curriculum workshop under the auspices of the college or university met the needs of the local community. By this plan teachers are able to earn academic credit while making direct application of their study of modern curriculum theory and practice to their local situation. It is common practice for teachers to be subsidized for such study by the school and for their tuition to be paid when they attend a workshop under the auspices of a teacher training institution. In addition many schools encourage selected teachers to attend workshops in various university centers, or to take special work elsewhere so that they may be able to give special assistance in certain phases of reorganization of the local school curriculum.

A device now coming into favor, even in schools not committed to a definite curriculum innovation plan, is to bring the faculty back one week to ten days in advance of the opening of school. If part of the faculty has been in attendance at a curriculum workshop during the summer and has worked out specific proposals for modification of the curriculum, this is an excellent time for all to plan together so that whatever plans are finally adopted are all-faculty plans understood by everyone.

If possible, it is desirable for schools that are eager to launch a program of curriculum change leading toward some form of core curriculum to encourage as many staff people as possible to attend a summer curriculum workshop, or to have at least a week or ten days of institute period for the entire staff immediately preceding the opening of school in September.

The administration should assume that for any in-service plan to be successful, the superintendent, principals, and supervisors should attend and be part of faculty study programs during the school year, and should participate in workshops specially attended by any large part of the school staff. They should also be active during the period when the faculty is together immediately preceding the opening of school. Too many efforts at curriculum modification have been stymied by failure of the administration to be a part of the study. Generally, when proposals for changes are made by the hard-working faculty under these circumstances, the school leadership does not understand the proposals. Many staff members are given the false feeling that the leadership is giving only lip service to new ideas but is not genuinely interested.

One school launching a curriculum revision program had over half the teaching staff in attendance at a summer workshop from which all elementary school principals were conspicuous by their absence. When school opened and proposals for modifications were suggested to the principals the teachers met with puzzled unwillingness to make the changes. Two things were obvious: first, the principals did not understand what the teachers were talking about; they talked a different educational language. Second, since they did not understand, they were unwilling to agree to changes. The teachers were frustrated and became irritable. The second summer workshop was attended by all administrative staff members. From then on, change toward the core curriculum was rapid.

A curriculum specialist was asked to participate in the in-service program of a staff that met for a week before the fall opening of school. The staff was especially interested in introducing the core program and had begun intensive faculty study the winter before. At this meeting the school administrators were present long enough to introduce the speaker, but most of the day they were busy with other things. The staff was discouraged. A couple of them asked the visitor: "How can we do anything when the administration won't take time to join us and find out what this is all about?" Launching a program of curriculum change is an all-staff proposition.

Teachers, in summary, should be constantly encouraged to assume leadership in keeping with a democratic philosophy of administration. Provision of time and opportunities for leadership training can provide an incentive for teachers to assume unusual responsibilities in curriculum modifications throughout the school.

democratic leadership

The fifth principle listed earlier states that the program must be centered on problems identified by the group concerned. This principle implies a basic democracy in school planning, following a philosophy that is gradually modifying our earlier concepts of administration. Studies have shown in recent years that unification of thinking, cooperative planning, and direct participation of all teachers hinge upon their being consulted as to the agenda of any meeting. It must be *their* meeting, not the principal's or the curriculum director's. A recent discussion of secondary school administration includes the following statement on this point:

It is probable that cooperative planning will seldom succeed when the problems under study are not real to all participants. At this point some administrators have made a costly mistake. Many school principals have entered upon their new positions with a considerable number of ideas and goals. They have studied the existing curriculum and have made a list of the outstanding problems that seem to them to need some attention. They may be quite right in their selection of the problems that are most urgent.

Yet these particular problems may have no significance for the faculty group. Because of the prestige of the leaders, teachers may go along with a program of study; sometimes they may even give the appearance of accepting the leader's proposals for study. If their interest and concern are not rooted more deeply than that, however, the study has little chance of success. The problems on which teachers spend themselves must be real to them.[4]

A bulletin on supervision has summed up the role of the status leader in group planning as follows:

1. Discover group goals sufficiently vital so that they will call forth a maximum of cooperative effort

2. Set up a system of values enabling the group to define, select, or choose the needs and interests of first priority

3. Instill in others a desire to "belong" and take active part in group action

4. Discover their skills, competencies, interests, and abilities so that each, while taking part in group processes, may gain the maximum security which results from each having a part to play and a contribution to make

5. Develop good human relationships and satisfactory personal interactions, so that a cooperative, permissive atmosphere characterizes group functioning.[5]

The function of leadership, in brief, must be deliberately and skillfully shared with teachers if the program is to be significantly improved.

use of resources

Many resources exist for help in in-service programs. The most important of these are, of course, available in the local school. The students themselves are our first resource, both as keystones of curriculum planning and as planners themselves, at their own level of interest and skill. They should be involved in the planning activity at the earliest appropriate time. The parents and other lay citizens can contribute much to any curriculum develop-

[4] Roland C. Faunce, *Secondary School Administration*. New York: Harper and Brothers, 1955, p. 70.

[5] Association for Supervision and Curriculum Development, *Group Processes in Supervision*. Washington, D. C.: The National Education Association, 1948, p. 59.

ment program. Any school staff which ignores them does so at the risk of having the program attacked and perhaps lost through misunderstanding of its goals. Besides, the ideas of lay citizens are likely to improve any curriculum program. The understanding and support of those who own the schools can only come about through their involvement in planning, implementing, and appraising the school's program.

There are place- and material-resources in every community which can be useful in any program of in-service curriculum planning.[6] Acquaintance with these, systematic listing and filing of them, and their use in curriculum planning is an important phase of any in-service education program for core teachers.

The teachers and administrators are themselves resources for the program. This fact is a truism often overlooked. Any real cooperative planning must make significant use of all the participants. Each of them is a unique organism with a rich background of experience which should be shared. In a staff of 100 teachers with an average of ten years of teaching experience, there is a reservoir of 1,000 years of professional backgrounds, insights, and values, just waiting to be shared. When the channels of communication are opened, so each person's ideas can be heard, a real resource for planning will be released. A good test of any in-service program is the extent and reality of such sharing.

Finally, some resources for in-service education exist outside the local community. The county school staff may include specialists who can be helpful in local planning. The state education agency is likely to have professional consultants available, as are colleges and universities. Not only curriculum experts, but specialists in other fields can be secured as consultants for the local program. These outside visitors should not be expected (or indeed permitted) to dictate the program's goals or to evaluate its effectiveness. Those who cannot be responsible for continuing local leadership should not permit themselves to fall into the roles of deciders, checkers, or appraisers. They should come in on invita-

---

[6] These resources have been discussed in detail in Chapter 9, in connection with their use in core classes.

tion, should start where people are, and should earn their local status by performing a needed service. They can help with small group planning, furnish stimulation, help locate resources for solving local problems, and encourage teachers and administrators to become more professional, more creative people. Miel has pointed out that the outside expert must know how to work with local teachers on their level of development:

> There is increasing recognition of the value of the outside expert who has "specialized" in being a general consultant. Often this person can render the best service by helping school faculties and other working groups in a community to learn useful techniques of group problem-solving. Such a consultant should be an expert in social processes with particular reference to curriculum change.[7]

growth in service

We have noted that core teachers learn how to become more effective teachers while they are experiencing the core assignment. They are aided toward self-improvement by their participation in curriculum planning, by workshops, school visits, and conferences, and by simply being useful members of a cooperative planning effort in which their own ideas count. Outside consultants, too, have furnished help in their growth.

One study of core teachers in eight schools cited certain direct benefits from their involvement in in-service programs:

1. Teachers became more active as participants and leaders in local and state committees, conferences, and workshops.
2. Teachers wrote more for publication.
3. Class groups became easier to work with; students were increasingly cooperative; the longer you worked in core the more fun it was.
4. Teachers became more interested, more sympathetic, and more understanding of growth problems.
5. Teachers became more skillful in planning and discussing with other teachers.
6. Teachers had more creative experiences in common; they became

---

[7] Alice Miel, *Changing the Curriculum, A Social Process*. New York: Appleton-Century-Crofts, Inc., 1946, p. 131.

more alert to world and local events and more aware of new materials and methods.

7. Teachers became more active in research activities.
8. Teachers became more interested in graduate study.
9. Teachers observed needs of child more skillfully.
10. Teachers became more capable at teaching discussion skills.
11. Subject matter became more meaningful to teachers.

These eleven items present a well-rounded portrait of the effective teacher. It is evident that these administrators and teachers believed the core assignment, with its unique purposes and special challenges, to be rewarding and enriching professional experience.

The reasons for these achievements are not hard to discover. In the first place, it has been pointed out earlier that time for planning was deliberately included in the teachers' schedule. There was released time for preschool conferences and workshops throughout the year, and daily periods together were assigned in most cases.

A further releasing factor lies in the reduced number of different pupils per day characteristic of the core assignment. A typical class load for a teacher in a departmentalized program involves from 150 to 200 different pupils each day. A teacher with two half-day core sections, on the other hand, may deal with about 60 different pupils in all. This sharp reduction in the number of different personalities to be studied, children to be helped, and different backgrounds, problems, hopes, and plans to be understood, makes a real difference in professionalizing the teacher.

Finally, and perhaps most important, a stimulating atmosphere develops in a school where core classes meet. The feeling of being an important link in an experimental program has an exciting effect upon teachers. The interest and enthusiasm of the principal or supervisor are contagious. The students and their parents are aware of the importance of the program's goals, and this keys up teachers. There is discussion with other teachers, with parents, and with students about the techniques being used and their effectiveness. Visitors come in to observe and discuss the teaching situation. Teachers are invited to speak before groups or to write articles about their work. They meet other teachers at workshops and compare problems and techniques.

This is not an easy way to teach, but it is a challenging experience. It results in the development of a basically experimental school climate. There is always the possibility that teachers in such a climate may discover some really important things, and they know it. The development of this atmosphere is basic to any program of school improvement. That it characterizes the core curriculum programs may partly account for the unusual professionalization of core teachers.

SELECTED REFERENCES

A Study of In-Service Education. Chicago: The North Central Association, 1944.

Association for Supervision and Curriculum Development, *Preparation of Core Teachers.* Washington, D. C.: The National Education Association, 1955.

————, *Group Processes in Supervision.* Washington, D. C.: The National Education Association, 1948.

————, *Action for Curriculum Improvement.* Washington, D. C.: The National Education Association, 1951, Chapters I, III, and IV.

————, *Toward Better Teaching.* Washington, D. C.: The National Education Association, 1949, Chapter 1.

Commission On Teacher Education, *Teachers for Our Times.* Washington, D. C.: The American Council on Education, 1944, pp. 17-26.

————, *Helping Teachers Understand Children.* Washington, D. C.: The American Council on Education, 1945, Chapter 1.

Faunce, Roland C., *Secondary School Administration.* New York: Harper and Brothers, 1955, Chapters 4 and 5.

Kelley, Earl C., *The Workshop Way of Learning.* New York: Harper and Brothers, 1951, Chapter 1.

MacConnell, Charles, Ernest Melby, C. O. Arndt, and Leslee Bishop, *New Schools for a New Culture,* Revised. New York: Harper and Brothers, 1953, Chapter X.

Michigan Secondary Curriculum Study, *Organization of School Staff for Evaluation*. Lansing, Michigan: The Department of Public Instruction, 1950.

Miel, Alice, *Changing the Curriculum, A Social Process*. New York: Appleton-Century-Crofts, 1946, Chapters IV and V.

Spears, Harold, *The Teacher and Curriculum Planning*. Englewood Cliffs, N. J.: Prentice-Hall, Inc., 1951.

Sharp, George, *Curriculum Development as Re-education of the Teacher*. New York: Bureau of Publications, Teachers College, Columbia University, 1951, Chapter 1.

Wiles, Kimball, *Supervision for Better Schools*, Second Edition. Englewood Cliffs, N. J.: Prentice-Hall, Inc., 1955, Chapter 1.

Yauch, Wilbur, *Human Relations in School Administration*. New York: Harper and Brothers, 1949, Parts 4, 5.

Chapter 12

The Role of the Administrator

At least one conclusion emerges clearly from most of the curriculum programs of the past fifteen years: the most important single factor in effecting continuing improvement in school programs is the quality of administrative leadership available. Teachers at schools involved in curriculum programs have usually identified the principal as the key figure in the initiation of the program. In smaller systems, the superintendent of schools is likely to be the key figure. As the size of the school system increases, the mantle of leadership falls increasingly upon the building principal. However, no principal can be expected to give effective leadership without the aggressive support of the superintendent. It has been noted in the preceding chapter that teacher-leadership, too, depends for its emergence upon the calibre of administration. This is especially important in light of the principle of centering study, in local in-service programs, on problems that are of real concern

263

to participants. This places a real responsibility on the principal to involve teachers in the planning of these programs.

WHAT IS THE ROLE OF THE ADMINISTRATOR
IN A CORE PROGRAM?

In view of the importance of the administrator, it may be useful in this chapter to examine some of the qualities that make for success in administering any program of curriculum improvement. We shall then investigate some of the special problems and challenges that the core curriculum, as one kind of curriculum improvement, presents to the building administrator.

sharing leadership

The effective administrator is defined as follows by a recent state curriculum guide:

> The effective administrator is he who challenges teachers and parents to develop into leaders by inspiring and leading them to participate in planning, executing, and evaluating activities within a school. Furthermore, the effective administrator is one who is himself continually inspired and guided into participating as one of the group, by the leadership which emerges from teachers, parents, and students.[1]

This principle of shared leadership has been emphasized by Kilpatrick, Lewin, Miel, and others as a significant element in increasing the productivity of group work.[2] Groups which have chosen curriculum change as their goal present an even greater need for shared leadership. With the growing recognition that effective learning is evidenced by changes in behavior, the curriculum is now being defined as experiences the learner has through

---

[1] *Planning and Working Together,* Bulletin 337. Lansing, Michigan: State Department of Public Instruction, 1945, p. 154.

[2] Kilpatrick, William H., "Principles of Community Learning," in Samuel Everett, Editor, *The Community School.* New York: Appleton-Century-Crofts, 1938, p. 20; Kurt Lewin, "Dynamics of Group Action," *Educational Leadership,* Vol. I, January 1944, p. 199; Alice Miel, *Changing The Curriculum.* New York: Appleton-Century-Crofts, 1946, pp. 158-159; see also W. A. Yauch, *Human Relations in School Administration.* New York: Harper and Brothers, 1949.

which the school seeks to change his behavior. Thus the curriculum may include both in-school and out-of-school experiences which are so built into the child's learning that he is never again the same organism as he was before he had these experiences.

It is clear that this notion of curriculum places a significant emphasis on real, as opposed to planned-for experiences. The pupil's experiences are influenced by the teacher's behavior more than by any other single factor. The attitudes and relationships of teachers tend to influence, directly and sharply, the attitudes and relationships of pupils. Indeed, all human experience is conditioned by attitudes and relationships. As Sharp has pointed out, however, "The teacher is the key figure in the process of guiding children in their experiences, for it is he who has direct and prolonged contact with them. The quality of these experiences rests largely on the kind of person the teacher is. His background, his insights, his sensitivity, and his effectiveness determine to a great extent the caliber of the work accomplished in the school." [3]

In Chapter 5 herein the concept that learning is a product of experience has been explained and supported. This concept gives a crucial importance to the relationships and attitudes that exist or develop among the learners, and between them and their teachers. This experience concept also complicates the process of curriculum development. It leads us to view the teacher not as a purveyor of subject matter but as the planner of situations in which attitudes and relationships are to be changed for the better.

Thus the teacher is the architect of the social learning situation. It is his task to arrange the total learning environment in such a way that relationships will be friendly and strong, that attitudes will be constructive, and that the individual learner will be strengthened, supported, and challenged. For this task, the teacher's own attitudes, and his own relationships with others are of immense significance.[4]

---

[3] George Sharp, *Curriculum Development as Re-Education of the Teacher*. New York: Bureau of Publications, Teachers College, Columbia University, 1951, p. 2.

[4] Roland C. Faunce, *Secondary School Administration*. New York: Harper and Brothers, 1955, p. 64.

Thus the administrator who sets out to improve the curriculum is confronted by a highly complex task, summarized by some such a conceptual outline as this:

1. The curriculum consists of people, more basically than it consists of content.
2. Changing the curriculum really amounts to changing people.
3. Teachers are the first subjects for change, since they are central to the real curriculum.
4. Teachers, like persons generally, do not welcome change in themselves.
5. The principal has no one's sanction to change him.
6. It is impossible to change another person without his volition.
7. Teachers must be involved in the process of changing themselves.

Thus we have before us the real reason for involving teachers in the process of curriculum planning. By no other than cooperative means can attitudes and relationships be improved. This axiom lies at the heart of teacher-pupil planning of classroom experiences. It also supplies the rationale for involvement of teachers in curriculum planning.

some handicaps

The administrator confronts certain handicaps that he must surmount if he wishes to achieve success as a status leader in democratic planning. Chief among these is the tradition of line and staff responsibility and authority that has predominated in our schools for many years. This tradition places the administrator of a school in the middle of a hierarchy of authority. It assumes that plans and policies must be handed down from the superintendent to the building principal or supervisor, and from them to the teachers, sometimes through a department head.

The principal, indeed, suffers a special kind of handicap from his very status in a line-and-staff administrative organization. His position is one of responsibility to the superintendent's office for the operation of his school. He has power and control over people in the building. He can make their daily lives more pleasant or more difficult by his decisions and assignments. He is an important link in a chain of authority. He may have some difficulty escaping from this power role, even if he wishes to do so. It may be hard for him to see how he can share his responsibility for planning when the tradition of his position holds him responsible for the outcomes of such planning.[5]

This authoritarian tradition has been so thoroughly built into our administrative philosophy that even the well-intentioned administrator is often perplexed as to how to operate democratically within the existing structure. Many a building principal has pondered the problem of harmonizing his own impulse to share responsibility for planning with the tradition that holds him responsible for the outcome of such planning. In the back of his mind lies the uneasy thought that the faculty may make a decision that will cause trouble, a decision to the enforcement of which he may be committed because of his position. He fears that he may lose a measure of his control by sharing it. As a result of the line and staff tradition, the building principal faces a further handicap because of the power he wields over his colleagues and the resulting deference they pay him. Even when he shares this power as fully as he knows how, the halo effect of his position still hovers about him with devastating damage to his relationships with his colleagues. There is a barrier between him and the group that sometimes proves surprisingly hard to surmount.

The administrator may discover a further handicap in his lack of know-how. It is fairly easy to learn administrative procedures concerned with buying supplies, constructing a budget, or maintaining the building. It is quite another thing to learn the techniques of group process and the methods of leadership in cooperative planning. But courage and security in sharing his leadership will come with continued success. First, however, he must develop the insights to make beginnings and the techniques that spell success in those beginnings.

there are assets, too

Fortunately, the administrator has certain assets that can help him to overcome his handicaps. The first of these is a basic good will, a desire to develop the best possible program, that usually charac-

---

[5] Faunce, *Secondary School Administration*, pp. 5-6.

terizes not only the administrator but the faculty as a whole. The discovery that all of the staff are interested in doing a good job can be a tremendous stimulus to the administrator. He will not usually discover this encouraging attitude until he lets himself get acquainted with the staff members as individuals. The collective good will of the staff and administrator can be a significant force when it is articulated through a common attack upon mutual problems.

The example of other schools can be an asset, too. Successful curriculum programs in neighboring or similar schools have proved helpful in developing insights as to what can be done and in giving courage to make a start.

Professional writings and in-service courses in leadership have their place. The group dynamics movement, while still in its infancy, has had a profound effect upon the contents of professional journals and the kinds of courses and workshops now available through teacher-educating institutions. Many colleges of education are offering courses in local school curriculum planning, evaluation of curriculum change, leadership in curriculum programs, and similar fields. Schools of social work and departments of sociology are giving courses in group dynamics and social psychology. Articles on the role of the status leader appear in a dozen national professional journals. The state and national organizations that serve the school administrator have reflected these trends, also, in their conference programs and workshops.

The goals and techniques of group process have profoundly influenced education in recent years. The results of field research in this area are available to school leaders and can be extremely helpful as the administrator seeks to clarify his role in curriculum developments like the core curriculum.

But the most valuable asset of all is the collective power of a faculty that has learned to share in curriculum planning. The autocratic administrator never realizes what a tremendous resource he is wasting when he does not utilize the leadership of the entire professional staff. No democratic enterprise can be efficient in any real sense unless it makes full use of the good will, the enthusiasm, the ideas, and the evaluative judgment of all its participants. The administrator who once discovers this resource by instituting a genuine program of shared planning will seldom go back to the autocratic method.

stimulating group action

The administrator will find himself faced with the task of stimulating group planning and group action. Just as the teacher must arrange the social situation of the classroom so that it challenges the learner, in the same way the administrator is the architect of a social climate for group action. Teachers should see the building climate as one in which they will enjoy working and living with others. This climate includes the physical aspects of the building, which should be such as to encourage group interaction. It includes also the provision of means whereby teachers can get acquainted, dissolve the barriers that separate them from their colleagues, discover their mutual needs, and learn of resources that can be helpful. Each new school year presents a new challenge of social orientation, since the group is never exactly the same as last year's staff.

The problems or concerns on which the staff members are to spend themselves must be real—they must make sense to the participants. It is not easy to confess your most urgent problems or concerns to strangers. It is at this point that we often cherish our barriers and build them higher. Until we have got acquainted with others, until we have moved toward firm friendship with them, we are not ready to share in expressing common needs or problems. It is therefore important to provide an adequate social setting in which these barriers are reduced. Individuals should be encouraged to move about, and meet others. Name-tags are helpful. Games, dancing, group-singing, coffee hours, picnics, and other forms of social activity assume a new significance—as means of making communication possible and natural. Eating and drinking together seem to make such communication more easy. Each new school year should begin with a series of well-planned social events.

The administrator has a contribution to make in this socializing process. He can reduce social intercourse by controlling the agenda of the meetings himself, or he can encourage lively interaction by helping to develop a program and a setting which make it possible. His example can hinder or help, too. A warm, friendly way of treating other persons is contagious. Of course, there are others on the staff who can assume leadership in social activities. Some of these persons are better qualified than the principal for this role, an intelligent administrator may soon discover. Still, the principal's example and assistance are of crucial importance in this business of getting better acquainted. He sets the tone of attitudes and relationships within the staff group. Miel has observed that "real progress toward a better curriculum will not be made until all persons concerned with curriculum development are treated with respect, until it is demonstrated in countless ways that their opinions are valued." [6] Hence, the administrator treats teachers with genuine respect, even when he may disagree sharply with them. "He works constantly to keep the way open for continued discussion and appraisal. He seeks always to release the power that is in other people, by reducing the barriers to group unity and group action." [7] In short, the administrator uses techniques that stimulate teachers to renewed group activity through reducing the barriers between them.

An important aspect of this stimulation is the extent to which the leader is able to interpret to his colleagues the results of their group work. This role stems from a genuine respect for the contributions of each individual. The Educational Policies Commission posed the following questions on this point in *Learning The Ways of Democracy*:

Does your school morale improve with every expansion of the base of participation in policy making? Do teachers feel that their opinions really count on important questions? Do the teaching and administrative staffs work in harmony because they have a common vision of the job to be

---

[6] Miel, *Changing the Curriculum*, p. 170.

[7] Faunce, *Secondary School Administration*, p. 69.

done, a generous sharing in deciding the best way to do it, and mutual respect for each person's contribution? [8]

In stimulating group planning in the manner suggested by these questions, the administrator will need to help his colleagues to discover what has been happening to them, both as individuals and as a group.

the role of participant

Not only is the administrator a *leader,* and *stimulator* in group planning. He must also be able to *participate* effectively in group situations where other leaders have emerged. This means that he must become, on occasion, a follower, too. When leadership is shared, the administrator must accept the leadership of others. Kurt Lewin has pointed out the significance of this role for the status leader:

Establishing democracy in a group implies an active education: The democratic follower has to learn to play a role which implies, among other points, a fair share of responsibility toward the group and a sensitivity to other people's feelings.

What holds for the education of democratic followers holds true also for the education of democratic leaders. In fact, it seems to be the same process through which persons learn to play either of these roles and it seems that both roles must be learned if either one is to be played well.[9]

The administrator can only learn to follow by experiencing it, by entering into the role with sincerity and adhering to it with consistency. If he attempts to mix the roles of leader and follower in the same group situation, he is likely to lose all that he has gained by sharing the responsibility for planning. For example, the administrator who has "permitted" the faculty to elect a discussion chairman for a committee or faculty meeting, and who then runs the meeting from the floor, is not fooling anyone. Worse yet, he is perpetuating the very status barriers that he has

---

[8] Educational Policies Commission, *Learning The Ways of Democracy.* Washington, D. C.: The National Education Association, 1940, p. 475.

[9] Lewin, "Dynamics of Group Action," p. 199.

set out to overcome. The administrator who really means to develop cooperative planning must be prepared to accept group decisions, to participate at the discussion level as one of the group, and to find himself in the minority upon occasion.

In the role of follower the administrator has an excellent opportunity to demonstrate to his colleagues his readiness to accept leadership from teachers who are elected or appointed to leader positions. This is especially significant because of the importance of teacher leadership in curriculum development programs. Teachers have often furnished more positive leadership than administrators in such programs, possibly because of their freedom from some of the status barriers that handicap administrators.

liaison with community

The responsibility for interpretation of the program goes beyond the faculty involved in a particular school's program. The building administrator has a further role in *interpreting the program* to other administrators, to the board of education, and to the public through all possible channels. It is desirable that there be general understanding of school programs. This need for understanding becomes acute when changes are under way, and there is a particular responsibility for the administrator to insure understanding of the program by all persons and groups concerned. This can be really achieved only by involving everyone concerned in the planning of the program. Again, if he is wise, the administrator will share with other staff members and community representatives this planning role. Students, too, need to be brought to understand what is being done through having a part in making decisions. They are the most significant public relations agents in the school. The principal is assumed to be capable of spear-heading the continuous task of interpretation to the community. He should never look upon himself as the sole interpreter of the school. He should constantly look for ways of sharing this role, but also be ready to assume it when he is needed. He can be of great help to teachers if they feel that he shares their goals, that he has faith in them, and that he can help them to secure solid community support for the program of the school. Further treatment of this matter of interpreting to and involving the community will appear later.[10]

analyzing group dynamics

The administrator has a focal role as an *analyst of group dynamics* involved in faculty planning. He must become a student of the interpersonal relationships that affect every aspect of total staff planning. He must understand and appreciate people and their motives. He must, above all, believe in the value of their unique contributions. It is a part of his task constantly to explore the ways in which these contributions can be released for the good of all.

The alert administrator is aware of the barriers that keep persons and groups apart. He knows the faculty cliques and their leaders, and he seeks intelligently for ways to resolve social conflicts and unify the staff. He does not exploit the leaders for his own ends, but enlists their cooperation in working toward the achievement of group unity. He knows that barriers are maintained and intensified through lack of communication, and this knowledge leads him to devise ways of bringing people and groups together in work and play. He recognizes and helps the group to make allowances for individual differences in its membership. He understands that the establishing of a common ground for group planning is a difficult technical task, and he is conversant with the techniques of problem census, definition of problems, devising of plans for attack, evaluation, and the other procedures that a group must employ in its work together.

Above all, the administrator sets the tone of relationships in a building staff. He demonstrates through all his daily contacts a fundamental faith in his colleagues and a skill in human relationships. Wiles has called attention to the importance of this faith and respect:

---

[10] See Chapter 14.

The basic way for a supervisor to help create a satisfying emotional tone is by respecting the personality of all individuals with whom he comes in contact. . . . [This] involves being concerned about them and their problems, being willing to place their desires ahead of his own, giving full consideration to their ideas and suggestions, creating the type of staff meetings in which each teacher has an opportunity to make his opinions known, encouraging socializing activities that build friendly relationships among the staff, providing working conditions that are comfortable and attractive, and such commonplace things as maintaining an even disposition and showing courtesy.[11]

The administrator therefore treats others with respect, and maintains a free channel for communication with them, even when their educational philosophy is not in harmony with his own. He earns the respect of all members of the staff by the integrity with which he deals with them. Thus he keeps the way open for continued discussion, planning, and group action through which new insights can be developed and goals can be modified.

It has been pointed out earlier that staff planning must begin with matters that are of real concern to the participants. However trivial or irrelevant these problems may appear to the administrator, they will still furnish a far more dependable base for group planning than purposes, program, or problems that are the unique property of the leader. Teachers must begin where they are.

Even when the administrator is concerned to discover the real concerns of teachers, the process is not an easy one. A small group of staff members, or an influential individual, may succeed in imposing on the rest of the staff a problem in which there is no genuine interest. This kind of domination of the problem census can be fully as disastrous as that exerted by the principal or supervisor. It often requires a complex process to discover the real concerns of a large group of persons. Yet the productive quality, the morale of a group depend so directly on their identification with

---

[11] Kimball Wiles, *Supervision For Better Schools,* Second Edition. Englewood Cliffs, N. J.: Prentice-Hall, Inc., 1955, p. 20.

the group problem that a leader will find it worthwhile to work and wait for reasonable consensus. Sometimes anonymous listing (and later rating) of individual concerns must precede open discussion. The process will be much more rapid and efficient if the staff has had previous, successful experience with group planning. The problem census is also simplified and quickened by previous social experiences which have created a friendly climate. One essential, of course, is a feeling of freedom to express any views, regardless of their unpopularity with the administration or with the majority of staff members.

In spite of the difficulties often involved in the planning process, it has been successfully accomplished by hundreds of staff groups. Again and again, teachers have justified their leader's faith in their ability to:

1. Develop values and goals
2. Recognize problems that prevent attainment of goals
3. Share problems and answers with others
4. Find resources
5. Arrive at consensus about what should be done
6. Try solutions
7. Appraise results[12]

Inexperience with group processes is still common among faculty groups; but those who have once had a successful experience of this kind have discovered for themselves a capacity and an appetite for further planning experiences. Their skill increases with their self-confidence, and they are soon ready to tackle any group problem.

The building administrator, then, must be a student of group action techniques and a humanitarian in his philosophy. He knows that programs change only as persons change, and that there is vast power for constructive changes inherent in any faculty. It is a part of his task to release this power through his skill in reducing the barriers that separate people.

All that has been said in this chapter regarding the role of the

---

[12] Faunce, *Secondary School Administration*, p. 72.

administrator applies with equal force to other status leaders responsible for curriculum programs. Supervisors and consultants must play these same roles in their efforts to help develop programs. Some school systems are now employing core supervisors who have a special responsibility for the development of the core curriculum. Such consultants or supervisors have a special challenge to operate in such a way as to evoke leadership in others. The same principles apply also to curriculum directors, program coordinators, and similar status leaders in curriculum programs.

an expediter of plans

The administrator has a further function: *expediter* of the plans that a faculty develops. The administrator is a crucial agent in achieving the purposes of the core curriculum. The core teacher is dedicated to the task of individual and group guidance through his classroom assignment. It follows that the administrator must believe in the possibility of achieving such guidance. He must go beyond this faith to active support and implementation of the program of guidance by core teachers. If he acts as though he believes that guidance can be performed only in the office of a specialist in counseling, it is not likely that core teachers will achieve any permanent results in better guidance.

Again, the core teachers are seeking to achieve a democratic classroom experience as a means of producing effective citizens of a democracy. It is possible for such a goal to be achieved in a single classroom operating within an administrative autocracy. In the long run, however, teachers tend to treat children as they themselves are treated. If there is a climate of autocracy in the school, teachers will usually extend that climate to the pupils in their classes. If there is a climate of democracy in the school, it has a tendency to permeate the classrooms, too. If administrators show a consistent respect for personality, an interest in and command of the processes of group planning, and the courage to share with teachers the development, implementation, and evaluation of school policies, these same qualities will probably be found in the teachers' classroom approach.

For the core teacher, who is committed by his assignment to provide real experiences in democratic living for his pupils, the example and support of a democratic administrator are especially important. Without that support, he will not be likely to improve his techniques; he may even lose the courage and faith out of which his techniques must be developed.

One persistent problem confronting every core curriculum is that of instructional materials, discussed at some length in Chapter 10. It was pointed out there that the core class, more than any other class, depends upon varied and rich instructional resources. In many schools, teachers report that they are unable to secure administrative support for their requests for materials. Even in those classes that appear to be well provided with classroom materials, the demand for additional resources persists, for it appears to be characteristic of the core class, and constitutes good evidence of the effectiveness of the core method. Requests for resources do not emanate from a static program. It is a common occurrence for students in core classes to become keenly interested in a given problem and to ransack the school and community for more help and information on the problem. Textbooks and ordinary library references are quite inadequate to meet this kind of demand, which every experienced core teacher has repeatedly witnessed.

The administrator has a primary responsibility to assist in every possible way in providing instructional materials and resources for core classes. Without his help it may prove difficult or impossible for the core teacher to secure such resources.

Some things which the administrator can do to help secure instructional resources are:

1. Help teachers to anticipate the annual cost of such resources and have it included in library budgets, with adequate amounts reserved for standing orders.
2. Subscribe for the school to one or more free-materials indexes.
3. Provide adequate shelving facilities in the core classrooms.
4. Help the teachers to establish a student materials fee plan, if that is legal and acceptable in his school district.
5. Devise plans for making materials kits available from one classroom

to another. Such floating kits can be based in the high school library but be constantly on the move as core teachers reveal their needs in planning sessions.

6. Aid teachers by coordinating their requests for outside resources in the community.
7. Constantly interpret this unusual demand for materials to the superintendent, to the board of education, and to other teachers who may think they are being discriminated against in the matter of materials.
8. Help teachers by removing from them commercial pressures that would channel all instructional materials into one direction—for example, the adoption of a single basic text for all pupils.
9. Aid in securing funds for the more expensive resources that take long-range planning. An example is the local film library.
10. Help to make it possible for students to move about the school and the community more freely in search of resources.

In short, the building administrator can become so keenly interested in the core classes and their learning experience that he will go all-out to assist students and teachers in their search for help. Such interest, and such faith in the program, will pay rich dividends to the administrator. Without such administrative leadership, the core curriculum is unlikely to succeed.

In most high schools, the administrator is still responsible for the development of the schedule of classes. This is a task that offers rich dividends when it is submitted to the faculty to be developed cooperatively. As long as the final decision regarding the schedule remains in the administrator's hands, it is obvious that not even a beginning can be made at block scheduling for core classes without his full support. In fact, he usually either initiates the necessary schedule changes himself or is pressured into doing so by the requests of teachers.

in summary

We have explored in this chapter some of the important roles that the administrator or supervisor should assume as a leader in democratic planning. There is no intention of representing these roles as the exclusive prerogative of the administrator. On the contrary, every participant in a group process may effectively assume any of these roles at various times. But a special challenge is presented to the administrator or supervisor to employ his status leadership in such functions as these:

1. He *leads* the group in social orientation and in planning desirable program changes, especially during initial stages.

2. He *participates* in such planning and action as one of the group.

3. He *follows* cooperatively the leadership of his colleagues when they emerge as leaders.

4. He *stimulates* them to renewed group activity.

5. He *interprets* the effects of the group's efforts to the faculty members and to the community.

6. He *analyzes* the quality of group dynamics and human relationships, which constitute the matrix of program change.

7. He *expedites* the plans that he and the faculty develop.

Our next chapter will present some transitional steps in schedule building that may be helpful as administrators and teachers work on the task of evolving a core curriculum from the existing departmentalized schedule.

SELECTED REFERENCES

Alexander, William M., and J. Galen Saylor, *Secondary Education*. New York: Rinehart and Company, 1950, Chapter IX.

Anderson, Vivienne, and Daniel Davies, *Patterns of Educational Leadership*. Englewood Cliffs, N. J.: Prentice-Hall, Inc., 1956, Chapters 2 and 8.

Association for Supervision and Curriculum Development, *Leadership Through Supervision*. Washington, D. C.: The National Education Association, 1946, Chapters I and II.

Bossing, Nelson L., "Wanted: A New Leadership for the Secondary School," *Bulletin,* National Association of Secondary School Principals, No. 138, 30:92-100, April 1946.

Educational Policies Commission, *Learning the Ways of Democracy*. Washington, D. C.: The National Education Association, 1940, Chapter VI.

Faunce, Roland C., *Secondary School Administration*. New York: Harper and Brothers, 1955, Chapters 4 and 5.

French, Will, Dan Hull, and B. L. Dodds, *American High School Administration*. New York: Rinehart and Company, 1951.

Johnston, Edgar G., and Roland C. Faunce, *Student Activities in Secondary Schools*. New York: The Ronald Press Company, 1952, Chapter 14.

Kelley, Earl C., "The Function of the Principal in a Modern School," *American School Board Journal*, June 1947, pp. 27-28.

Koopman, G. R., Alice Miel, and Paul Misner, *Democracy in School Administration*. New York: Appleton-Century-Crofts, Inc., 1942.

Menge, J. W., and R. C. Faunce, *Working Together For Better Schools*. New York: American Book Company, 1953, Chapter 4.

Miel, Alice, *Changing the Curriculum, A Social Process*. New York: Appleton-Century-Crofts, Inc., 1946, Chapter 6.

Mackenzie, Gordon N., Stephen M. Corey, and associates, *Instructional Leadership*. New York: Bureau of Publications, Teachers College, Columbia University, 1954.

Sharp, George, *Curriculum Development As Re-education of the Teacher*. New York: Bureau of Publications, Teacher College, Columbia University, 1951.

Wiles, Kimball, *Supervision For Better Schools*, Second Edition. Englewood Cliffs, N. J.: Prentice-Hall, Inc., 1950, Chapter 1.

Yauch, Wilbur A., *Human Relations in School Administration*. New York: Harper and Brothers, 1949.

Chapter 13

Procedures in Developing
a Core Curriculum

Those who have initiated the core curriculum in their schools are fully aware of the difficulties to be encountered. Simple reorganization of even the traditional curriculum involves problems of adjustment. To shift from the traditional subject-matter type of curriculum to the core curriculum is an adventure; but it is an exciting and rewarding adventure.

In this chapter, some cautions and guide lines will be offered to help those who have educational vision, a professional sense of obligation, and the courage to follow their ideals. There are no ironclad rules and there is no suggestion of finality in the ideas offered. A substantial body of educational writings based upon extensive experience is available to guide the curriculum innovator. This wealth of experience, if properly used, may enable the curriculum worker to circumvent many pitfalls that others through unfortunate experience have learned to avoid. Out of these successes and some failures have emerged some promising general lines of approach to this problem. They are included here in the hope that boys and girls may sooner experience a better way of education, and the democratic way of life may more surely be promoted.

While certain procedures are indicated in moving progressively from where we appear to be to where we wish to go, they are not hard and fast. The present advance of some schools in educational thinking and the level of their practice may make some introductory phases unnecessary, or may suggest telescoping them, which would be wholly inadvisable for most schools. Schools are likely to be at different levels of educational thinking and attainment, and there are other considerations that make each school unique in matters of curriculum reorganization. The age of the staff, the recency and nature of their professional contact, the size of the community in which the school is located, and the level of educational and social thinking of the community will determine in no small measure the rapidity of progress and the specific nature of the procedures taken.

Not only are no two schools alike, even in the same community, but also, no two schools progress at the same rate in all respects. The human element makes this inevitable. One hesitates while another moves too fast. This means that broad phases in curriculum development are often irregular, cross one another, or become twilight zones of transition.

1. *taking stock of the situation*

Only in the most exceptional situation should the core curriculum be introduced in full bloom. These situations are so rare that they may be disregarded for purposes of discussion. However, in spite of the tragic failures that litter the path of hasty curricular changes, the number of attempts to make overnight changes in the school curriculum, as in the social set-up in general, is appalling. A study made before World War II of proposed curricular changes revealed that more than a score of schools contemplated the initiation of radical curricular changes at the September opening of schools without proper orientation or tryouts.

The type of reaction that may be encountered in a too-hasty effort to upset practices of long standing is reported in a medium-sized city. A conservative community where little change in the school curriculum had taken place in over two decades employed a new superintendent with advanced educational ideas; he was impatient to get these ideas into practice in the school. Before he had been in the community three months, he sought professional counsel on a program of curriculum reorganization. It was obvious that he had his heart set on drastic changes in the curriculum, and so on. After a week or ten days a plan of curriculum study by staff, school board, and community leaders was submitted. The plan called for intensive study of modern educational and curriculum developments throughout the year, with the possibility that by spring some concrete suggestions for most urgent and agreed-upon changes might be forthcoming, and ways and means determined for the initiation of these changes during the next year. The administrator remonstrated at the slowness of change likely under the plan, which called for intensive in-service education, as the logical first step, to occupy most of the year. However, by the end of the first year a curriculum director was decided upon and hired. It was not until the second year that concrete curriculum changes began to be proposed. The teaching staff, old in years, settled in their ways through years of unchanged practice, and largely lacking in recent study of modern educational developments, began to manifest energetic if subtle opposition. Teachers with roots deep in the community as a result of long years of residence began, through relatives, friends, and organizational contacts, to arouse public opinion against the new fads and frills being imposed upon them and the schools. In short, the superintendent lasted out his three-year contract, but the board of education, filled by election with members opposed to curriculum innovation, eliminated the curriculum project at the end of the second year and fired the curriculum director after one year of service.

Another city with a generally average staff that was educationally conservative and not alive to modern educational developments, but with a strong nucleus of progressive teachers and leadership, brought in some new top administrative officers. Steps were immediately set in motion to attack the curriculum through in-service committees. In this situation more attention to the *how* than the *why* characterized teacher participation in the program. This program, while democratic in intention, did by bandwagon appeal get into the core program teachers who were not eager for it or did not know exactly what it was all about. The result was some excellent core work, spotted by ragged, disjointed, hybrid work called core but not understood by the teachers. Criticisms from vested-interest teachers, and from confused teachers and laymen who saw only the grotesque aspects of the many unfortunate attempts at core work by teachers who admittedly did not know what they were about, placed a cloud over what should have been recognized as an educationally sound program. The core curriculum in that school system has experienced a slight, temporary setback.

It is of the utmost importance, not only for the advancement of desirable educational practices, but even more for the protection of the right of our children to the best in education, that progress be made slowly but surely.

School leaders contemplating the introduction of the core curriculum should be very conscious of the human equations involved. They must keep in mind that the introduction of the core curriculum into a school system operating with the traditional subject curriculum is a major undertaking. To most schools and teachers it means a drastic change in educational outlook and classroom procedures. Teachers, particularly the older ones, have been trained to think and teach subject matter. It was the kind of education they experienced from the first grade to college graduation, and it represents the skills they have developed over the years in classroom teaching. It is all they know; they have had no practical contacts with any other type of education.

It is not surprising that teachers are honestly hesitant to be rushed into radically new educational ideas that require drastic changes in classroom procedures, especially where guideposts are still too few and rule of thumb techniques do not fit. Although the public sometimes seems to disagree, teachers are human— very human. Like other people, they want security. And unlike most other people, after once being labeled a failure, a teacher has great difficulty in getting a new start. Experienced teachers who have achieved success with the traditional curriculum have demonstrated to themselves and to the community their ability to succeed. They have established in themselves a sense of assurance and security. As a teacher remarked a few weeks ago when she was about to return to her school for the second year: "How different I feel as I look forward to my work this year. Now I know I can do it. I have made good; I am accepted. Getting started made last year a trying one." This sense of security is not lightly cast aside.

For older teachers, habits of thinking and doing are hard to change. Legitimate question of their ability to make the change-over haunts many of them. They need careful orientation to the new, the unknown; they need every assurance that the adventure is experimental and that complete success at first is not expected. Some are more adventurous than others and display more flexibility or adaptability to the changes required. Some may not appear to be advisable risks because the adaptability demanded by the new may be beyond them.

Clear thinking is important as stock-taking proceeds. It must be kept in mind that there are certain definite personality traits or characteristics indispensable to success in the core curriculum. Although enlightened educational theory has stressed for a quarter of a century the introduction of more democratic procedures in the school, the subject curriculum bears within it the spirit of authoritarianism. Many older teachers have been trained and employed largely on the basis of their possession of the personality traits or characteristics appropriate to the older conception of education. These teachers need to be evaluated carefully in terms of their possible adaptability to the new patterns of teaching behavior required by the core curriculum. This may have much to do with questions of how to begin, where to begin, and how far the program can reasonably be expected to advance with the teacher resources at hand.

Young teachers are more flexible and do not have deeply fixed habits. What they may lack in experience they may more than make up by adaptability. Their educational training, being recent, is likely to be in harmony with the core curriculum, at least in spirit. Although it is true that teachers are made, not born, it is also true that many bring to their position a well-developed pattern of social traits or characteristics ideally suited to the core idea. These teachers become the potential assets as the situation is carefully surveyed.

Another aspect of teacher availability for the core curriculum is that of the balance and breadth of the training of the staff. Fortunate is the school contemplating the introduction of the core curriculum that has a staff of teachers with broad backgrounds of training rather than limited intensive training in a single field. More than a decade ago a school system intent on developing a more general educational program for its high school literally had to canvass the teacher training schools to find a teacher with a double major in English and social studies and a fair background in science. Extremely narrow specialization in its teaching staff has blocked effective introduction of the core curriculum in a number of schools. Even at the elementary level the emphasis a few years ago on arithmetic or reading specialization made core development in the grades difficult. The problem of integrating the special-interest areas of music, art, and physical education, for example, is made exceedingly difficult where teachers in these fields have little breadth of education or interest beyond their specialties. It is a real advantage to the school to take practical stock of its personnel availability for such a program. With a full knowledge of its weak spots, replacements and staff enlargements can be handled by the selection of teachers of broad educational background, social sensitivity and understanding, and training in modern educational thinking.

However, before plunging into the core curriculum a careful

appraisal should be made of other factors important to its success. Successful core curriculums have been found under conditions of adverse building facilities and shortages of equipment and supplies, but it takes an unusual staff of competent, loyal, devoted people to succeed under conditions in which teachers are asked "to make bricks without straw." It is difficult to create a wholesome working environment in poorly lighted, dingy rooms, with desks fastened to the floor and little else in the room to work with. A teacher assigned to a room of this sort once asked, "How can I conduct a core class in such a room, with its poor lights, poor seating facilities, and little material outside of the traditional class textbooks? It is bad on the eyes of the pupils. This room was made to recite in, not for study purposes." She was right. But being a highly creative person, determined to make the core idea work, this teacher did succeed in spite of the obstacles.

The conventional, narrow, rectangular rooms, with lights on one side and desks anchored to the floor in straight rows, were designed for lecture or recitation purposes, for which they are admirably adapted. But they are not adapted to a workroom situation, where flexibility of interior arrangements is desired to meet different types of workroom needs as they develop day by day or within a core block period. These are the handicaps with which new educational ideas must cope. New buildings cannot often be built; and although new lights and movable tables and chairs are not immediately available, ingenuity and determination can accomplish much. Some schools facing these conditions have mapped out a schedule to run several years within the budgetary limitations of the school, whereby new seating and equipment replace the old. One of the most successful core curriculums is carried on in a school where each year a certain number of new tables and chairs replace fixed desks. Complete replacements may be achieved in five years. About a third of the fixed seats in each room have been replaced by tables and chairs so far. A small school set a policy of room-by-room replacement of old desks by movable tables, on a yearly basis. This may be slow, but it keeps up morale. Another school, by special budgetary increases, made the change-over in seating and other room equipment a two-year plan.

The school must not forget that any departures from traditionally accepted practices must take into account community attitudes. At no point do school administrators fail more often than here. The wise school leader properly estimates possible community reaction and plans accordingly. Some communities may be expected to accept curriculum change eagerly, or, with little educational effort, to cooperate warmly. In others a careful program of enlightenment will be necessary, and a cautious program of change will be required. Wise administrators involve the community in a cooperative study of possible major curriculum change.

With these preliminary considerations in mind the school leadership has an intelligent basis on which to propose a tentative program. It can begin to assess its assets and liabilities with some confidence in the success of the venture. Out of such stock-taking the school should have a reasonably good idea of where and how to start.

2. launching an in-service study program[1]

There is a common saying that "to begin one should begin." But where and how is not always a matter of general agreement. In an earlier era of concern for curriculum change it was assumed that modifications of the curriculum should take place at the behest of subject experts or at least at the hands of the administrative leadership of the school. It was not uncommon for the curriculum to be determined and the texbooks to be selected by the school administrator, and by fiat imposed upon the school. The concepts basic to the subject matter curriculum appeared to be consistent with the ideas of authoritarianism then prevalent in school administration.

In a democratically conceived and projected program it is essential that the community and the school staff determine co-

---

[1] Certain aspects of this problem are discussed in Chapter 10.

operatively what curriculum changes are to be brought about. This is a test of the educational leadership of the school. Modern education assumes that teachers cannot effectively put into practice educational ideas they do not understand or plans they have had no part in creating.

Thus the second phase in a well-developed plan is to interest the staff and the community in a study of why curriculum change seems desirable, if not imperative. Although there may be a firm conviction that the end product of such a study will be the emergence of the core curriculum, it would be a violation of sound educational processes and thus of sound educational procedure deliberately to structure the community and staff study to insure that result. If, after a careful study of the reasons for a change in the curriculum, the community and staff decide on modifications short of a complete core curriculum, well and good. Whatever adjustments in the curriculum that result from a careful study of contemporary educational problems will no doubt result in marked improvement of the curriculum. There has been an impatience on the part of some to get to the practical matter of tinkering with the machine before discovering what was wrong with it and what ought to be done about it.

Older procedures in curriculum reorganization tended to follow a well-defined, sequential pattern of curriculum development— a somewhat stereotyped pattern of curriculum production which seemed appropriate to a subject matter type of curriculum, but now is considered inappropriate for a curriculum form based upon the conception of experience learning. Whereas the subject matter type curriculum often was characterized by exact identity of fixed patterns offered the schools, the experience-core curriculum is characterized by its flexible differentiation and adaptation to particular school communities and the learning needs of their children.

Contemporary thought and practice, therefore, favor beginning where curriculum problems make themselves evident. Thus, the initial point or points of attack upon the curriculum may vary widely between communities, and even between schools within a school system. Thoughtful efforts to find solutions to recognized curriculum problems, it is held, inevitably will lead to a consideration of the larger curriculum issues involved.

At this point it is important to suggest a danger, at least a caution, to curriculum workers. Although the principles of experience learning applied to modern curriculum-making indicate the value of beginning curriculum study where problems appear, it does not follow that such an approach inevitably leads to a critical overview of the curriculum in relation to the problem attacked. The very nature of the core curriculum concept makes imperative the need for all participants to see the curriculum as a whole in relation to its parts. All problems pinpointed for study should be so attacked as to involve a consideration of the immediate problem in the context of the total curricular concept.

The approach of two small school staffs in the organization of an in-service program may be suggestive. In both cases, the school leaders had aroused in a majority of the teachers a sense of dissatisfaction with the curriculum as it existed; the interest manifested by a large majority of the groups in a serious study of desirable curriculum changes initiated the study. The larger school system, with the advice of a consultant, organized a directing committee consisting of representatives of each school faculty in the system. This group met each week until a study plan agreed to by all was under way. After that the directing committee met every second week during the first year. The faculties met to listen to and discuss reports on phases of the curriculum taken from educational writings by selected teachers of the staff, or to carry on an open discussion after initial presentation of some curriculum issue by an educational authority brought to the meeting for the purpose. The second year, one of the local staff with special curriculum training, a person respected and accepted by the group, was made director of the study and freed for a couple of class periods to carry this extra work. The directing committee then met monthly to consider matters of general policy. It was not until the fourth year that the core curriculum was started in the secondary division, although by that time many elementary school teachers had shifted from subject to problem-situation emphasis.

The smaller school system, with elementary and secondary divisions housed in one building, had a similar beginning but made a more rapid change-over to the core curriculum. In contrast with the larger school system, this school of some thirty teachers had at the beginning of the study a young, alert staff, most of them doing advanced graduate work. Little initiating was required of the school principal, who had hired practically all the staff in several years at the head of this school. Several of the teachers were already innovating in their own fields. The staff agreed immediately to begin a sustained group attack upon the problem of curriculum. One consultant served both schools, and was thus in a position to note the evolution of curriculum change in both places. The high school principal served as a leader, and for all practical purposes the entire staff functioned as its own directing committee, often meeting twice a week to plan and study curriculum problems.

Almost from the outset, this staff began to apply new curriculum theory to the local situation; here and there the staff suggested modifications in practice as they saw more clearly the implications of educational philosophy and psychology for the local school curriculum. The following summer a majority of the staff attended a workshop at which there were representatives of the larger school systems. By the end of the six-week session, an advanced reorganization plan for the core curriculum to be introduced in much of the school at the fall opening had been worked out.

These schools may represent extremes in the initiating of a core curriculum. The authors are not familiar with any situation in which two schools have followed the same time sequence or identical procedures in introducing a core curriculum. The most successful have followed over-all plans that are basically similar but, in important respects, reflect the unique dissimilarities of the school communities.

An intensive, in-service educational program should keep in

mind that the average staff is already carrying a heavy teaching load. Teachers can be expected to add to their heavy schedule some extra time for a curriculum study project, but it helps morale and is simple justice to the teacher if planning reduces this time to a minimum. Much of the time devoted to faculty meetings is wasted in announcements and details that could be handled more expeditiously through mimeographed bulletins or small committees. This time could be appropriated for the study of modern education and the curriculum.

Launching a program of possible curriculum change is a matter of community concern. While the school staff is encouraged to study the why's and wherefore's of curriculum change, there should be a simultaneous effort to inaugurate a similar plan of study in the community, beginning with the school board. Certainly, little beyond the stage of faculty study of the curriculum can be done without the consent and support of the board. Although the board, theoretically, is the intermediary between the community and the school staff, the responsibility for educating the community in matters of education and curriculum rests with the leadership of the school.

The wise school leader has predisposed the members of the school board to favorable interest in a study of the curriculum before the matter has been seriously raised with the staff. As far as possible, the members of the school board should be in close touch with what is being studied by the staff in general. Some schools have brought at least one or two members of the board into the faculty study groups. It has been a common practice to have faculty-board-community dinners where specialists in curriculum discuss new developments in curriculum thinking and practice. Selected articles or books dealing with the core curriculum and related educational ideas should be placed in the hands of board members to read. The school board should be kept always fully informed and should give intelligent support to the program.

The same, of course, holds true for the community.[2] The necessity for full cooperation of the community in all school

_____
[2] See also Chapter 14, "The Community Can Help," in connection with this point.

matters has been repeatedly stressed. It is a *sine qua non* of the successful core curriculum. Learning through experience, an idea basic to the core curriculum, makes full community co-operation essential if boys and girls are really to have learning experiences in democratic living. Every member of the community should somehow be informed of new curricular developments and the lay leadership brought into active, cooperative study of the curriculum and its implications for the core curriculum. Through articles in the local papers and radio talks or interviews on modern educational developments, large sections of the public may be reached.

In one small community school, board members and members of different influential organizations were invited to attend faculty meetings on a given date. They were urged to return whenever they wished, but for the next faculty meeting other individuals were invited so that a wide range of representatives of these groups was brought in touch with the curriculum study project of the school. In another small school community, a dozen of the most influential and alert women became very interested in the school's study of the curriculum. They organized a study club and invited one of the leading young members of the school staff, who was studying for his doctorate in the curriculum field, to serve as their leader. He did this in addition to his regular participation in the faculty study. Later, when some criticism of the core curriculum came from newcomers to the community, these women were its most intelligent defenders. The ways in which the community can be involved in the study are legion. The success of the introduction of the core curriculum is dependent upon the extent to which the community is informed about it. Further, wherever there has been some opposition to the introduction of the core curriculum, it is largely the result of misunderstanding and ignorance of the meaning of this radical curriculum innovation.

3. *beginnings of the core*

However long or short the time taken for the two preceding phases, most schools find that after distinct periods devoted to deciding to launch a curriculum revision program and to careful study of what changes should take place, the time arrives when the core curriculum must be initiated— if it is the pattern of curriculum development decided upon by the staff. How to begin the core curriculum is a critical question. Getting off to a good start may have much to do with the success of later efforts toward complete change-over.

Usually it is easier to get started in the elementary school, where difficult administrative adjustments of time schedules are not involved. With teachers generally assigned all day to one grade class the shift to core is largely one of personal adjustment of the teacher to the organization of her work around problem situations based upon life needs rather than subjects. Her room schedule no longer will read "9:00-9:15 reading; 9:15-9:35, arithmetic" and so on. The teacher will have in mind some plan that will insure achievement of the competencies that were supposed to follow from an isolated study of these subjects. The problems most pressing in a life-needs program will be the vehicle used by the teacher with the introduction of different problem-situations as need and interest dictate. Frequently, by the time a beginning can be made in advanced elementary and secondary groups, the lower elementary classes have begun the use of the core. Many elementary school teachers may already have their classes organized with flexible programs on the problem basis, without benefit of "core" designation, when the issue becomes one of general school concern.

The difficulties in initiating a core curriculum are most serious at the secondary level, where class periods for specific subjects and teachers are the tradition. For that reason much of the discussion of this and succeeding steps will center around the difficulties encountered in shifting from the traditional subject-scheduled program to the flexible core curriculum.

Where it is necessary to readjust from a lockstep schedule of subject classes, it is important to select one or two places to make a beginning. A few very strong teachers with a broad background of training and successful teaching experience possessed of great leadership, tact, and social sensitivity, thoroughly sold on the new core idea, and eager to try the idea out, should be given the go-ahead. Weak or narrowly specialized teachers are not good risks to start the program.

Better than average physical facilities should probably be provided these pioneering teachers. If movable tables or movable unit desks are available, so much the better. It is often a question, in a school where the old fixed seats, limited equipment, and poor lights will take several years to replace, whether especially favorable conditions should be provided for the teachers who initiate the program. It is sometimes better to allow good teachers to demonstrate that it can be done under the less-than-ideal conditions they will be asked to face. It is much more important that library supplies be supplemented, as a large supply of different materials is essential to the core curriculum. Also the provision of a flexible time schedule through setting up of blocks of two or three hours is an absolute must to a real core atmosphere of flexibility and enlarged community resource opportunities.

It is important, too, that only in exceptional cases should teachers be expected to begin immediately in core classes. Even the most competent normally need to begin gradually in a transition from traditional teaching. Teachers should be encouraged to move over to life-needs problem situations as rapidly as possible. Some teachers with ingenuity and experience have begun at once by throwing textbooks aside and then, together with the class, mapping out a list of vital problems to study and moving forward from there. Once in a while an exceptional new teacher with an excellent background of training for core teaching can go ahead without subject crutches to lean on. But these teachers are few. The authors have in mind a fine young man, inexperienced but with much ability, who came from the training school and was eager to try out his ideas about the core in a new situation. Unfortunately, he was assigned two core groups and began each with a clean slate. Before he realized his difficulty, he was overwhelmed with his tasks. In that school he was without supervisory help, and consequently did such a poor job of teaching during the first semester that he did not regain his confidence or the administration's favor for the remainder of the year. A promising prospect, he is no longer teaching. A young but experienced tenth grade teacher, brought into a school already employing the core curriculum, approached the consultant with considerable anxiety and said: "I was brought here to handle tenth grade core classes but I do not understand how to start." She was advised to stay with the textbook used the previous year, before the two classes in this grade were put into the core, until some likely problem-situation arose in the class, and then to enlist class enthusiasm and eagerness to find an answer to the problem. After a few such experiences in helping the class attack some live problem, she would probably forget the texts and become absorbed with the class in their eager adventure in finding solutions to life-need problems of vital concern. In the meantime she was given help in understanding the core and how to teach it.

Most core curriculums, in fact, have begun by a slow, transition process. It seldom happens that a block of time in which vital problem situations alone are considered can be created without some transition interval to move from the familiar subject curriculum. Both parents and pupils are used to certain course requirements, which often have acquired a prestige far beyond reality. Sometimes it is forgotten by administrators that pupils' sense of security may be jeopardized if they are plunged into a core program. They have developed habits of reacting to a subject curriculum and have achieved some confidence in their ability to do so. Teachers have been surprised to discover that pupils did not react with enthusiasm to the first introduction of the core curriculum. The brighter the pupil, the more likely he will be to favor the old. But this should be expected. Not only do pupils want a sense of security, but the more efficient they are in the old, the greater their hesitancy to venture into the new lest they prove to be less efficient. In the long run, however, pupils once initiated into the core do not want to go back.

It is so with teachers also. They are seldom ready to accept a full core curriculum. Their own hesitancy to step off the deep end means that they must develop their skills and their sense of security through successful experimentation. During such an experimental or innovating transitional period, they may wish to retain recognizable course titles and patterns of course organization. Some overcautious teachers and schools have desired to begin with fusion and unified studies courses. Some have felt it desirable to begin even more cautiously, as is reported by Wright: "We have been working slowly toward this objective [core] by assigning 'blocks of time' to seventh- and eight-grade teachers—approximately one half day each with the same pupils. We hope to break down overdepartmentalization."[3] Other examples of the way successful core curriculums were initiated are typical and suggestive:

1. In one junior high school, a forty-five minute class period was combined with a thirty-five minute home room period. A core class developed within the resulting eighty-minute block after six years of persistent experimentation.

2. In another school, the ninth grade social studies and English were combined into a unified studies course. Later the home room period was added. Later still, the lines between the three periods were eliminated, teacher-pupil planning was perfected, and a core curriculum developed.

3. In a third school, a skillful sixth grade teacher was asked to continue into the seventh grade with her group, substituting her unit-type teaching for the separate subject program previously used in the seventh grade.

4. In another school, a team of three ninth grade teachers undertook a unified approach with three sections of students numbering about 100. The course titles were English, civics, and science. A fourth period was assigned for teacher planning and for counseling students. In effect, the three conventional subjects tended to become blended into core classes.

All of these devices, and many others that might be cited, have been used as means of launching core curriculums on the basis of conventional course titles and modified subject organization. In some schools a combination of subjects such as American

---

[3] Grace S. Wright, *Core Curriculum in Public High Schools, An Inquiry into Practices, 1949.* Washington, D. C.: U. S. Office of Education, 1950, p. 15.

history and American literature has been effected for the initial purpose of better correlation of the content of these courses. Where such correlation has been achieved within a two-hour block of time, it is very easy to shift over to the core idea. In fact, that has been a recognized way for cautious teachers to make the transition.

Needless to say, there are hazards as well as benefits involved in efforts to launch a core curriculum while retaining the conventional structure and nomenclature. Experience in many schools has indicated that correlation or unified studies programs may never lead to anything else. Unless these stepping-stones on the way to the core curriculum are labeled for what they are, and not permitted to be loosely or carelessly classified as core, they may lead to great confusion. Many people who are not technically grounded in educational terminology, and who visit schools that claim to be on the core basis but are actually at the level of correlation or unified studies, come away confused, and often comment: "There was nothing wonderful about that. Why all the fuss about the core curriculum?" If too many concessions are made to the insecure teacher, or administrator, it may turn out that security has been achieved at the expense of everything else. If the same old things go on in the larger block of time, the program will not have been basically improved for pupils. Indeed, it is possible that some of the students may find themselves in a worse plight than in the single-period program. They can scarcely be blamed if they prefer not to be tied to an inferior teacher for more than a single period if there is no compensating improvement in the curriculum.

In spite of these hazards, many schools have been able to develop an effective core curriculum by beginning with subject combinations. It would appear that progressive improvement takes place when certain factors obtain:

1. A strong democratic, liberal leader must be present, usually in the administrative staff of the school. In very rare cases this leadership has developed among teachers when the administrator was merely permissive or acquiescent.

2. An intelligent program of community interpretation is required.
3. Resources and opportunities for in-service education of teachers are a necessity.
4. The total staff of the school must retain a definite orientation to the core curriculum and sympathy toward its goal.
5. A climate of experimentation must characterize the teaching in the school.
6. Teachers must come to set more store upon human values and social adjustments goals than upon mastery of any given area of knowledge or skill.

If these conditions obtain, the core may emerge from a combined subject beginning. The nearer the school starts to a life-needs problem situation basis in core classes, the more assurance there is that the core curriculum will be utilized.

The in-service education of teachers needs to be continued and intensified during this brief period. More teachers should be getting ready to begin core teaching. Workshops, extension courses, ten-day institutes preceding the fall opening of school, and special faculty study of the further implications of modern education for the core curriculum should go forward. The community should be increasing its participation in planning the program. By this time, the older pupils should be sharing in the study of the significance of the core for them. Modern curriculum theory and practice include the pupil as an important element in the scheme of school-community cooperation.

At this point, before classes are actually initiated into the core, it may be well to find out what the attitude of the state department of education may be toward such innovations. These departments are rapidly introducing flexibility into the regulations governing the school curriculum, in conformity with modern educational theory, and in keeping with research studies that have shown there is no justification for rigid subject prescriptions. Recent studies also reveal that the attitudes of state officials are far ahead of prevailing school practice, and are favorably disposed toward the core curriculum. Nonetheless, it might avoid embarrassment if the local school checked to be sure it was not going beyond curriculum changes that would be approved by the state educational officials.

4. *increasing the tempo of core change*

It is important that the school move forward as rapidly as the mood of the staff and community permits. After a brief try-out period of one semester or one year by one or two selected teachers, the program should expand rapidly from the elementary school through the senior high school and into the junior college, if such exists.

The staff should begin planning the reorganization of the more academic phases of the school curriculum to better serve the educational implications of the core curriculum. If, for example, the school under the core curriculum, is realistic about its essential guidance function, it must make adequate provision for every core teacher to have the time and facilities for personal conferences with boys and girls, and with their parents as well. This has not been a function of the teacher in the traditional subject curriculum, but it is the very heart of the core curriculum. The organization of the core in large blocks of time serves many purposes, not the least important of which is guidance. Providing time for a more informal attack upon problem situations that develop competencies to make adequate personal adjustment is one important aspect of the guidance function of modern education made possible by large time blocks within the core organization.

Further, the core organization makes the home room of the traditional curriculum a part of the core. The home room has never functioned as a real guidance center. It is extraneous to the subject curriculum concept of education. Meeting for twenty, forty, or even fifty minutes in formal classrooms, with no real ties between teacher and pupil, does not provide the environment of the core situation. The teacher with two core groups totaling 50 to 70 pupils, instead of the 150 to 200 found under the old plan, can come to know each pupil and his needs much more profoundly. Ordinary guidance of the pupil can take place to best advantage where informality of the program enables the teacher to deal with pupils individually.

However, to carry through successfully the modern idea of educational and personal guidance means that the teacher must have additional free time to talk with pupils on extraordinary phases of their personal adjustments and needs. Then there are parents who must be brought into the picture if the needs of children are to be fully met. Too, modern education within the core curriculum envisages extensive community relationships. The teacher from elementary through secondary school must have free time for conferences to this end. At this stage, the school should be planning and effecting a change in schedule organization to provide an extra hour for the teacher to meet pupils, parents, and public, as well as to have some time to plan and care for details of the general program.

Likewise, if the educational guidance function is to be realized to best advantage, provision must be made for contact of a teacher with core groups over longer time intervals than are possible in a one-semester or one-year subject course of the traditional school. The school must plan the reorganization of its program to increase the length of time teachers remain with their core groups to two or three years. This has already been discussed.

The experience of schools operating on the core plan indicates that more time is needed for general and special faculty group consultations to implement the guidance function. A flexible program subject to frequent changes necessitates constant group planning and frequent opportunity for consultation. One large junior high school carrying on a successful core curriculum has found it necessary to have lengthy faculty meetings one afternoon a week, and a shorter meeting each week in the morning, before the opening of school. The morning meeting sometimes involves the entire faculty, but usually the faculty meets in smaller groups concerned with more specific problems of coordination of the general guidance program. On the morning the faculty meets, school begins a half-hour later than usual and the faculty comes to school a half-hour earlier, providing a full hour for consultations. In the afternoon the pupils are dismissed forty-five minutes early so that additional time is provided for a longer faculty meeting. A certain small school faculty, during this stage in their developing core curriculum, often met every afternoon after school until the dinner hour. Scarcely a week passed that this group did not meet two or three times. However, this was a highly motivated group; it effected a complete shift of program in an unusually short time. This phase of the emerging core should be carefully planned by the school staff at this stage in the developing program. Otherwise, the curriculum is likely to lack that coordination so necessary for the proper guidance of the total learning activities of the pupil.

At the junior and senior high school levels, attention should now be directed to what aspects of the total school curriculum should be given over to special-interest areas, and in what way these areas are to be related to the basic core program. Although the core program is specifically concerned with the aspects of behavioral competencies that all should possess in some degree, it cannot be developed in isolation from these special-interest areas of avocational, special aptitude, and vocational life. Education must be a total pattern that meets all the needs of children, and must be fully integrated. There is general agreement in educational circles that the core concept should involve the entire elementary school program. Educational and curriculum leaders are in general agreement that special avocational interests should begin to receive attention at the junior high school level. Probably 80 per cent of the curriculum should be essentially core in nature.

Interests of a more technical vocational nature, all agree, must make up part of the senior high school curriculum. As one phase of modern education, stress upon adjustment competencies for life needs obviously involves development of the more specific behavioral competencies needed to make a living. Whatever conflict in theory and practice at the junior high school level still exists on this score is largely a holdover from the theory behind the establishment of this division of the school around 1910. Now that the conditions that justified a vocational emphasis at that time have ceased to exist, educators see no justification for provision of technical vocational work at the junior high school level.[4]

At any rate, the school staff must now begin to think of what part of the total schedule of the school at the various educational levels should be devoted to the core program, and how the core program and special-interest areas are to be integrated. The ideal is, "every teacher a core teacher." Ultimately, every teacher in the school should be tied into the core program by teaching at least one core group. This would guarantee that special-interest areas would be taught by teachers who understood the relation of common competencies for all to individual avocational and vocational interests. It would insure continuation of the basic methodology of the experience-learning process into the entire school experience of the pupil. At present, there is no reason for the absence of such integration throughout the junior high school, and in time it should include all vocational teachers in the senior high school.

At this stage of the developing core curriculum, if this problem has not previously arisen, schools should come to grips with the problem of how to evaluate learning as now conceived, and how such learning progress is to be reported to parents and defined for the school records. Even the tryout teachers in the previous step faced this question. It can no longer be sidestepped when much of the curriculum is being organized on the core basis.

Educators are agreed that the concept of learning as change in behavior through experience requires a fundamentally different approach in evaluation from that required of the traditional concept of information learning. It is not achieved by simple pencil and paper tests of information acquired. These tests, however, may be used judiciously to check the adequacy of the factual basis for understanding the kind of behavior appropriate in a given situation, and how this behavior may be modified. It is, of course, necessary to remember that behavior changes do not occur in an

---

[4] See Educational Policies Commission, *Education for All American Youth,* Revised. Washington, D. C.: The National Education Association, 1952, pp. 45 and 220 ff for a consideration of the core curriculum through the junior high school.

intellectual vacuum. Data are essential in the determination of needs, goals, purposes, and rational planning for their realization. But the focus of evaluation of learning as change in behavior must be on the degree of behavioral change that takes place. A more detailed discussion of the problem of evaluation will be presented in Chapter 15.

5. completion of the change-over to the core curriculum

It may take from three to five or even eight years to effect a complete reorientation of the secondary school program and organization. At the secondary level, the traditional segmentation of the program organization into watertight compartmentalized subjects, specialized teachers, and fifty-minute class schedules, makes complete change-over a process of years. In fact, few if any senior high schools have yet made the complete change visualized in the previous discussion.

Whatever degree of ultimate change-over the school staff and community consider possible within a reasonable time period should now be effected. It must never be lost sight of that a completely effective core curriculum involves the totality of the educational program.

It is in this period that final decisions must be made on what part of the total program of the school is to be devoted to core and what part to special interests. For example, what changes in proportional emphasis between core and special-interest areas are to be made at different grade levels through the twelfth grade, or the thirteenth and fourteenth, if these are present? What possible consolidations or eliminations of special-interest areas need to be made? How can an over-all, flexible but guiding schedule be worked out to care for the program adjustment contemplated? Some administrators hastily conclude this cannot be done; others with imagination and courage are making satisfactory adjustments in school schedules.

Attention is called to an over-all division of time for the core and special-interest areas for Grades 10 to 14 suggested as a practical beginning by the Educational Policies Commission of

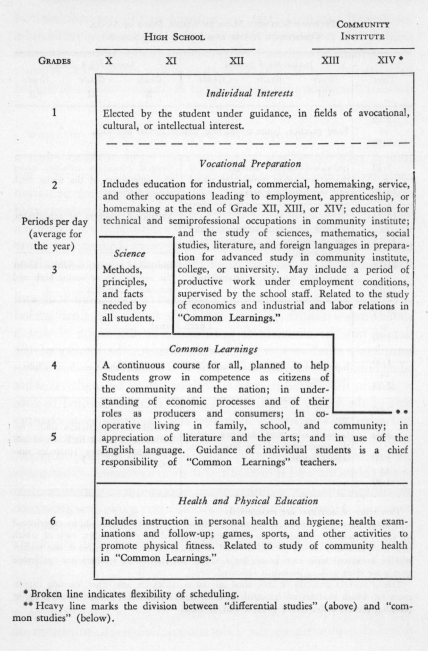

| | | HIGH SCHOOL | | | COMMUNITY INSTITUTE |

GRADES | X | XI | XII | XIII | XIV *

Individual Interests

1 Elected by the student under guidance, in fields of avocational, cultural, or intellectual interest.

Vocational Preparation

2 Includes education for industrial, commercial, homemaking, service, and other occupations leading to employment, apprenticeship, or homemaking at the end of Grade XII, XIII, or XIV; education for technical and semiprofessional occupations in community institute;

Periods per day (average for the year)

Science

3 Methods, principles, and facts needed by all students.

and the study of sciences, mathematics, social studies, literature, and foreign languages in preparation for advanced study in community institute, college, or university. May include a period of productive work under employment conditions, supervised by the school staff. Related to the study of economics and industrial and labor relations in "Common Learnings."

Common Learnings

4 A continuous course for all, planned to help Students grow in competence as citizens of the community and the nation; in understanding of economic processes and of their roles as producers and consumers; in cooperative living in family, school, and community; in

5 appreciation of literature and the arts; and in use of the English language. Guidance of individual students is a chief responsibility of "Common Learnings" teachers.

**

Health and Physical Education

6 Includes instruction in personal health and hygiene; health examinations and follow-up; games, sports, and other activities to promote physical fitness. Related to study of community health in "Common Learnings."

* Broken line indicates flexibility of scheduling.
** Heavy line marks the division between "differential studies" (above) and "common studies" (below).

PROPOSED SCHEDULE MADE BY SCHOOL STAFF OF SMALL
COMMUNITY JUNIOR AND SENIOR HIGH SCHOOL

Time	Junior High School			Senior High School		
	Grade VII	Grade VIII	Grade IX	Grade X	Grade XI	Grade XII
8:45 to 9:30	Band practice, home room, and certain special activities.					
9:30 to 10:30	Individual-interest activities under the supervision of junior high school and vocational teachers.			General education activities under the supervision of the senior high school teachers.		
10:30 to 11:15	General education activities under the supervision of the junior high school teachers.			Vocational teachers as consultants.		
11:15 to 12:15	Vocational teachers as consultants.			Individual-interest activities under the supervision of senior high and vocational teachers.		
12:15 to 1:00	Lunch Period					
1:00 to 2:00	Individual activities under supervision of all high school teachers. Clubs— Intramurals.					
2:00 to 3:00 3:00 to 4:00	General education activities under the supervision of the junior high school teachers.			Special-interest activities under supervision of senior high school and vocational teachers (includes athletics).		

Two types of activities are recognized:

General education activities represent those learning activities that should be experienced by all. The school is divided into seven groups labeled by year number, each of which will work as a unit during periods devoted to general education. In general, one teacher will be associated with each group for a school year, although teachers may exchange groups for short or long periods if indicated.

Special interest activities or individual-interest activities are any other learning experiences for which students are grouped on other bases: vocational, college preparatory, or remedial classes, clubs, hobby groups, and so forth.

the National Education Association. This commission believes the core program should utilize the complete time of the junior high school.[5] Their plan for Grades 10 to 14 appears on page 233.

CORE PROGRAM PROPOSED IN A LARGE CITY
JUNIOR AND SENIOR HIGH SCHOOL

Class Periods	Seventh Grade	Eighth Grade	Ninth Grade	Tenth Grade
I	Core	Core	Core	Core
II	Core	Core	Core	Core
III	Core	Core	Core	Core
	Lunch	Lunch	Lunch	Lunch
IV	Arithmetic	Arithmetic	Applied Mathematics, Algebra, or General Science	Elective
V	Gym and Health	Gym and Health	Gym and Health	Gym and Health
VI	Ind. Arts Food and Clothing	Ind. Arts Home Making	Ind. Arts Elective	Ind. Arts Elective
VII	Music and Art	Music and Art Speech	Elective	Elective

On pages 305 and 307 are examples of efforts to develop the core program into the total curriculum pattern of the school within the practical limitations imposed by local conditions. These schools would represent the fourth phase in their stage of development, with the first example approximating the organizational ideal of Phase Five.

PROCEDURES IN DEVELOPING A CORE CURRICULUM

Similar schedules have been employed in larger high schools, both the four-year and the three-year types. Space limitations prevent

[5] Educational Policies Commission, *Education for All American Youth,* Revised, 1952, p. 233. For the Commission's position that common learnings should make up the entire program of the junior high school period, see this same work, p. 220.

the reproduction of these more complex schedules here, but it should be pointed out that many large schools employ schedules that are broken down into more manageable units, some of which provide for core classes for students of a given grade level. The reader may be interested in examining sample schedules of larger high schools, such as are included in French, Hull, and Dodds, *American High School Administration*,[6] and Faunce, *Secondary School Administration*.[7]

At the beginning of this chapter it was said that no two schools or communities were alike. While the broad procedural phases outlined are essential to the successful development of a core curriculum in any school, the way in which each phase is carried forward must be adapted to the local situation. These points are again emphasized in conclusion not only because of their importance, but also because these apparently obvious truths are often ignored in practice.

SELECTED REFERENCES

Alberty, Harold, *Reorganizing the High School Curriculum,* Revised. New York: The Macmillan Company, 1953, Chapters VIII and XVI.

Alexander, William, and Galen Saylor, *Secondary Education.* New York: Rinehart & Company, 1950, Chapter XV.

American Association of School Administrators, *Public Relations for America's Schools,* The Twenty-eighth Yearbook. Washington: The National Education Association, 1950.

Anderson, Vernon E., *Principles and Procedures of Curriculum Improvement.* New York: The Ronald Press Company, 1956, Chapters VIII-XI.

Bossing, Nelson L., *Principles of Secondary Education,* Second Edition. Englewood Cliffs, N. J.: Prentice-Hall, Inc., 1955, Chapters XII-XIII.

Caswell, Hollis L., and associates, *Curriculum Improvement in Public*

---

[6] Will French, Dan Hull, and B. L. Dodds, *American High School Administration.* New York: Rinehart and Company, 1951, pp. 328-332.

[7] Roland C. Faunce, *Secondary School Administration.* New York: Harper and Brothers, 1955, Chapter 13.

School Systems. New York: Bureau of Publications, Teachers College, Columbia University, 1950.

Doll, Ronald C., and others, *Organizing for Curriculum Improvement.* New York: Bureau of Publications, Teachers College, Columbia University, 1953.

Douglass, Harl R., Editor, *The High School Curriculum,* Revised. New York: The Ronald Press Company, 1956, Chapters XVI, XVII, and XX.

Educational Policies Commission, *Education For All American Youth,* Revised. Washington, D. C.: The National Education Association, 1952, Chapters V-IX.

Faunce, Roland C., *Secondary School Administration.* New York: Harper and Brothers, 1955, Chapter 13.

French, Will, J. Dan Hull, and B. L. Dodds, *American High School Administration.* New York: Rinehart & Co., 1951, Chapter 16.

Gwynn, J. Minor, *Curriculum Principles and Social Trends.* New York: The Macmillan Company, 1950, pp. 167-176.

Jacobson, P. B., W. C. Reavis, and J. D. Logsdon, *The Effective School Principal: In Elementary and Secondary Schools.* Englewood Cliffs, N. J.: Prentice-Hall, Inc., 1954, VII.

Krug, E. A., C. D. Babcock, J. G. Fowlkes, and H. T. James, *Administering Curriculum Planning.* New York: Harper and Brothers, 1956.

Leonard, J. Paul, *Developing the Secondary School Curriculum,* Revised. New York: Rinehart & Company, 1953, Chapters XII and XIII.

Menge, J. Wilmer, and Roland C. Faunce, *Working Together for Better Schools.* New York: American Book Company, 1953.

Mudd, Dorothy, *A Core Program Grows.* Bel Air, Maryland: The Harford County Board of Education, 1949, Chapter II.

Noar, Gertrude, *The Junior High School—Today and Tomorrow.* Englewood Cliffs, N. J.: Prentice-Hall, Inc., 1953, Part II.

Planning and Working Together, Bulletin 337. Lansing, Michigan: Department of Public Instruction, 1945, Chapters X, XI, XIII.

Romine, Stephen A., *Building the High School Curriculum.* New York: The Ronald Press Company, 1955, Chapters XV and XVI.

Spears, Harold, *The High School For Today.* New York: American Book Company, 1950, Chapter VII.

310 PROCEDURES IN DEVELOPING A CORE CURRICULUM

The Core Program. Howard County, Maryland: Howard County Public Schools, 1949.

The Story of Holtville. Holtville, Alabama: Southern Association Study, 1944, pp. 5-20.

Youth Learns to Assume Responsibility, Michigan Secondary Curriculum Study. Lansing, Michigan: State Department of Public Instruction, 1944, pp. 66-77.

Chapter 14

The Community Can Help

Fear of public opinion has forestalled much educational progress. School administrators and teachers frequently act as though the public were the school's enemy and that the school's activities should be kept secret. It is common for school people to become cautious, even reactionary, in their conceptions of what parents and the community in general will think of new ideas that the school would like to initiate. But few school people have actually tried to discover what the community thinks. They seem to forget that the schools belong to the community.

In many situations where the opinion of lay citizens about curriculum revisions has been sought, it has been found that their collective judgment is considerably in advance of that of the local school personnel. It is a discredit to the leadership of our schools that so many significant advances in educational practice have been forced upon them by the public rather than instituted by adventurous local school leadership. It is true that some school programs have foundered on the rocks of public opinion, largely because of misunderstanding of the nature of the programs; many

311

more have never been launched because of fear of public opposition. The core curriculum, like many another educational innovation, has suffered from the habit of presupposing public opposition and failing to interpret school programs to the public intelligently. It is important that the schools become aware of the actual sentiment of the communities they serve. It is equally essential that there be much better rapport between the school and the public, so that the school can render its most effective service to the community. Modern education cannot be effective without full cooperation of the community and full awareness of the resources available in community cooperation.

What Do People Think of the School Program?

Although every school should seek to learn what the particular community it serves thinks of its program, much may be learned from studies already made in other school-community situations. A few examples from among the many such studies available are given here to indicate that public thinking is generally in advance of school practice.

In 1938-39, parents and other lay citizens in eighteen school communities in Michigan were asked to respond anonymously to a questionnaire about the goals of the secondary schools. Part I of the questionnaire asked for judgments as to the relative importance of twenty common goals. The responses of 4040 lay citizens to this question are summarized in Table 1.

An analysis of these responses gives little support to the theory that the public is holding back curriculum improvement. In the column *Great Importance,* the ten items that received over 50 per cent of the votes were, in order of their ranking:

1. To make intelligent decisions for himself .... 92 per cent
2. To plan for himself ways of meeting his own problems . 90 per cent
3. To judge for himself whether his work in school is satisfactory or unsatisfactory .... 82 per cent
4. To understand and to meet the problems related to living in the home .... 80 per cent

5. To collect and use information about his own problems 70 per cent

6. To cooperate with other boys and girls in working on
their own problems .... 67 per cent

7. To cooperate with other boys and girls and with adults
in working on problems in the community .... 67 per cent

8. To take part in social affairs with other boys and girls . 65 per cent

9. To understand and make use of important principles of
science that he can apply in everyday life .... 63 per cent

10. To select and participate in satisfactory kinds of recreation .... 54 per cent

It may be observed that those ten goals regarded as of great importance are essentially social goals—the educational goals important to the success of a democratic society, and to the individual who would participate in the democratic way of living. These are the educational goals that the vanguard of educational leaders in America have been stressing for the past three decades; they are, regrettably, only slightly emphasized in the actual practice of the schools, often because of distrust or fear of public sentiment by local school leadership.

It is equally interesting to see the evaluation of the goals that the schools have traditionally stressed and have exemplified in practice. The ability to solve geometry and algebra problems was regarded as of great importance by respectively 21 and 28 per cent of the laymen; foreign language study was thought important by only 19 per cent; and the Quiz Kids type of memory learning (Question two) could arouse the enthusiasm of only 8 per cent of the respondents.

It appears that these 4040 lay citizens judged the traditional subject-matter goals of little importance in comparison with social goals. This survey of citizen opinion about the curriculum has been cited in some detail because five of these eighteen schools were organized on the core curriculum basis. The survey indicates that a large section of representative parents and lay citizens are ready to accept the goals of education emphasized in the philosophy and practice of core curriculum organization of the curriculum. For the most part, the educational thinking of these school

TABLE I

Questions	Degree of Importance				
Is it important that the school should help your son or daughter to learn:	Great Importance (per cent)	Some Importance (per cent)	Little Importance (per cent)	No Importance (per cent)	No Opinion (per cent)
1. To make intelligent decisions for himself?	92	6	1	1	0
2. To answer questions about famous authors of the past?	8	45	32	12	3
3. To enjoy music?	41	46	10	2	1
4. To plan for himself ways of meeting his own problems, both in school and out of school?	90	8	1	1	0
5. To solve algebra problems?	28	42	22	5	3
6. To select and participate in satisfactory kinds of recreation?	54	35	7	2	2
7. To be a scientist?	11	25	32	18	13
8. To enjoy art?	19	47	23	6	5
9. To read a foreign language?	19	42	23	11	4
10. To take part in social affairs with other boys and girls?	65	27	5	2	1
11. To understand and to meet the problems related to living in the home?	80	13	4	2	1
12. To solve geometry problems?	21	37	25	12	5
13. To be a skilled musician?	18	30	28	16	8
14. To collect and use information about his own problems?	70	20	6	3	1
15. To write in a foreign language?	17	30	28	19	6
16. To cooperate with other boys and girls in working on their own problems?	67	23	6	3	1
17. To be an artist?	15	22	30	23	10
18. To cooperate with other boys and girls and with adults in working on problems in the community?	67	25	5	2	1
19. To understand and make use of important principles of science that he can apply in everyday life?	63	28	6	1	2
20. To judge for himself whether his work in school is satisfactory or unsatisfactory?	82	13	3	1	1

communities is distinctly ahead of the educational practices of their schools.[1]

Another sampling of opinion of parents and citizens may be pertinent because of the type of community studied. It is a Minnesota community of average economic status, stable and conservative in its socio-economic attitudes. A questionnaire was sent to a representative selection of families in the community. One of the questions listed what were considered to be ten major purposes of schools in a democracy. The citizens were asked to indicate whether, in their judgment, the schools were achieving these objectives.

The percentages are shown for each question.

TABLE II

GENERAL PUBLIC'S EVALUATION OF SUCCESS OF THE SCHOOL
IN ACHIEVEMENT OF EDUCATIONAL PURPOSES

Question	Per Cent Voting		
	Yes	No	Un-certain
1. The achievement of proficiency in such basic skills as arithmetic, reading, writing, and speech	86.5	6.7	6.7
2. The development of physical and mental health knowledge and habits	76.2	11.4	12.4
3. The development of the ability to meet and effectively solve the usual problems of life	52.9	14.7	32.4
4. The acquisition of the desire and ability to spend one's leisure time for some desirable purpose	54.2	21.9	24.0
5. The appreciation of and ability to cooperate in furthering more desirable home and family life	49.5	16.2	34.3
6. The preparation of youth for successful vocational life	63.1	24.3	12.6
7. The development of a greater sense of the beautiful in life—music, art, etc.	68.9	12.6	18.4
8. The preparation of youth so that those who so desire may find ready admission to college	84.5	2.9	12.6
9. The development of useful work and study habits	64.7	17.6	17.6
10. The development of desirable social behavior	52.4	19.4	28.2

[1] This survey of lay opinion is quoted more completely, along with references to several other similar surveys, in *Youth Learns to Assume Responsibility,* Michigan Secondary School Curriculum Study. Lansing, Michigan: The State Department of Public Instruction, 1944, pp. 86-92.

The citizens were asked to indicate how well they thought the school was educating children in reference to the ten education purposes presented. Some idea of the value of these purposes is revealed indirectly by the number who were negative or uncertain. The three educational objectives the people thought the schools were achieving best were (1) teaching the three R's, (2) preparation for college admission, and (3) development of physical and mental health. On the other hand, the three objectives that modern educators generally would rate highest in importance were judged by the citizens to be poorly taught: the one rated lowest in achievement was that of desirable home and family life, the next-lowest was the development of desirable social behavior, and the third from the bottom was the ability to meet the problems of life.

To check the opinion of the community as to the relative importance of these purposes, the citizens were asked to indicate in order of importance what they considered to be the three major purposes of education. The combined ranking of the ten purposes is given below.[2]

TABLE III

CITIZENS' RANKINGS OF RELATIVE IMPORTANCE
OF EDUCATIONAL OBJECTIVES

Purposes	Combined Rank
1. Acquisition of skills	1
2. Physical and mental health	4
3. Ability to meet usual problems of life	2
4. Worthy use of leisure time	10
5. Desirable home and family life	7
6. Successful vocational life	3
7. Appreciation of the beautiful	8
8. Preparation for college	9
9. Useful work and study habits	6
10. Social behavior	5

It is interesting to note the traditional emphasis upon the three R's, and encouraging to note that the objective second-

[2] Adapted from Nelson L. Bossing and Leo J. Brueckner, *The Impact of the War on the Schools of Red Wing*, No. 5, The Community Basis for Postwar Planning. Minneapolis: University of Minnesota Press, 1945, pp. 86-87.

highest in importance is the ability to meet usual problems of
life. The low ranking of home and family life is surprising, but
the low rating of college preparation shows community discern-
ment. In the judgment of success of school practice, preparation
for college ranked second and was pressing the basic skills for
first place. Even in such a conservative milieu the citizenry in
general is ahead of school practice in its judgment of what the
schools should do. It is interesting to note that if desirable home
and family life were substituted for successful vocational life in
ranking, the first six purposes selected by the community would be
in full harmony with the general purposes of the core curriculum.

The *Minneapolis Tribune* conducts throughout Minnesota an
opinion poll covering major issues of general interest. The merits
of modern education, including sex education, have been brought
to the public attention by small but voluble groups. While interest
was high, these issues were featured in the Minnesota Poll of
Public Opinion. For the most part schools have been chary about
offering instruction in sex education for fear of public disapproval.
It is interesting that a newspaper, not the school, set out to find
out what the public actually thought about this supposedly ticklish
subject. The poll revealed that only five per cent of the parents
thought their children were getting sex education, while 68 per
cent of the parents with children in school and 65 per cent of a
cross-section of adults believed sex education should be taught in
the schools.

Again, with the question of the merits of modern education,
particularly the core or common learnings program, versus traditional education, the vocal minority usually tries to pass itself off
as a majority. The Minnesota Poll of Public Opinion revealed that
61 per cent of the citizens believe the schools of today do a better
job of teaching the basic skills, whereas 14 per cent think the
schools do a worse job of teaching these skills. On the issue of
whether today's schools do a better job of preparing boys and girls
to meet the problems of adult life, 64 per cent of the citizens
believe they do, and only seven per cent believe they do not.
Seventy-four per cent of the people either had never heard of or

did not know what was meant by the core or common learnings curriculum; of those who did, nearly twice as many favored it as were opposed.[3]

Many remember the "Pasadena" school affair of 1950, where a small vociferous group of ultraconservatives under the guise of opposition to modern educational ideas and increased school taxes stampeded the Board of Education into the removal of its superintendent. Later, when a careful community study was made, it was found that the solid citizenry in the ratio of six to one favored better schools at the cost of higher taxes, the desirability of teaching pupils how to deal with controversial issues, the teaching of morals and manners in the school, attention to world affairs, and by a ratio of more than four to one citizens urged the school's acceptance of responsibility for sex education.[4]

The findings of these studies are similar to those of many other studies that have been made. Our trouble lies in the fact that we often fail to seek the understanding and cooperation of the lay public. We even fail to find out what their opinions are.[5]

Community support for school programs must be based upon complete mutual understanding. Such understanding, in turn, can only be achieved by the involvement of parents and other lay citizens in planning, executing, and evaluating the school program. This is not true of the core curriculum alone. Any curriculum innovation lays an unusual burden upon the understanding of lay citizens, and accordingly presents school people with an unusual challenge to secure lay participation in the program. The introduction of the core curriculum, however, places unusually heavy emphasis upon a vigorous program of cooperative school-community planning.

[3] See *Minneapolis Sunday Tribune,* March 25 and June 11, 1950, for fuller details of the Minnesota Poll of Public Opinion on the issues of sex education and modern education.

[4] Clyde M. Hill and Lloyd N. Morrisett, *Pasadena Faces the Future: Survey Report,* Abridged. Pasadena, California: Geddes Press, 1952, Chapter 4; also David Hulburd, *This Happened in Pasadena.* New York: The Macmillan Company, 1951.

[5] A stimulating discussion of the importance and technique of getting valid opinion reactions concerning the schools, with samples of inventory questions for such polls, will be found in Harold C. Hand, *What People Think About Their Schools.* New York: World Book Company, 1948.

How Utilize the Community Survey
in the Core Curriculum?

One of the first steps in such school-community planning is a
survey of the community. A weakness of most school children,
even through secondary school, is ignorance of their own communities. They may know their neighborhood reasonably well
but they have only a very superficial idea of the structure and
functioning of their community. A survey of its governing
institutions, how they operate and how they affect the lives of the
people, is always a fruitful study. An inquiry into such matters
as the manner in which the water supply is provided, its whole-
someness safeguarded, its adequacy assured is valuable in developing appreciations of community living and of the interdependence
of the citizens for their general welfare. The fact that this is a
problem facing many communities can easily be illustrated by
pointing out the difficulties of some large cities in securing adequate water supplies.

Such surveys can furnish a rich basis of learning experiences
for core classes. They are naturally adapted to problem-situation
emphasis. Studies of this kind, properly made, alert the student
to critical appraisals of the merits of community activities and
functions. Shortages and needs within the community and weaknesses in the structure and functioning of existing institutions and
agencies are revealed. Students in core classes have made surveys
of such vital matters of personal and community concern as
occupational opportunities in the community, housing, health,
traffic, safety, parks and other recreational facilities, industries,
merchandising methods, community history and background,
labor-management relations, population trends, churches, schools,
municipal government, and politics.

Recurrent surveys of this kind can provide information, pose
problems, and point out community needs. They can furnish
vitally stimulating resource materials for learning activity. The
importance of such surveys to the classes concerned is brought

out in the summary of values a class felt it received from conducting an opinion poll on important current political questions. These values are listed in order of their importance as judged by the class.

1. Gained an understanding of current problems
2. Learned how to conduct a poll
3. Learned to write a clear and interesting letter
4. Discovered opinions of different types of people
5. Learned how to interview
6. Enjoyed meeting new persons
7. Enjoyed the change from regular class work
8. Found that people are cooperative and intelligent
9. Found it lots of fun
10. Would like to conduct another poll [6]

To the extent that valid information about the community is collected and used in core classes, the school and community will draw closer together and a base will be laid for strong community support of the instructional program.

As indicated above, a valuable by-product of the class study of the life of the community is the interest in the school stimulated in the community by these pupil-conducted surveys. Community contact with the school through pupils' personal visits and interviews with citizens in these various projects becomes in time quite extensive. In one way or another, many of these studies enlist the cooperation of community groups in correcting weaknesses brought to light. These groups will be keenly interested in the outcomes, and in student interpretation of the data. Often a fresh and guileless directness of approach in interpreting data of community significance is a characteristic of student thinking. The results of such studies can be used by core classes, by the school faculty, and by community groups, for an honest analysis of the needs of the community. Students, teachers, and lay citizens become joined in a common effort and the school program is energized by community interaction.

[6] John B. Learson, "Ninth Graders Conduct a Public Opinion Poll," *Social Education,* 12:166-68, April 1948.

An interesting example of this interplay of school and community through pupil study of community conditions resulted when a wide-awake science teacher in a small community supported the viewpoint that science was real and important to students and to the local community in their daily lives. As a result, class study in science was directed to matters of real pupil and community concern. As the pupils studied the health of the community, they found a serious condition of typhus infection and recurring illness. Students and teacher laid plans for a frontal attack upon this problem. They found out all they could about conditions causing typhus infection. The community was checked for these, and shallow open wells, often near sources of contamination, became suspect. The class learned how to take proper specimens of water from the wells in the community; they sent samples to the state board of health and analyzed duplicate samples themselves. They found that the water in a majority of the wells contained typhus germs. This led the class to a study of remedies, and finally to a study of a water-system project for the village. Armed with the data of their study, they presented their proposals to the village council, and the proposals were accepted. Today, this community is proud of its water system, and of elimination of typhus infection from the community.[7]

How Organize School-Community Cooperation?

Throughout this book constant emphasis has been given to the unique relation of modern education to its community environment in a democratic society. Learning through experience projects the thinking and activities of the school into the stream of vital democratic living that makes up the life of the community. This means that the school is immediately concerned with the other

[7] Help in conducting community surveys may be found in Roland L. Warren, *Studying Your Community.* New York: Russell Sage Foundation, 1955; E. G. Olsen and others, *School and Community,* Second Edition. Englewood Cliffs, N. J.: Prentice-Hall, Inc., 1954, Chapters 18 and 19; by same author, *School and Community Programs.* Englewood Cliffs, N. J.: Prentice-Hall, Inc., 1949, Chapter 6; Merle Sumption, *How to Conduct a Citizen's School Survey.* Englewood Cliffs, N. J.: Prentice-Hall, Inc., 1952.

educative influences the child is subjected to in his contact with his immediate environment. As society's official educational agency, the school carries the obligation of effecting some form of coordination of the educative influences of the community. The development of the experience curriculum and the core program as a means of educating for democratic living makes some form of community organization for educational cooperation imperative.[8]

Two practices commonly followed to secure school-community cooperation are the creation of lay committees to advise the school and the organization of more elaborate community coordinating councils. Both are frequently functioning simultaneously. The advisory committee is the simplest, most direct way of securing community cooperation in specific phases of the school program. It is therefore the one easiest to get started, and a natural way to experiment and lead into the larger, more complete community council.

Advisory committees are usually appointed by the superintendent of schools and charged with the responsibility of developing policies around specific school problems. Such advisory committees have helped to plan buildings, to provide for extracurricular enrichment programs, to initiate or improve school lunches, to secure needed equipment, to survey school building needs, to determine curriculum trends, and to solve other important school problems. These committees, as the name implies, are purely advisory bodies. In a democratic school system they furnish a broader base for policy planning, and can be utilized by core teachers to interpret the program to the general public.

An excellent example of the value to the school and community of an advisory committee was recently encountered. A citizens' committee of 25 members representing six geographical divisions of the community was asked to serve in an advisory capacity to the school. They met at the beginning of the school

---

[8] For a more complete discussion of this function of the school, see Nelson L. Bossing, *Principles of Secondary Education,* Second Edition. Englewood Cliffs, N. J.: Prentice-Hall, Inc., 1955, pp. 202-216; E. G. Olsen and others, *School and Community,* Second Edition, Chapter 17.

year in September, explored the types of problems confronting the school and community, and then divided into subcommittees to work on problems the committee had decided should be considered by them. As a result of the cooperative study by the school and the advisory committee, it was recommended that social studies should receive greater emphasis in a school that had been somewhat traditional in its program. Because of this recommendation, practically all students were enrolled in a social studies course. This advisory committee also felt that problems of family living were not receiving the emphasis their importance warranted. As a result of the recommendations of the Family Living Committee, the broad outlines of a course in family living, to include frank consideration of problems of sex and marital adjustment problems, were proposed. When the superintendent recommended to the board of education that provision be made for this and other similar additions to the curriculum based upon the combined approval of school staff and advisory committee, the board readily approved. It had a strong mandate not only from the school but also from an influential group of civic-minded laymen.[9]

In many situations that concern the immediate problems of the school in relation to the community, the advisory committee is the best and most easily obtained source of community help. Whatever other organizational set-up may serve the needs and interests of the community more extensively, the advisory committee is the most flexibly adaptable to specific needs of the school. But such a committee, by its very design, has a limited usefulness in the over-all integration of school-community activities. The community council, or community coordinating council as it is often called, is a policy-coordinating group that includes representatives of each major civic organization in the school community. The purpose of such a council is to acquaint citizens with total community needs and resources, and to coordinate those resources in an attack upon community problems. These general purposes are more definitely stated thus:

[9] Reported by Dr. George Sharp, Coordinator of Curriculum, Tenafly, N. J.

1. To promote cooperation among organizations and citizens interested in community improvement.
2. To foster the coordination of efforts of the foregoing organizations and individuals in community betterment.
3. To sponsor the study of conditions, needs, and resources.
4. To develop public understanding and support.
5. To secure democratic action in meeting local needs through existing agencies, organizations and institutions.[10]

Since the school should play an important role of leadership in such an organization, it has been recommended that the school should provide a person with social understanding, imagination, and social skills, to serve as its leader. Such a council would be advisory in nature; in any action it thought desirable for the community welfare, it would function through the collective organizations represented. This council would offer a ready-made opportunity for the school leadership to carry issues and problems to the public and secure lay participation in planning on a large scale.

An interesting example of the way in which an advisory committee leads to the organization of a community council occurred in a small Michigan community. When the new superintendent of schools arrived, he invited some prominent citizens of the town to advise him on a few items of school-community interest such as observation of American Education Week. This group met three or four times the first year. The next year every important group in the town was invited to participate. After these groups had considered the possibilities of united community activities, a council was organized. Each participating group has one representative on the council, and the superintendent acts as chairman. The policy of this council has been to consider matters of community concern brought to its attention by groups rep-

---

[10] For more detailed discussion of the work and organization of community councils, see E. G. Olsen, and others, *School and Community*, Second Edition, Chapter 17; L. A. and E. F. Cook, *A Sociological Approach to Education*. New York: McGraw-Hill Book Company, Inc., 1950, Chapter 17; *Organizing a Community Council*. Lansing, Mich.: Michigan Council on Adult Education, 1953; Roland L. Warren, *Studying Your Community*. New York: Russell Sage Foundation, 1955, Chapter 17; *Community Council Handbook*. Pittsburgh: Association of Community Councils, 1950.

resented on the council. The council serves as a means of integrating the activities of the member groups through suggestion as these groups carry out community-wide projects.[11]

specific sources of community help ✓

Parents, of course, are always a prime source of community help in the school program. Wide-awake classes have always made use of the varied backgrounds parents represent. They offer unusual opportunity for core classes. In one school, a class was studying the ways in which our social customs are like and unlike those of other peoples of the world. The parents of one member of the class had served for many years as missionaries among tribal groups in Africa. Their travels had brought them in contact with many other cultures. They had an unusual collection of motion pictures showing strange customs of peoples they had met. Because of the nature of these pictures, several other classes were invited to see them and to hear the informative talk of the mother, who presented them. It is interesting to read about strange wedding ceremonial customs, eating rituals, and social conventions, but much more impressive to see them and to hear them explained by a first-hand observer. Another core class was considering the problem of communication through the press, how papers get the news, why some things that appear in one paper are not reported in all papers, and scores of other vital concerns of press reporting. The father of one of the boys in the class was editor of the local paper. He gladly consented to come and discuss with the class the problems of publishing a daily newspaper, and to answer questions submitted in advance and impromptu questions following his talk.

The possibilities of parents as sources of help to the school are almost unlimited in the average community. One class requested that parents cooperate in providing needed equipment or other types of materials. Another class was trying to appreciate the artistic contributions of peoples of other cultures represented

---

[11] W. C. Morse, "Community Coordination in Mason, Michigan," *Community Coordination,* 9:8-11, March-April 1941.

in the parental background of its members. Because it drew upon the immigrant parents of other children in the school, this class project gained the interest of the entire school. A feature display of artistic production of all kinds—weaving, needlework, painting, basketry—mostly proud family heirlooms collected from parents, were shown in a special room; refreshments were served and many parents were present to explain the history and use of certain rare articles displayed. Cooking special dishes or helping with picnics has frequently been a contribution of mothers to group activities in which their children participate.

Besides the almost unlimited help individual parents can give to core classes, much use has been made of small parent groups in the school such as the room mothers' clubs common in the elementary school, and, more recently, room parent groups in the upper elementary and secondary schools. These room groups grow up naturally around the core class, since the parents of such a group have a common focus of interest in the school program. In many cases, these room groups have originated from a P.T.A. committee composed of parents of a given grade level who were gradually drawn into active planning with the teachers of the grade. In other cases, the groups have developed because of repeated invitations by the pupils of a core class to their parents to attend programs or exhibits of work. The groups have even originated as planning committees for a core class party or picnic.

However developed, a strong, continuing organization that gives parents a real role to play in the school can grow out of the room mothers' club or the room parent groups. Parents in such groups have a real feeling of identification with the school. When such a feeling exists, parents will be ready to make constructive suggestions for the improvement of the school program. They will give freely of their time and energy to assist in the actual conduct of the core class, helping in a dozen ways in the living and learning of students in class. In schools like these there is little need for concern about public opinion. The class and school program has become the concern and pride of parents as well as of students and teachers.

The most inclusive parent group is the Parent Teacher Association. It is without doubt the most important resource group available in the average community, since parents make up the largest single group in any community. The school deals with the matter of greatest concern to the parent—the welfare of the children. There is scarcely any personal sacrifice parents will not make, scarcely any effort they will not put forth if they are convinced it is for the good of their children. It is most unfortunate that so many schools do not recognize this element among community resources available to the school. The purposes and program of the National Congress of Parents and Teachers are too well-known to require their presentation here.[12]

What has already been said of parents as a community resource can be said with double emphasis here. Many of the parents who are most helpful as individuals or in limited group activities are or should be a part of the larger P.T.A. organization. The parents of a community, acting in a cohesive group, can have for their children what they will. They represent the voting power of the community. They represent the potential educational interest of the community.

Parents must, however, be intelligently informed on modern issues in education and made fully aware of the why's and wherefore's of contemporary developments in educational theory and practice. This can best be insured by seeking their cooperation in various studies of changing educational practice and community educational problems, and their cooperative planning in the solution of problems and the projecting of educational programs for the common good.

If the school sought the cooperation of P.T.A. groups and shared with them the problems of the school in relation to the community, it would be possible to reduce very sharply the cultural lag between educational social knowledge and practice. It was startling to discover in the opinion poll referred to earlier in this chapter that 74 per cent of the public had never heard of or did

---

[12] See "Four-point Program of the National Congress of Parents and Teachers," *National Parent Teacher,* 41:17-18, March 1947, and other publications of this organization.

not understand the meaning of the core curriculum, which was under fire by a minority group in the community. Had the school been enlisting the aid of parents, and particularly the P.T.A., in solving its problems, such a condition would not have existed. In one school community largely devoted to the core curriculum, the opposition could scarcely create a ripple of concern because of a very active and informed parents' organization.

Teachers in core classes have a special reason to become active in the P.T.A. They have a real motive for becoming acquainted with the parents of the children in their classes, and they are in a position to win the confidence and enlist the help of the parents in educational concerns. In one school, for example, the core class in grades seven, eight, nine, and ten took over successive meetings of the P.T.A. Each month the core students of one grade planned the program and personally invited all the parents to come to the meeting. They even followed up their written invitations by telephoning parents who had not responded to the invitation. This series of programs was so well attended and so interesting to the parents that a noticeably better spirit of understanding and cooperation between parents and school prevailed thereafter.

A certain large high school serves a community of low economic status made up for the most part of immigrants from southern Europe. The school, organized on the core curriculum basis and thoroughly alive to the need of making democracy operative, has organized what is known as a P.T.S.A.—a Parent-Teacher-Student Association. This brings the staff, the students, and the parents into close contact and gives them a feeling of equality. This alert school discovered that pupil choice of lunch items was poorly balanced and very heavy for students' sedentary work. A careful check of lunches selected over a period of time provided the data, but how to use them was the question. It was decided that this was a problem for the P.T.S.A. to study. Therefore, a meeting of representatives of this group was called and the facts were laid before them. It was concluded that there was no chance to correct the lunch habits of students without the cooperation of the homes. The meeting agreed upon a program to be referred back to the constituent groups. It included a presentation of the problem and recommendations of the kinds of foods that homes should stress for their children and that children should select at the cafeteria. The program was proposed before sectional meetings of the P.T.S.A., and letters were sent to the homes, explaining the kind of breakfast and lunch children should eat.

Aside from parents who occupy a key place in the community-school relationship, there are many specialized individuals who can be of help to the schools. They may or may not be parents; their potential contribution to the school is in their specialty. In many of the middle western or western sections of the country there are still old pioneers who followed the trails westward in search of home, adventure, gold. These men and women can help boys and girls to see the contrast between life as it is now and as it was then better than any textbook can.

A core class was studying the personality characteristics that make for success at a job. A personnel director from a nearby airplane factory was brought in to discuss job personality. Another group was making a study of comparative religion because of differences in church affiliations within the class. In order to get a clear idea of religious similarities and differences, the class arranged to have ministers of different churches come to explain the creeds of their respective churches. Two core classes exploring the way in which local governmental bodies carried on the city's business decided to get their information first-hand. One class interviewed the mayor and two council members about community planning, while the other spent a half-day visiting a council meeting to see the way the city's business was handled.

how communities have helped school programs

In addition to these types of community resources available for core class use, there are many other school-community cooperative projects that may be used as a basis for core and other class participation by the wide-awake school and teacher. Many of these school-community cooperative projects have been overlooked.

A school faculty became interested in making the school more community-centered. The problem of delinquency was much in the press at the time. It seemed desirable to investigate the reasons for delinquency, the evidences of delinquency in the community, the recreational activities of children, and what recreational facilities were actually available in the community. Classes began a study of these areas. To enlist the cooperation of the community, certain civic-minded groups including the Women's Club, which had community-wide influence, were invited to participate. After the combined study of students, faculty, and community, questionnaires were drawn up to find out from children and young people how they spent their leisure time, to determine community reaction to the prevalence of delinquency in the community, and to elicit suggestions as to what might be done about the recreational opportunities afforded in the community.

The faculty and certain classes joined in working out the questionnaires, and with the cooperation of community groups saw that a proper sampling of community reaction to the problem was made. When the results were tabulated, students in classes tried to interpret the findings while the faculty and representatives of the community met in the school library to study the data. As a result of this study, initiated by the school and joined in by the community, it was decided that the community needed additional recreational facilities. The possibilities for outdoor and indoor recreational facilities were explored, and the most feasible place for indoor recreation was found to be the partially unfinished basement of the community's combined elementary-secondary school building. Money was not immediately available without involved financial procedures. At this point the American Legion stepped in and agreed to underwrite finishing off the basement. A beautiful Teen-Age Canteen now serves the youth of the community. To give the young people a real sense of ownership, the responsibility of the canteen was placed in the hands of the student council of the school; an adult was employed to supervise the canteen, and parents served as chaperones during evening open-houses.

A young woman fresh from teacher training school, eager to put into practice her new ideas of education for democratic living, and possessed with creative imagination, accepted a position in a one-room school in a poor, logged-over district of a once-rich timber area. She found a school with not a single window unbroken and with seats and desks in various stages of disrepair; the building was dirty and unpainted inside and out, with virtually no equipment or supplies. Such a picture would be enough to dishearten a veteran teacher, but this girl was not discouraged.

She studied the community, its background, its needs, and the needs of the children for several days before school was to open in September. When the children came to school, she and they planned together how to improve their school living conditions. Children were sure their fathers and other men in the neighborhood would help repair the seats and desks and put in the window lights. They knew their mothers and other women would gladly help make curtains for the windows. It was not long before the men and women of the little community, shy at first, were earnestly at work making the school a more comfortable place for the children of the community. It was the first time many of the adults had ever been in the schoolhouse. As they talked to the teacher about the needs of the children and the school, things began to happen. They made suggestions for the improvement of the physical facilities of the school and playgrounds. Paint was secured and willing hands painted the schoolhouse. Since hot lunches were desirable as a health measure, a table was made out of waste lumber at the mill; pans, dishes, and other necessities for hot lunches were collected. These items were not fancy, but they were adequate for a one-room school of 15 or 16 youngsters. Before the year was over, there were frequent community meetings in the school to consider matters of school and community interest, and there was community entertainment. In consequence of the fine spirit developed around the school, a wealthy former member of the community provided money for the erection of a new brick school building to provide more adequate school-community facilities.

A community with an active community council was holding its first meeting of the new school year. This community was in a state of transition. Once a wealthy residence district of the city, it had become a mixed community. Near the business part of the city, large homes had been transformed into rooming houses or multiple dwellings. Sections of this large district had become the living areas of underprivileged groups of low economic status, while middle-income families made up the rest. The council had met to consider some problems that needed attention, and the question of continuing the extensive recreational program for the children that had been carried on in previous years was raised. The community justly prided itself upon having the lowest delinquency rate in the entire city, and the council was sure that this was largely due to their program of using vacant lots, basements of neighborhood churches, and low-rental old houses as recreation centers. They took up the question of the current need for such centers. The program involved a lot of work and they were only representatives of interested community groups. The principal of the two schools that serve this community, who was in many ways the kingpin of the council, was quick to suggest that some of the core classes in his school would welcome an opportunity to make this a study project.

The next day an observer at this council meeting was being shown about the school by this principal. In a couple of core classes visited, the principal described the problem the council had considered, and mentioned that he had assured the council some of the core classes would no doubt like the opportunity to make this a study project for the council. He suggested that they think over whether this would interest the class.

It is this fine spirit of cooperation between community and school that has made possible a high level of social life within a community very difficult to work with. The school has found its educational program greatly vitalized by this practical, direct interplay with the community.

In another large community a referendum vote was set for the middle of September, shortly after school opened, on the question of substantially increasing the school tax levy. There had been several unsuccessful attempts to get the school tax limitation statute changed. The school had not been able to increase its tax assessment for twenty-nine years, and it was in desperate financial straits.

Finally, a Citizens' Committee on Education, which had been created about a year previously, became very much interested, then deeply concerned about the financial condition of the public schools. A subcommittee, known as the Vote Yes School Committee, was formed to wage an active campaign in favor of the referendum to increase the school tax. This committee in turn organized with vice-chairmen to represent the following important group interests in the community: business, labor, P.T.A., and the over-all citizens committee, which itself was widely representative of community leadership.

The campaign was well organized and had excellent cooperation from the newspapers and radio. Important groups in the city endorsed it, with the sole exception of a small diehard group of taxpayers habitually opposed to tax increases of any kind.

The P.T.A. organized open-house programs and assisted in block work. The administrative elements in the school system worked with the P.T.A. and the various committees of the citizens' group.

An important feature of the campaign, from an educational point of view, was the enlistment of junior-senior high school students. They distributed colored tickets in the downtown area the afternoon and evening before election day and covered other areas of the city that were not covered in the intensive block campaign. They assisted in organizing programs in the schools and in getting pupils to take home data on the campaign and to urge parents and friends to vote. A campaign song was sung in the schools, and television programs were presented. It was the first time the schools had actively enlisted pupils for such a campaign.

The vote was overwhelmingly in favor of the increased tax levy. The campaign brought school and community together as nothing else had in years. Its effect upon the pupils was to identify them with the community and awaken in them a high sense of responsibility as citizens of the community.

How Does Community Service Help?

During the World War II it was not unusual to see collections of scrap in many communities. One large scrap pile boasted a sign that declared in bold letters, "Collected by the School Children of Our City." It was the grateful tribute of its citizens to the services rendered by the school children at a time of crisis and need, when the usual manpower was sorely needed elsewhere. It was customary to draw heavily upon the schools for services in many phases of community life at that time. In many ways the stress of war and the lack of manpower created opportunities of the highest educative values for practical sevices of children to the community.

A once-rich farming area near a small city was rapidly becoming a wasteland because of faulty methods of farming and severe erosion. The entire community became aroused and took practical interest in proposals to set conservation plans in motion. Through a publicity build-up, most of the younger business men, the junior-senior high school boys and girls, and the school faculty joined in a tree-planting holiday. Several thousand trees were planted under the direction of the state conservation service. The school children who participated in this program had the rich experience of observing first-hand, in a way not easily forgotten, what conservation of our natural resources means, and how these resources can be saved by cooperative community effort.

A typical way in which schools can become effective in improving the beauty of a community was exemplified in a project carried out by the student body of the high school of Moultrie,

Georgia. This project, which involved the participation of nearly all of the student body, was a community beautification plan. Over 11,000 trees were planted on vacant lots, around the school, and around homes. A nursery was established under the school's agricultural department to provide plants for future use.[13]

In some classes beautification became a subject of special study. As a result, special projects were undertaken in landscaping, planting trees, making rock gardens, and so on. The girls became interested in beautifying their homes by refurbishing and rearranging furniture and by properly using curtains.

A type of community service that gives students practical experience in local government grew out of a class study on municipal government. Since the school was located in a sizable city, it presented many of the problems that all American cities face. After intensive study of the various theories of government with particular reference to their own city council type, the class became convinced that the city manager form of organization was best adapted to the modern city. This was not just an academic question for them. They organized, carried on a campaign, and were able to have the issue submitted to the electorate for their decision.

One core class conducted a study of the parks and picnic places in their community. They also took note of the ugly and unsanitary areas. Through their student council representative, they aroused the interest of the whole school in a clean-up campaign. The city loaned trucks and drivers. The newspaper gave the drive much publicity. Not only were the public alleys cleared of unsightly and unsanitary debris, but private citizens also cleaned up their backyards and alleys. For a day the whole town rolled up its sleeves and house cleaned—all because of a study made in a core class.

A partial list of community service activities performed in

---

[13] See account reported in much detail in S. M. Corey and others, *General Education in the American High School*. Chicago: Scott, Foresman and Company, 1942, pp. 224-225. A rich source of similar illustrative materials is to be found in Lloyd A. and Elaine F. Cook, *A Sociological Approach to Education*, Revised. New York: McGraw-Hill Book Company, Inc., 1950.

recent years by core classes is offered below as a source of imaginative stimulation to core teachers and others:

Mapping the school area for the city planning commission
Developing a park along a river bank
Securing a new traffic light near the school
Landscaping the school-yard
Building a school camp
Developing a school nature trail
Painting fences
Conducting salvage drives
Sending CARE packages to Europe
Supporting a family in Europe for a semester
Mapping a community as an aid to the city airport committee
Preparing Thanksgiving and Christmas baskets
Organizing a program bureau for the use of community organizations
Submitting to the city council data on types of heating used in homes

The list could be considerably extended. The possibilities for community service are almost unlimited. Every community needs the help of its young people. The young people need the exhilaration, the practical experience, and the sense of reality that these activities make possible. Core classes are especially likely to perform such services because of their interest in the study of the real problems of the here and now.

Community service makes a rich contribution to the enlistment of public support of education. It gives the lay citizen a chance to learn by first-hand contact what the schools are doing, and how they may contribute to community welfare. It represents a dynamic kind of public relations program, one that invites the participation of all citizens in its planning and execution. In short, it epitomizes the good community school at work.

SELECTED REFERENCES

Alexander, W., and G. Saylor, *Secondary Education*. New York: Rinehart and Company, 1950, Chapter 19.

American Association of School Administrators, *Lay Advisory Committees*. Washington, D. C.: The National Education Association, 1951.

————, *The Superintendent as Instructional Leader,* Thirty-fifth Yearbook. Washington, D. C.: The National Education Association, 1957, Chapter 7.

Anderson, Vernon E., *Principles and Procedures of Curriculum Improvement.* New York: The Ronald Press Company, 1956.

Bossing, Nelson L., *Principles of Secondary Education,* Second Edition. Englewood Cliffs, N. J.: Prentice-Hall, Inc., 1955, Chapter 16.

Campbell, R. F. and J. A. Ramseyer, *The Dynamics of School-Community Relationships.* New York: Allyn and Bacon, Inc., 1955.

Dahir, James, *Communities for Better Living: Citizen Achievement in Organization, Design and Development.* New York: Harper and Brothers, 1950.

Davies, D. R., and K. F. Heller, *Citizens' Committees.* New London, Conn.: Arthur C. Crofts Publications, 1954.

Educational Policies Commission, *Strengthening Community Life: Schools Can Help.* Washington, D. C.: The National Education Association, 1954.

Gwynn, J. M., *Curriculum Principles and Social Trends.* New York: The Macmillan Company, 1950, Chapter 19.

Hamlin, Herbert M., *Citizens' Committees in the Public Schools.* Danville, Illinois: Interstate Printing Company, 1952.

Hand, Harold, *What People Think about Their Schools.* New York: World Book Company, 1948.

Hillman, Arthur, *Community Organization and Planning.* New York: The Macmillan Company, 1950.

Ivey, John E., and others, *Community Resources.* Philadelphia: John C. Winston Company, 1951.

King, Clarence, *Organizing for Community Action.* New York: Harper and Brothers, 1948.

Melby, Ernest O., and Morton Puner, *Freedom and Public Education.* New York: Frederick A. Praeger, Inc., 1953, Chapters III, IV, and V.

Menge, J. W., and Roland C. Faunce, *Working Together For Better Schools.* New York: American Book Co., 1953.

National Citizens' Commission for the Public School, *How Can Citizens*

Help Their Schools? New York: National Citizens' Commission, 1954.

National Society for the Study of Education, *Citizen Cooperation for Better Schools*. Chicago: University of Chicago Press, 1954, Part I.

Olsen, E. G., and others, *School and Community*, Second Edition. Englewood Cliffs, N. J.: Prentice-Hall, Inc., 1954.

Pond, Millard Z., and Howard Wakefield, *Citizens Survey Their School Needs*. Columbus, Ohio: College of Education, The Ohio State University, 1954.

Romine, Stephen A., *Building the High School Curriculum*. New York: The Ronald Press Company, 1954, Part 4.

Sander, Irwin T., *Making Good Communities Better*, Revised. Lexington, Kentucky: University of Kentucky Press, 1953.

Warren, Roland L., *Studying Your Community*. New York: The Russell Sage Foundation, 1955.

Chapter 15

Evaluating Progress
in Core Classes

In classes devoted to the mastery of a subject, evaluation is a fairly simple process. If the goal of the course is the development of a specific skill such as shorthand, it is not difficult to discover by performance tests whether or not students have achieved the desired speed and correctness. If the goal is the mastery (at examination time) of facts, a test may reveal the extent of the student's achievement.

Of course, good teachers do not generally confine their goals to subject mastery. They are also interested in the total development of the student. They would like to see improvement in his attitudes and understandings, in his social adjustment, and in the important collection of traits commonly labeled "citizenship."

In practice, however, we seldom succeed in emphasizing the measurement of these personal and social traits in a subject-matter class. There is not enough time, there are too many faces confronting us, and it is so much simpler to discover achievement in skills or areas of knowledge than it is to measure all-round development. For every hour that we devote to the evaluation of social and civic development in our students, we spend many more hours in having them write examinations based on subject-matter mastery.

The core teacher, however, is compelled to attempt this more difficult kind of evaluation. His purpose, as set forth in Chapter 4, is not the mastery of facts or the development of routine skills. He has set himself to the challenging task of helping his students to achieve a more desirable social and vocational adjustment through guidance, of developing well-rounded individuals through a correlated learning experience, and of teaching democratic attitudes and abilities through the provision of a democratic classroom experience. He therefore cannot avoid the implications of these goals when he sets out to evaluate. Since new purposes require new evaluative techniques, the core teacher is challenged by the nature of his assignment to develop procedures for evaluation.

The core teacher usually has a further motive for evaluation. An experimental program is expected to justify itself in contrast with whatever program has preceded it in a school. If such expectations express themselves in nagging or negative fashion, or result in a divided faculty, little progress may be expected in the development of a core curriculum or in the improvement of the program in any other respect. It is true, however, that the search for a better way is inherent in the very nature of the core curriculum. Whether it is justifiable or fair to expect one kind of instructional program to show such improvement while ignoring the accomplishments of the rest of the school program is beside the point. Good core teachers cannot help evaluating, because the impulse to seek improvement is an important part of their daily task. The search for a better way challenges students as well as teachers almost every day, when they have launched a cooperative attack upon a group problem.

The evaluation process is a perplexing and frustrating experience, from which many class groups would gladly escape if they could. Evaluation has not always been done with skill. It frequently takes the form of self-analysis, which is never a comfortable business. The techniques for measuring the goals of a core class are still far from perfect, even in the hands of experts. Yet core classes and core teachers continue to experiment with evaluation devices and seek constantly to discover ways of measuring their progress.

It is sometimes assumed that the only genuine evaluation is based upon purely "objective" data. But core teachers are discovering that significant data about changes in people can be drawn also from the judgments of people themselves and from those of others who live with them, both inside and outside the classroom. Such data acquire increased validity when the purposes of the program deal with changes in human behavior, as they do in the core class.

The two basic questions that evaluation procedures are designed to answer are: (1) in what ways is the individual in a core class developing into a more competent person? and (2) in what ways is the core class changing its pattern of relationships and its group behavior in desirable ways? In this final chapter, the techniques that have been used by core teachers in seeking evidence on these two questions will be described.

How Evaluate Individual Growth?

some common devices

The core teacher makes use of many conventional kinds of data that are usually to be found in the high school files. Among these are the students' scores on intelligence tests, aptitude tests, and achievement tests. There are usually data available on the student's health, his marks in school, and his participation in school activities. Sometimes his work record is also on file, if he has held a part-time job while in high school.

Core teachers are likely to be interested in their students' test scores, not only as a means of knowing more about each individual at the beginning of a semester, but also as a means of checking progress in some of the commonly accepted skills. In this connection, reading scores have been used as an index of academic progress in many core programs. For example, Myrtle Toops, a core teacher in the Burris Laboratory School at Ball State Teachers College, Muncie, Indiana, has described the growth in reading of her two core classes:

> Sixty children were divided into two matched, heterogeneous groups of thirty each for core groups in the fall of 1949. They were matched as evenly as possible according to the intelligence quotients revealed by the California Test of Mental Maturity, Long Form for Grades Four to Eight. . . . The Stanford Achievement Tests in Reading, Forms G, H, and M, were administered to both groups in September, 1949; May, 1950; and May, 1951, respectively and a complete tabulation of all results was made. . . . The mean gain in total reading (the term total reading means the average of paragraph meaning and vocabulary meaning) for the entire time was 2.15 years, while the approximate median was 2.2 years. The range in gain in total reading was from 0.2 years to 4.8 years in grade levels. The mean gain in comprehension was 2.33 years, and in vocabulary the average gain was 2.05 years . . . An examination of the medians made by these cases in total reading showed them to be slightly above or at the standard norm.[1]

In some schools, only part of the students at a given grade level are enrolled in core classes. This fact has made it possible for teachers to conduct comparison studies, using the method of matched pairs or matched groups. Capehart, Hodges, and Berdan have reported such a study of core and non-core students in the Oak Ridge (Tennessee) High School in 1949-50. The 225 students in core classes were matched with non-core students in intelligence, sex, age, and reading-grade equivalent. The following tests were then administered to both groups in December and in May:

Cooperative English Test
   Mechanics of Expression
   Effectiveness of Expression
Wrightstone Scale of Civic Beliefs

---

[1] Myrtle Dewey Toops, *Working in the Core Program in Burris Laboratory School.* Muncie, Indiana: Ball State Teachers College, 1955, p. 47.

Wrenn Study-Habits Inventory
Heston Personal Adjustment Inventory:
  Analytical Thinking
  Confidence
  Sociability
  Personal Relations
  Emotional Stability
  Home Satisfaction

The authors report that the core students made gains in all areas tested except one, between December and May. The single exception was "analytical thinking," which showed a very slight loss. The researchers then applied criteria of statistical significance to their data, and drew the following conclusions from the study:

1. On the average, pupils enrolled in the core curriculum made significantly greater gains on effectiveness of expression than did the pupils not enrolled in the core curriculum.

2. On the average, pupils enrolled in the core curriculum showed significantly higher gains than did pupils not participating in the core curriculum within the area of self-confidence.

3. It is also probable that sociability was developed more fully in the core curriculum than in the non-core curriculum. This conclusion is tentative, however, and must be tested by further study.

4. The probability of finding large changes or significant differences between the control and experimental groups is not too great because of the many uncontrollable factors involved in studies of this kind. . . .

5. The experimental (core) group showed marked improvement in study skills. . . . . . . The core group also showed greater growth in civic attitudes, as measured by the Wrightstone Scale of Civic Beliefs. . . . This may be explained in part by the considerable use of library and other resource materials by the experimental (core) group.[2]

Other studies using similar techniques have shown similar results. Gale's study of 269 core curriculum students in the Highland Park (Illinois) High School has been, in part, summed up as follows:

---

[2] Bertis E. Capehart, Allen Hodges, and Norman Berdan, "An Objective Evaluation of a Core Program," *The School Review*, February 1952, pp. 84-89.

The objective tests administered to 269 core-curriculum students revealed that statistically significant gains had been attained during the year 1953-54 in the basic mechanical skills of English; in the mastery of subject matter in the fields of biology, American history, and American literature; in the fundamental concepts and attitudes involved in effective citizenship; and in personal and social adjustment.[3]

Core teachers may be interested in these uses of individual test data as one means of evaluating progress of students. Care should be exercised, however, that the testing project does not shift from the laudable goal of evaluating individual growth to that of proving one part of the school's program to be superior to others. The implication of this "proof"—namely, that core teachers and their methods get better results than do teachers not involved in the core program—is essentially divisive. Such comparisons will create hostility within the school staff unless the core program, and the evaluation process too, are psychologically owned by all the teachers. When all members of the staff think of the core program as *theirs,* even though they do not all have core classes of their own, it may be possible to conduct controlled research based on comparison between contrasting methods. Meanwhile, core teachers should recognize the fact that one may analyze individual test data for the purpose of more effectively guiding individual growth, but without attempting to prove the superiority of the core program over other programs within the school.

Another kind of caution may be in order. Achievement tests may be useful as base-line data about an individual, but basically they represent subject-matter goals. New goals, we have emphasized, call for new methods, including new methods of evaluation. Core classes which employ the problem-solving method and which have relative freedom of choice as to what problems they will study may not, at any given semester-end, have mastered the sequential details of world history, or of American history, or of

<hr>

[3] Raymond F. Gale, "The Progress of Students and Graduates of a Core Curriculum," *The School Review,* October 1955, pp. 384-387.

literature or science. Over a period of two or three years the members of a core class are likely to learn even more in such fields than those in a separate-subject class; at any given test-point, however, their understandings and skills may be in areas not tested by the usual achievement battery. It would be unfair and unwise to test the validity of what might be called the "core method" by measures appropriate mainly for subject-matter classes.

anecdotal records of individual growth

The cumulative record varies in form and length from school to school. In some schools it consists merely of a card on which are recorded periodically the student's school marks and activity record, and which contains also such vital facts as his name, address, age, and family. In other high schools a rather extensive developmental record book is kept and passed on from kindergarten through the twelfth grade. Some of these lengthier record books are thirty or forty pages long, and have space for semi-annual posting of the anecdotal information collected by the homeroom or core teacher. Some of them are book-folders in which anecdotal material, written or typed on a separate form, is inserted whenever it is recorded.

The use of anecdotal records is not a simple business. It involves a considerable amount of work and is subject to certain hazards of misinterpretation or misuse. Yet the information contained in such records is so valuable that core teachers have devoted many hours to the process of learning how to develop and use them intelligently.

The anecdotal record is an objective report of a single incident or of a closely-related series of incidents which reveal significant or characteristic behavior of a student. It is not the teacher's unguided judgment, but a simple, factual story that reveals the student's traits. Judgment or interpretation is left to the reader. The 1950 Yearbook of the Association for Supervision and Curriculum Development provides much valuable help on the writing and interpretation of anecdotal records.[4] It includes the following criteria of a good anecdotal record:

A criterion for recording skill is the extent to which the teacher lets the child tell his own story. A good record is one which includes specific details, a wide selection of behavioral incidents, actual conversations, samples of written or other creative expression, descriptions of behavior in formal and informal situations, behavior with friends and relatives, and behavior in and out of the classroom. A good anecdotal recording is specific, factual, descriptive of what was actually seen to occur, devoid as much as possible of subjective terms. The recorder should indicate time of day, central focus of the incident, beginning, middle, and end. The data so introduced give more meaning when later interpreted for the bearing they have on one or more phases of the child's development.[5]

With some help from persons who have had experience in the use of the anecdotal record, core teachers have developed considerable skill with this kind of evaluation. It should be noted that the nature of the core teacher's typical assignment reduces the number of students for whom he would be writing the anecdotal records. He is also apt to have the same groups for two or more years. At the end of his period of years with a class, the core teacher may summarize many of the anecdotes in a brief case study for the use of the next teacher. He should be careful at this point to insure that the file tells a true and adequate story of the child, which will help the next teacher to gain a better understanding of his over-all patterns of behavior and growth.

work-samples and self-analyses

The core teacher's files often contain actual dated samples of the student's written work or art work, which reveal to student and teacher alike a helpful picture of his progress and his needs. Autobiographies written at various stages of the student's development

---

[4] Similar helpful material on anecdotal records may be found in *Helping Teachers Understand Children,* Washington, D. C.: The American Council on Education, 1945, pp. 1-41.

[5] Association for Supervision and Curriculum Development, *Fostering Mental Health in Our Schools,* 1950 Yearbook. Washington, D. C.: The National Education Association, 1950, pp. 197.

are often kept on file because of what they reveal about his insights, interests, and problems. Other kinds of introspective writing may also be kept on file for their interpretative value. They may simply be bits of creative writing—stories or poems or essays; they may be responses to such leads as, "If I had one hundred dollars to spend . . . ," or "If I had three wishes . . . ," or "What I want to be. . . ." There may also be self-analyses, written as such by the student at various stages in his high school career. Many core teachers use such self-analyses as a regular part of the evaluative process.

The following excerpts from a self-analysis are illustrative of the usefulness of this device for individual evaluation:

I don't think the class is perfect but we have a grand start and next semester I intend to put my nose to the grindstone—we know where we stand now.

Now that I have the opportunity to help make decisions in class, I use it to the best advantage at times, and at other times I abuse the privilege, I am sorry to say. But I have learned to do things on my own initiative, develop my thinking power, if any, improve my speaking ability, broaden my scope, improve my personality, enlarge my friendships, learn to know people better, and I have learned to distinguish between that which is best for me and that which I want to do.

Core has done a lot for me. It has helped me to overcome being frightened in front of a group. In this class we have more of an opportunity to express our opinions than we do in an ordinary class.

I have learned to rely on myself, not to talk out of turn whenever I please—if you make such a mistake the whole class jumps you!

I have found many new interests and learned about more things. This makes the class more interesting.

The class is very informal, it seems as if I belong here or as if it was a home or headquarters from which I go to other classes.[6]

opinions of teachers

Teachers' judgments, too, have an important role to play in evaluation. Copies of such statements, written regularly as a phase of the home report, have a place in the file and may contribute much

---

[6] Unpublished report, Michigan Secondary Curriculum Study, 1944.

to the over-all picture of the student. Such statements should be objective and as unprejudiced as possible. If the student is to be transferred to another core teacher, the teachers' judgments should be carefully studied and perhaps summarized to give as much helpful information as possible without creating an initial prejudice against the student.

The following brief letter to parents was written by a core teacher in the Burris Laboratory School of Muncie, Indiana. A copy of this letter went into the student's file.[7]

Dear Mr. and Mrs. ————————

Henry shows great improvement in his ability to share and work with the other children in his group. There is still some evidence of always wanting to be first to use a book or a map. He has accepted responsibility for clearing up after a work period in good style.

He shows much more respect for the suggestions and opinions offered by the other members of his class. He was chosen leader for group discussion yesterday and did a good job; however, he finds it difficult to listen to others' discussions when he is not a leader.

Henry reads well. He is able to spell most of the words he wants to use in his written work. His writing is still quite illegible.

Will you please stop in at school, soon, so that you, Henry, and I can plan further? I believe our earlier efforts have helped. Henry seems very willing to cooperate in every way.

Sincerely,[8]

sociograms

The student's file may also contain data derived from sociograms, posted for the class at various intervals. Much significant information about the individual can be derived from group sociograms. It is possible, for example, to trace in them his developing friendships, his status with his peers, his roles as leader and follower, and the ways in which he is resolving conflicts or changing social status.

---

[7] Other examples of teacher-judgments, expressed in letters to parents, appear in a later section of this chapter, pp. 365-368.

[8] Myrtle Dewey Toops, *Working in the Core Program in Burris Laboratory School,* p. 45.

Further discussion of the uses of the sociogram in evaluating group progress will appear in the next section of this chapter.

peer judgments

The opinion of his fellow students, too, has a bearing on evaluation. Summaries of such judgments are often kept in the files for comparison purposes, and they sometimes reveal much about the student's development. This technique of seeking judgments about a student from his peers must be handled with some skill. Core teachers are often able to develop these skills because of their longer period of relationship with the group in an informal, guidance-centered classroom climate.

Sometimes these judgments are expressed in a brief "Guess Who" paragraph, written by a fellow student and used in class as an identification game. Some of these "Guess Who?" paragraphs are so insightful that teachers have added them to the subject's file. Similarly, some core classes write on such topics as "I like —— because . . ." or "My favorite person in this class is —— because . . ." It is possible to learn much about a student from the opinions of his peers.

other data

Core teachers often add to the student's file a record of interviews held with the student himself and with his parents. If personality adjustment tests or interest inventories are used, their results are filed. The results of questionnaires about study habits, hobbies, or jobs are useful. The student's attendance record and his record of participation in extra-class activities are also kept on file.

All these efforts at individual appraisal are directed toward the goal of helping the individual to make an effective adjustment. Elizabeth Brady has suggested that a teacher ask himself such questions as the following about each student in his class:

Has he had a chance to learn what the school takes for granted—especially language, manners, ways of playing with others, obeying rules, concepts, like "cooperation"? If not, what has he learned in these and related areas?

What particular expectations and pressures has he had to meet thus far, particularly in his family and play group? To what special pressures has membership in a minority group subjected him? What values has he taken on? What does he consider success? [9]

As a summary of this description of devices used to evaluate individual growth, the following list of such procedures used in the core classes of one high school may be helpful:

WAYNE HIGH SCHOOL PARENT-FACULTY COMMITTEE
TYPES OF EVALUATION USED

(Activities engaged in from which we make judgments of students.)

1. Course content exams: written; oral; check lists; multiple choice.
2. Informal observation: appearance; general attitudes and reactions; participation in class discussions; study habits; associations with other children—acceptances, rejections; social adaptability; acts of aggression; withdrawing tendencies; nervous habits; physical weaknesses; satisfactions—dissatisfactions; attitudes toward parents, brothers, sisters, home.
3. Teacher, self, and peer evaluation registering opinions on the basis of: leadership qualities; degree of participation; type of discussion; changed behavior; conduct; respect for others; willingness to listen; personal growth; change in personality; open-mindedness.
4. Sociograms (group adjustment).
5. Group evaluation about: group feeling; self-discipline; discussion technique; planning, making choices; attitudes.
6. Problem census: Mooney Check List; California Test of Personality; autobiographies; discussions; etc.
7. Growth in reading: reading tests (Traxler Reading Test); Maturation of intelligence (PMA Test); screening special aptitudes (see senior plans for this spring).
8. Personal interviews and conferences with student: teachers; counselors; administration.
9. Participation in activities.
10. Anecdotal records.
11. Parent conference and parent evaluation.
12. Opinions about attitude toward: peers; school; teachers; family; money;

---

[9] Elizabeth H. Brady, "Children Bring Their Families to School," in *Fostering Mental Health in Our Schools,* 1950 Yearbook. Association for Supervision and Curriculum Development. Washington, D. C.: National Education Association, 1950, pp. 27-28.

morals; opposite sex; sex; nutrition; movies; radio; race; reading; religion; class procedures; etc.

13. Interest check lists: Kuder Test; Calif. Personality Test.
14. Cumulative records: data on family health, work, etc.; classroom; counselors; administration, official office records.
15. Attendance: school in general: particular activities.
16. Case studies.
17. Informal contacts with students.
18. Aptitude Tests. (USES Battery)
19. Miscellaneous: time budget; follow-up data; socio-drama; panel discussions; group thinking; drop-out data; etc.[10]

How Evaluate Group Progress?

A second kind of evaluation to which core teachers are committed involves the measurement of progress toward the goals of each succeeding class group and of the program as a whole. An important phase of this kind of evaluation is the development of group judgments as to the progress they have made. Such evaluative judgments are sought by the core teacher as an integral part of the group's work together. Not only at the end of a unit or a semester of study, but continuously as a part of the regular work of the group, such questions as the following are framed and answered by the core class:

1. What have been the best features of our work together?
2. In what ways are we becoming more effective in our work as a group?
3. In what ways have we failed in our objectives?
4. How could we improve our ways of working together?
5. How can we make more effective use of each other, and of other resources?

Many variations of the above questions have been developed and used by core classes as they seek to evaluate their work. In some of these classes the basic questions are worked out through group discussion and a consensus or group answer is arrived at by a

---

[10] Unpublished report, Wayne High School, Wayne, Michigan, February 13, 1950.

committee of the whole. In other cases several of the questions are pointed at individual evaluation of the effectiveness of the program and of the individual's contribution to it. A committee then sifts these answers, which may be signed or unsigned, and compiles a summary of them, which is then used as a basis for class discussion. Finally, group answers may be developed.

The following description of the evaluative process used by core teachers in one high school illustrates some of the techniques thus far described.

Evaluation Techniques for Core Classes
1947-1948

At the present time, the evaluation program relative to core classes in high school is carried out by the individual teacher. There are plans for a follow-up study of graduates since core work was instituted here and a comparative study of students who have participated in such classes and those who have not, none of whom is enrolled in combined classes at the present time. These studies will be carried out through the combined efforts of all the core teachers.

In the sections of core several methods of evaluation have been used on a small scale. These evaluations are, with one exception, carried out as a joint project—teacher and students working together on them at all times.

1. Toward the end of the first and second semester, we discuss the purposes for study we set up at the beginning of the year in order to discover whether these goals are being met and what we need to do to accomplish these purposes. This usually results in a revision of purposes and renewed interest in accomplishing goals. It shows us, too, where we have failed, and helps us to better our planning for the future.

2. Before beginning a new unit, we discuss purposes for studying the unit and put a copy of these into our folders for future reference. Methods for discussing purposes may vary; small, random groups, the class as a whole, or the steering committee follow these purposes closely in their planning and the class as a whole, at the completion of the unit, evaluates the work on the basis of achievement of goals by answering the following questions:

(1) Do you feel that we have accomplished these purposes? Explain your answer.

(2) In what ways have we done this?

(3) In what ways have you benefited personally as result of this study?

(4) What contributions did you make to the study?

(5) In what ways could the work on the unit be improved?

3. Near the beginning of the year, the students made an outline of classifications they considered important in connection with their six-weeks' grades. The students grade themselves in the space provided and the teacher follows suit. Grades are averaged for the final mark. Any wide differences of opinion are discussed in private conferences with students.

4. On small cards we keep an anecdotal record of the students' personality and behavior. We are concerned with their success or failure to get along well with the group, and make notation relative to this at least once each month. The students do not see these cards, but they have proved very helpful in private conferences. The results will be summarized and made a part of the students' permanent office records.

5. As we work with students on their projects, hear reports, or check papers, we keep a record in a notebook of progress in basic skills. This is helpful in grading and in discussing problems with a student. He reads the record and together we check his improvement.

6. At the end of the first six weeks this year, we sent a questionnaire to the students in one core class of last year. The questions were as follows:

Looking Back Over Our Year's Work

I. What are some of the things—topics, projects or ways of doing things —we have done this year that you feel were important or interesting?

II. Have our core classes helped you to improve personally in poise, confidence, or in getting along with others? What activities do you think helped in any of these?

III. Do you feel that our class as a whole has improved any in the following:

Cooperating   Courtesy   Enthusiasm   Carrying out
                                                responsibility

IV. Has the class helped you to learn to think for yourself?

V. Do you think we have contributed to a feeling of better "world friendship" in our class or school? Explain.

VI. Do you feel that you have learned "English and World History" in this class?

VII. Do you like the combined class meeting for two hours instead of one?

VIII. In what ways do you think our class might have been improved?

IX. Have any of the things you learned in this class helped you elsewhere in or out of school? For example?

X. Do you feel that any phases of our classes have contributed to the outstanding reputation of your sophomore class? Which ones in particular?

XI. If there are any things you especially liked about your time in the core or any comments you would like to make about the year in general, please feel free to write them here.

These are some of the methods used for evaluation purposes in our core classes. There are other ways that are used almost every day in discussions of how we could improve our work and in the attempts the steering committees and class officers make to include everyone in the activities of the group. There is a great deal more that could be done both in single classes and in core classes. We realize the need for concrete, constructive, meaningful evaluation of our methods, and are making definite plans for the future along this line.[11]

group appraisal is an educative experience

It has been noted earlier that this process of developing group evaluative judgments is not an easy one. It cannot be avoided, however, because it is a basic part of the group planning process. Even when it is poorly done, much can be learned from these judgments. As a class continues its work and matures in its critical judgment, the group often become extremely skillful in the important business of reaching a true consensus as to the strengths and weaknesses of their work together. In view of the importance of critical judgment as an educational goal, the process of group evaluation can scarcely be overstressed. It provides a means whereby the evaluative procedure can become educative in the sense that it helps to change the learner's behavior. Indeed, the development of the skills involved in self-appraisal by individuals and by groups can hardly be brought about in any other way than through continued experiences in self-appraisal. By the same token, the exclusive use of methods involving appraisal by

---

[11] Unpublished report, Dowagiac High School, Dowagiac, Michigan, 1948.

the teacher can only result in the development of feelings of dependence upon others and helplessness in self-analysis.

follow-up

Many core teachers continue to seek group and individual judgment about the core curriculum, even after students have left the class. In some cases students have been asked to evaluate their core experience in retrospect each year until they graduate. One school asked the graduating seniors to respond to the question, "Would you advise a younger brother or sister to take a core class?" [12]

In many schools, a continuous follow-up study is made of both drop-outs and graduates. Some of these studies are designed to follow the student three, five, or even ten years after he leaves school. The questions asked of the former student in follow-up studies are likely to include one or more evaluative judgments about their high school courses, including the core class. The data from these studies have provided significant information with reference to particular core curriculums.

group relationships

Core teachers use other means of measuring group progress besides the judgments of the core students during and at the end of the class. Sociograms, which have been mentioned earlier in connection with the measurement of individual growth, also have a story to tell about group progress. The pattern of group relationships revealed by the Friendship Scale or Work Scale is highly revealing to the thoughtful core teacher. It is possible to trace in these patterns the evolution of leadership, the emergence or disappearance of cliques, the acceptance or rejection of individuals, and the constantly evolving peer relationships of the class. These data are highly significant in view of the effect of interpersonal relationships upon the learning process.

Not only group behavior, but also the effective development of

---

[12] In the high school referred to here, the core curriculum was on an experimental basis and not open to all students.

every individual is influenced directly by the nature of group relationships. The "friendship" sociogram is a pattern obtained by plotting, on either a bar graph or a scattergram, the answers to such a question as "Who is your best friend in our class? Who is your next best friend?" The "work" sociogram is similar, but worded in relation to "Whom would you prefer to work with on the next project in our class?" In the bar graph the names of all the students are placed across the top and down the left side of the graph. Connections are then drawn between the student chosen and the student choosing. The scattergram arranges these same data but in clusters of circles with connected arrows that show the direction of the choices. It is thus possible from analysis of a given sociogram to discover cliques and their centers, fringes, and overlaps; mutual choices limited to two persons; isolates who are chosen by no one; and the differences in choices based respectively on friendship or on work-relationships.

holding power

One purpose often expressed by core teachers is that of aiding students to adjust successfully to school. One evidence of adjustment may be the number of students remaining in school until graduation. It is therefore common for core teachers to engage in studies of the number of drop-outs, both current and in earlier years. The results of such studies can be compared with other analyses of school holding power.[13] Allowance should be made for the fact that there are numerous and complex reasons for quitting school. Careful follow-up studies of school-leavers must be made before generalizations about cases can be validated.

There seems to be some evidence that students who have spent one or more years in a core class are less likely to drop out of school. There are at least two powerful influences at work to induce them to remain in school—a friendly, understanding teacher and a group of peers who seem to need and want them.

---

[13] See, for example, Charles M. Allen, *How To Conduct the Holding Power Study*, Illinois Secondary School Curriculum Study, Bulletin No. 3. Springfield, Illinois: The State Superintendent of Public Instruction, 1949.

These influences will need to be intensified, however, in the case of students whose families and out-of-school friends are urging them to quit school.

teachers' opinions

The judgments of teachers and administrators responsible for a core curriculum are probably the most valid single measure of group progress. They are always being expressed, at least informally, but some faculty groups are using an organized plan for securing and recording periodically the opinions of core teachers about their groups. They may be expressed in anecdotal fashion in a class diary or plan book; or they may be brought out in discussion at regular meetings of core teachers and recorded under appropriate question headings. In one study of eight programs, the teachers and administrators concerned were asked through a group interview to arrive at a consensus in answering the following questions:

(1) What, in your opinion, appear to have been the outstanding strengths or advantages of the program in comparison with conventional organization for instruction?

(2) What were its chief weaknesses, in comparison to whatever program preceded it?

(3) What, in your opinion, could have been done to remedy the weaknesses of the program?

(4) What do administrators think about the program as regards its comparative cost, schedule difficulties, demands upon teacher personnel, effect upon the total school program?

(5) Did teachers become more effective as they worked in the program?

(6) What has been the effect of the program on teachers' growth in service?

(7) What relationships developed between the teachers involved in this program and other teachers in the school?

The responses to the first question—the outstanding strengths or advantages of the core curriculum—indicated that all eight faculty groups agreed on two advantages:

"Enabled us to understand the needs, interests, abilities, and problems of the individual pupil better."

"Facilitated a real homeroom feeling among pupils—a sense of security and a family feeling for their group."

Seven school staffs agreed on a third advantage, summed up as follows: "Enabled pupils to learn democratic citizenship by practicing it, making decisions and governing themselves, free from teacher domination."

Six school staffs were in agreement on two other advantages:

"Taught pupils to work with others and to adjust to group situations."

"Gave pupils a better chance to develop through individualized and small group activities fitted to the learner."

Krug and others have reported a series of evaluative interviews with 41 teachers of "multiple-period" classes in 15 Wisconsin schools. Their summary follows:

The teachers interviewed see value in multiple-period classes. They feel particularly that this organization seems to help establish closer personal relations between students and teachers. In large and medium schools where impersonal relationships are more likely to prevail, this would seem to be an especially important result of the multiple-period program. Teachers in the small schools also stressed the role which such organization plays in helping the class to become more closely identified with the school-community relationship.

There is some expression on the part of the teachers to the effect that they have not been helped to see clearly the basic objectives of multiple-period organization. This points to the need for in-service education opportunities which might be developed in local school systems and in teacher-education institutions.

The interviewer was especially impressed by the seriousness with which the teachers have approached their responsibilities in multiple-period organization. These teachers are most earnestly concerned with trying to find means of working with their students to improve the educational offerings of the school and to help students to grow into responsible citizens in our democratic society.[14]

---

[14] Edward A. Krug, Clifford S. Liddle, and Quentin Schenk, *Multiple-Period Curricular Organization in Wisconsin Secondary Schools.* Madison, Wisconsin: The University of Wisconsin, 1952, p. 32.

Equally serious attention should be given to teachers' judgments about the weaknesses of the core curriculum, and what should be done to remedy these. Care should be observed that these judgments are not directed at any individual on the staff, but rather are expressed as friendly agreements among teachers as to how a "good curriculum can become a better curriculum."

parent opinions

Parent judgments can also contribute significantly to the evaluative process. Well-planned core curriculums will involve parents in the establishing of the goals and in the measurement of progress toward these goals. In the next section, descriptions will be given of ways in which parents can participate in evaluation of individual progress. Parents can help to evaluate the curriculum as a whole, too. To this end, they should be involved in its planning from the beginning.

We have too often worried about real or fancied parent opposition to curriculum programs that are new or changing. We have seldom actually explored parent opinion, involved parents in our planning, or taken any similar steps that would enable us to know their opinions instead of merely wondering about them and fearing them.

The following devices have been reported by one or more school core groups as a means of involving parents in the evaluation of the core curriculum:

(1) Surveys of parent opinions regarding curriculum and the purposes of education.

(2) Public forums in which the purposes and techniques of the core classes are freely discussed in split or random groups.

(3) Open nights, teas, or parent nights, in which parents come to the core classes instead of the pupils. The time is then used to discuss the purposes and achievements of the class.

(4) Letters to parents, and the replies received, help in some schools to build up a body of data about parent judgment.

(5) Questionnaires of parent opinions have been used by many core teachers several times during the school year.

(6) Room parent clubs serve in some schools as evaluative opportunities. These clubs, organized for each core class, serve many valuable purposes.[15]

(7) Discussions held before luncheon clubs, P.T.A.'s, and church groups are reported by a number of schools.

(8) The use of film strips and moving pictures to stimulate evaluations by parent groups has been occasionally reported.

(9) A planning committee involving representative parents has been used, in some cases for total program planning for all core classes in the school, and in some cases for each core class.

(10) At the end of each year parents of core students in many schools are asked for an evaluation of the core class, and for their response to the question of whether or not they wish their child to continue in a core class. (This question is obviously limited to experimental programs involving only part of a given grade.)

(11) In a few schools, parents have been so actively involved as resource helpers in the day-by-day work of the core classes that they have become closely identified with the goals of the program.

All of these devices, and any others that can be developed, should be employed to insure that parents have a real voice in the evaluation of core classes. This is of importance in order to insure continued parent support for the program. An even better reason for involving parents is that they have an important contribution to make—and good schools will become better schools if all possible resources are utilized.

A further important role of parents in evaluation will be discussed as we turn to the perplexing problem of school marks.

What about Marks?

Probably no problem has been so vexing to core teachers as that of what to do about school marks. In the first place, it seems clear that the conventional competitive, symbol marks are quite inadequate for reporting the kind of growth that core teachers seek to achieve in their students. Marks not only fail to describe

---

[15] Room parent clubs are discussed at greater length in Chapter 14, pp. 326-329.

the many aspects of development to which core classes are devoted; they also actually violate certain important purposes of the core curriculum unless their use is carefully guarded. Compare the following list of purposes that have been discussed at various points in this book with the list of attributes that usually characterize the use of symbol marking:

The core class seeks:	*Symbol marking tends:*
To learn the skills of cooperative planning.	—To encourage competition.
To learn the skills of self- and group appraisal.	—To place evaluative responsibility solely upon the teacher.
To help students to adjust more successfully to their peers.	—To erect barriers between peers.
To provide a well-rounded learning experience.	—To place undue emphasis on subject mastery.
To make evaluations continuously, as a part of group planning.	—To emphasize terminal evaluation.
To help students to grow from where they are.	—To force all to meet minimum standards, or quit.
To provide learning experiences deriving from the intrinsic needs and desires of the learner.	—To serve as an extrinsic motivation, thus helping to perpetuate poor teaching.

It appears that the use of symbol marks is invalid as a measurement device for core classes. It does not usually measure the kinds of growth that have been advanced as purposes of the core curriculum. As a matter of fact, many teachers are aware of various research studies that have demonstrated the invalidity of symbol marks, even for the purposes they were designed to serve. Wrinkle lists six beliefs on which symbol marks are based, all of which can be demonstrated to be fallacies by research:

Fallacies About Symbol Marks

1. Anyone can tell from the mark assigned what the student's level of achievement is or what progress he has made.
2. A student can achieve any mark he wishes if he is willing to make the effort.

3. The student's success in his after-school life compares favorably with his success in school.
4. The student's mark is comparable to the worker's pay check.
5. The competitive marking system provides a worthwhile and justifiable introduction to competitive adult life.
6. School marks can be used as a means to an end without their becoming thought of by students as ends in themselves.[16]

Basically, the inability of marks to serve the various functions which they are supposed to serve lies in the fact that they do not represent fixed values in terms of which they may be interpreted. The assumption that you or I or anyone else, except the person who gives a mark, can look at it and tell with any degree of accuracy what it means is the No. 1 fallacy involved in the conventional marking system.[17]

The facts are that the conventional system of symbol marking is invalid (in that marks do not measure what they purpose to measure), unreliable (in that they do not agree and cannot be compared), and non-descriptive (in that they convey no helpful information about the person marked).

In the light of the growing conviction that symbol marking is a completely inadequate means of recording and reporting growth, it is not surprising that core teachers have generally tried to find other devices. They have not been completely successful in such attempts, partly because of the difficulty with which educational change is often attended. We have "sold" marks to parents for many years. It is often their only contact with the school. They are sometimes reluctant to see this one contact removed *unless they have been helped to find a more satisfactory one.*

Another difficulty at the high school level comes from the demand of colleges and of some employers for a transcript of marks. This difficulty can also be overcome when the secondary school is ready to present more valid and more descriptive data than marks.

---

[16] William L. Wrinkle, *Improving Marking and Reporting Practices in Elementary and Secondary Schools.* New York: Rinehart & Company, 1947, pp. 36-49.

[17] Wrinkle, *Improving Marking and Reporting Practices in Elementary and Secondary Schools,* p. 35.

In the face of these difficulties, few basic changes have as yet actually been made in the marking systems of high schools. In most cases the studies made by core teachers and their colleagues have resulted instead in one or another of the modifications that will now be discussed.

SELF-EVALUATION	I	II	III
	S-U	S-U	S-U

I. Accepting Responsibility
   A. Getting work done on time
   B. Paying class dues
   C. Bringing library books
   D. Keeping files up to date			

II. Self-Control
   A. Committee meetings
   B. Class discussions and meetings
   C. When teacher is gone			

III. Attitudes
   A. Toward other students
   B. Toward school policies
   C. Toward work
   D. Toward teacher
   E. Toward responsibilities			

IV. Oral and Written English
   A. Spelling   D. Punctuation
   B. Grammar   E. Sentences
   C. Speaking F. Paragraphing			

V. Neatness of Paper
   A. Writing   C. Carelessness
   B. Form D. Condition of paper			

VI. Using Time Wisely
   A. Free time   C. Committee time
   B. Free reading D. Concentration			

VII. Contributing to Class Meetings and Discussions
   A. Participation   C. Being prepared
   B. Voting D. Paying attention			

VIII. Knowledge Gained
   A. Facts   C. New ideas and opinions
   B. Understanding			

pupil-teacher evaluation

The mark finally recorded is arrived at through a combination of self- and group-marking, and the core teacher's evaluation. This process is usually preceded by the development of criteria for such evaluation. The following instrument was used in one high school core class as a preliminary step, before a mark was arrived at through individual conferences with the core teacher.

In another school the form used for self-evaluation and teacher conference was worked out by the core class, as a phase of their effort to establish valid criteria for judging their own growth. They then rated themselves on a point scale, and this rating was

Ninth Grade Class Goals	Evaluation	
	Teacher's	Pupil's
1. Working together for the good of the class 　A. Respect each individual and his ideas 　B. Respect minorities 　C. Accept responsibilities 　D. Share ideas pertaining to the problem at hand		
2. Good group discussion 　A. Give whole attention 　B. Contribute worthwhile ideas to discussion		
3. Planning work well 　A. Planning each week's work 　B. Carry out plans on time 　C. Plan work in groups		
4. Use better methods to solve problems 　A. Use many sources of information 　B. Take good notes		
5. Good oral topic presentation 　A. Strive for better grammar 　B. Present work in interesting manner 　　1. Use different methods 　　2. Use pictures and illustrations 　C. Select important notes		
6. Better written presentation 　A. Strive for better grammar 　B. Express ideas in best way possible 　C. Neatness		

compared with the core teacher's evaluation. Conferences followed in case of disagreement between the teacher's rating and that of the student. No mark was recorded until a consensus was reached. The class used the following scale, for example, during one semester of their work.[18]

How Shall Progress Be Reported?

letters home

Many core teachers have supplemented the conventional marks by a letter to the parents at least once each semester. In a few schools, such letters have replaced the marks entirely. The letter to parents can become a burdensome responsibility upon teachers unless time is provided for writing them. It is possible also to supply core teachers with stenographic help from senior shorthand classes. These student stenographers should be carefully chosen for their discretion and responsibility.

In order to prevent these letters to parents from degenerating into stereotypes, cliches, or vague generalizations, some school staffs have held a series of meetings to provide in-service education in such reporting techniques. Released time for writing the letters is sometimes provided by early dismissal of students, by reducing or eliminating final examinations, or by the use of substitute teachers. Parents who have become accustomed to receiving these evaluative letters are usually reluctant to give them up in favor of symbol marks. They are keenly interested in home reporting devices and will often collaborate actively in developing better ones.

An example of a brief letter from a core teacher to parents follows:

Dear Mr. and Mrs. Jones:

Since my last letter to you, Mary has made some important gains which will interest you. She has made improvement in her silent reading rate, as our last test shows. Her art work and penmanship are both improving. I

---

[18] Rosalind Zapf, *A Core Curriculum Class in Action,* film strip. Wayne State University, Detroit, Michigan: Audio-Visual Materials Consultation Bureau, 1949.

know you have seen the design she made for her group mural during the unit on transportation.

As a result of a suggestion you made in your last letter, we managed for her group to put on a play about safety last Friday. Mary was active in all the arrangements, and actually took a part herself in the play. She did the part fairly well and we were all encouraged to see this effort on her part to overcome her shyness.

If it is possible for her to entertain her friends occasionally at home, I think this will help to give Mary additional poise.

I am glad the dental appointment is almost due. She complained of pain in her tooth yesterday.

In summary, Mary is making good progress.

If you could manage to visit the room the last hour next Tuesday, you'd see her in action as a Teacher's Aide. She performs this responsibility very well.[19]

There is a place for such a brief, friendly note in the total plan for reporting to parents. There is a place also for the longer letter which reflects more data and perhaps covers a longer timespan. In some schools the core teacher has the responsibility for incorporating in one summary letter the progress information forwarded to him by all the other teachers of a given member of the core class. Two examples of such summary letters are given in the Ohio State University School handbook for parents.[20]

One letter begins with an explanation of how often such letters are sent, and follows with several pages of description of procedures and recent activities of classes in English workshop, core, home arts, American history, and physical education. Each section reports the particular student's participation and achievement in such areas as discussion, writing, reading, social adjustment, crafts, interests, attitudes, and physical skills. These letters are therefore complete reports on a student's progress and, at the same time, interpretations of the program to the parents.

The letter is much more descriptive than are symbol marks, and

---

[19] J. W. Menge and Roland C. Faunce, *Working Together For Better Schools*. New York: American Book Company, 1953, p. 107.

[20] *A Handbook For University School Parents*. Columbus, Ohio: College of Education, Ohio State University, 1954.

need not involve comparison with other students. It tends to report progress of each student as an individual, mentioning his strengths and also his immediate needs for improvement. It sets the stage for enlisting the cooperation of the parents. It encourages letters from them in reply, as well as parent visits to the school.

The chief problem involved in the writing of such letters is provision of time for it. Of course, all letters need not be written at one time; they can be written at any time during the semester. They are more apt to be well-spaced, however, if some released time and stenographic help are provided for the purpose.

Students, too, can write evaluative letters to their parents. Such letters should report recent group activities in the core class, evaluate the student's own role in these activities and estimate his recent progress. Letters by students are supplements to those written by the core teacher. They provide a motive for many self-appraisal techniques which students in core classes have used. Toops quotes the following example of a letter written by one of her students:

Dear Mom and Dad:
Our class has studied Muncie this time. I learned a lot about Muncie that I did not know. I met lots of people and asked them to help me. Before we went on a trip we set up our problems and took them with us. We always tried to be polite and thank them for helping us.

In our group work I did not always do serious work. I tried to be funny. The group tried to help me see my mistake. This is something I must work on. I am doing better already.

I still have trouble with spelling my words in my written work, but I am using my dictionary.

I have read our book on Muncie. It is swell. My reading scores on my tests show that I have improved in reading this year.

Your son,[21]

Many school staffs that have been unable to solve the problem of providing the time required for writing letters to parents have

---

[21] Myrtle Dewey Toops, *Working in the Core Program in Burris Laboratory School*, p. 44.

provided parents with a comprehensive report in which there is space for free response on some items and provision for checking on others. An example of such a home report is given in Ruth Strang's book, *Reporting to Parents*,[22] together with suggestions for its development and use. If such a report is to be really descriptive, however, it is likely to take as much or more of the teacher's time than does the letter to parents.

conferences with parents

Perhaps most helpful of all reporting devices is the periodic conference with the parents, which is being increasingly used in elementary schools and in some high schools.[23] Time for the conference is usually provided by releasing pupils early. Such a conference may be scheduled for from 15 to 30 minutes, depending on how much time is made available for this purpose.

These conferences give parents and teachers a chance to see the progress made by individual children in terms of the total environmental pattern of their living in school and at home. This makes possible more complete diagnosis and plans for cooperative attack on behavior problems by school and home.

It is important that the parents are fully informed of and that they agree to proposed evaluation and reporting methods. The year before such a plan was put into effect in one community, every P.T.A. had several meetings devoted to this topic; their general approval was secured before the new reporting system was put into effect. Card reports on behavior characteristics were supplemented by parent-teacher conferences. Another small community school staff, at a summer workshop at which a majority of the teachers were present, decided to substitute a plan of parent-teacher personal conferences for the old report card. The matter was discussed at the first P.T.A. meeting of the year. It was too radical an innovation for many parents, so a compromise

---

[22] New York: Bureau of Publications, Teachers College, Columbia University, 1947, pp. 43-49.

[23] An issue of *Life* magazine devoted to education included a rating device by which to evaluate the merits of a good school. Emphasis upon teacher-parent conferences is one of the criteria given for a good school. *Life*, 29:54-55, October 16, 1950.

was necessary: some grades were to use parent-teacher conferences, and others were to send the old type of report card to parents who so desired; parent-teacher conferences were to be held when possible. Had the school taken time to educate the parents, compromise might not have been necessary. Within two years, parent-teacher conferences completely replaced grade card reports.

One high school staff of core teachers sent home the following letter, preceding their first parent conferences:

Mr. and Mrs. ——— ———

Dear Parents or Guardians:

The Basic Communications course which your child is taking is the result of the combined efforts of a parent-teacher-student committee formed last spring. This group agreed that our students need special help in these fields: reading, writing, speaking, listening, and observing.

Therefore, we are directing our efforts toward improvement in these five skills.

After numerous attempts, we find it impossible to satisfactorily inform you of your child's progress by means of a written report. Therefore, we are inviting you to come to Roosevelt School for an individual conference about your child's progress on Nov. 18th. Conference hours will be between 1:00 and 5:00 P.M. or 7:00 and 8:30 P.M.

All marks for other subjects will be sent home on report cards November 17 as has been done in the past.

In order to schedule the hours most effectively, will you list the time you can most conveniently come?

Sincerely yours,

Basic Communications Teacher

. . . .

(Please tear off lower portion of this letter and return to me as soon as possible.)

I shall come to Roosevelt School on November 18th at —— o'clock

(Signed) ————————————

This first schedule of conferences brought 68 per cent of the parents into the school. The following semester, the conferences were repeated, and over 75 per cent of the parents participated. All of the high school teachers participated in one way or another in this second set of conferences, although the invitation went out from the Basic Communication (Core) teachers.

It seems clear that the school faculties that have tried the parent conference have discovered certain significant values in it, as compared with the conventional report card. Some of these advantages are as follows:

1. The parent-teacher conference provided the opportunity for a clear, descriptive report of pupil progress.
2. It brings teachers and parents into contact, and provides a chance for them to get better acquainted.
3. It encourages parents to ask questions and get satisfactory answers.
4. It permits reporting to be made on the basis of the individual's own development in terms of his own potential, instead of forcing automatic comparison with other pupils.
5. It enables teachers to find out more about their pupils.
6. It strengthens the school-home tie, and thus makes a significant contribution to "public relations."
7. It challenges the teachers to do real evaluation. One cannot effectively participate in such conferences without first knowing something about pupils.

Teachers who try out the parent conference plan usually report that they would be reluctant to enter into such a conference without having at hand a considerable amount of information about their students. Thus the conference with parents presents a challenge to teachers to collect such data—in short, to *know* more about the progress of their students.

Trytten reports the following advantages of the plan, as used in the University High School of Ann Arbor, Michigan.

1. Communication was established with more parents than by any other activity—94 percent of all parents of the six grades.
2. The parents expressed almost unanimous approval of the procedure.

About 85 percent of the parents returned for the second series of conferences.

3. The homeroom teachers, without exception, said that the conferences had been very valuable, though strenuous.

4. The teachers made every effort to define their objectives and to observe behavior in order that their comments might be valid and specific enough to be helpful.[24]

There are problems that need to be solved in planning for parent conferences. Teachers must have some understandable data and must know how to present these data to parents. They also need to know how to answer certain questions that will be raised during the conference. Faculty meetings or grade level planning sessions might well be devoted to these problems. The conference plan is so valuable for reporting student progress that time and effort spent in mastering the techniques are surely well spent.

IN CONCLUSION

In this chapter we have analyzed the problems involved in evaluating success or failure in core curriculums. We have described some techniques that have been used for evaluating, recording, and reporting both individual and group progress in a core class.

It is clear that further procedures are needed for evaluation. New purposes, we have stated, require new evaluation techniques. Such methods are likely to emerge from the fundamentally experimental nature of the core curriculum. The drive to discover new and better methods is inherent in the core approach. Even though it is not an easy thing to achieve, core teachers will continue to seek better ways because they are committed to do so by the nature of their assignment. It is a part of their challenge to search constantly, with their students, for a better way of living and learning together.

Whatever steps are taken to correct the shortcomings of the

---

[24] John M. Trytten, "Parents Like the Conference Plan," *Bulletin of the Michigan Secondary School Association*, XVI:3, March 1952, p. 18.

modern school should be taken soon. The world today needs skillful, cooperative, integrated citizens as never before. In every city and town, we need schools that are developing such citizens. The purposes of the core curriculum represent basically the challenges that world conditions and the nature of learning present to education today.

SELECTED REFERENCES

Adams, G. S., and T. L. Torgeson, *Measurement and Evaluation for the Secondary School Teacher.* New York: The Dryden Press, 1956, Chapters 1, 2.

Allen, Charles M., *How To Conduct the Holding Power Study,* Illinois Secondary School Curriculum Study, Bulletin No. 3. Springfield, Illinois: The State Superintendent, 1949.

American Council on Education, *Helping Teachers Understand Children.* Washington, D. C.: The Council, 1945.

A Handbook for University School Parents. Columbus, Ohio: College of Education, Ohio State University, 1954.

Association for Supervision and Curriculum Development, *Fostering Mental Health in Our Schools.* Washington, D. C.: The National Education Association, 1950.

Chamberlin, Dean, and others, *Did They Succeed in College?* New York: Harper and Brothers, 1942.

Faunce, Roland C., *Some Went to College.* Lansing, Michigan: The State Department of Public Instruction, 1945.

Krug, Edward A., Clifford S. Liddle, and Quentin Schenk, *Multiple-Period Curricular Organization in Wisconsin Secondary Schools.* Madison, Wisconsin: The University of Wisconsin, 1952.

Leonard, John P., and A. C. Eurich, *Evaluation of Modern Education.* New York: Appleton-Century-Crofts, 1942.

MacConnell, Charles, Ernest Melby, C. O. Arndt, and Leslee Bishop, *New Schools for a New Culture,* Revised. New York: Harper and Brothers, 1953, Chapter V.

Mudd, Dorothy, *A Core Program Grows.* Bel Air, Maryland: The Harford County Board of Education, 1949, Chapter VI.

Noar, Gertrude, *Freedom To Live and Learn*. Philadelphia: The Franklin Publishing Co., 1948.

Smith, Eugene R., and Ralph W. Tyler, *Appraising and Recording Student Progress*. New York: Harper and Brothers, 1942, Chapters VIII, X, and XI.

Strang, Ruth, *Reporting to Parents*. New York: Bureau of Publications, Teachers College, Columbia University, 1947.

Toops, Myrtle D., *Working in the Core Program in Burris Laboratory School*. Muncie, Indiana: Ball State Teachers College, 1955.

Travers, Robert M. W., *How To Make Achievement Tests*. New York: The Odyssey Press, 1949.

Wrinkle, William L., *Improving Marking and Reporting Practices in Elementary and Secondary Schools*. New York: Rinehart & Company, 1947.

INDEX

Index